What to Sell on eBay®
and Where to Get It

What to Sell on eBay® and Where to Get It

Chris Malta
Lisa Suttora

McGraw-Hill

New York   Chicago   San Francisco
Lisbon   London   Madrid   Mexico City   Milan
New Delhi   San Juan   Seoul   Singapore
Sydney   Toronto

The **McGraw-Hill** Companies

McGraw-Hill books are available at special quantity discounts to use as premiums and sales promotions, or for use in corporate training programs. For more information, please write to the Director of Special Sales, Professional Publishing, McGraw-Hill, Two Penn Plaza, New York, NY 10121-2298. Or contact your local bookstore.

What to Sell on eBay® and Where to Get It

WorldWide Brands, Inc., Drop Ship Source Directory, and Market Research Wizard are trademarks of Chris Malta. Product Sourcing Mindset, Product Sourcing Notebook, Product Sourcing System, and Idea Hotspots are trademarks of Lisa Suttora.

1234567890 DOC DOC 019876

ISBN 0-07-226278-8

The sponsoring editor for this book was Margie McAneny and the project editor/ indexer was Claire Splan. The copy editor was Mike McGee and the proofreader was Paul Tyler. Composition and illustration by International Typesetting and Composition. Cover design by Jeff Weeks.

This book was composed with Adobe® InDesign®.

Library of Congress Cataloging-in-Publication Data

Malta, Chris.
  What to sell on eBay and where to get it : the definitive
guide to product sourcing for eBay and beyond / by Chris
Malta and Lisa Suttora.
    p. cm.
  ISBN 0-07-226278-8
  1. eBay (Firm) 2. Internet auctions. 3. Internet
marketing. I. Suttora, Lisa. II. Title.
  HF5478.M35 2006
  658.8'7--dc22
                    2005035697

To my parents, John and Mildred Malta, who showed me through their words and their actions that success in life and in business is not measured by how much others give to you, but by how much you give to others.

—Chris Malta

To my children, Noah and Gabrielle, for showering me with love and smiles each day as I wrote this book. You are the light of my life.

—Lisa Suttora

Contents

Foreword

If you're like most people I know, you've sold everything out of your garage, attic, closets, even all of your friends' stuff, and are starting to realize eBay is more than just a place to have fun and make a little pocket change—it's a bona fide business venture. But after you've sold off all of your own stuff, where do you find inventory to sell?

As I tour the country with eBay University, one of the questions I am asked most often is, "What do I sell, and where do I find it?" Many sellers who come onto eBay don't arrive with an understanding of inventory selection and the wholesale buying process. Instead, they throw away their money to middlemen masquerading as wholesalers, utilize drop-shippers who don't have products in stock (but find out too late), and think the products they want to sell online should miraculously make them money.

Another question I'm asked all the time is what I sell on eBay. My reply? "Anything that makes me money." Here are some of the truths about product sourcing that I have learned in my own online business:

1. You must understand your marketplace. Most sellers throw their items up on eBay and hope they stick to a buyer. I call this the "spaghetti factor." Instead, you should learn how to use the research tools that eBay and their certified providers offer to find out about the marketplace you are going to sell in. These research tools will tell you what buyers want to purchase, what the best pricing strategies are to use, the best date and time to end your listing, and the best category for your item. Too often eBay sellers treat the marketplace like a garage sale and then act shocked when they receive garage sale prices.
2. A wholesaler is rarely a wholesaler. Type the words "wholesale products" into Google—go ahead, I'll wait. Of the 38 million and growing links that show up, many are not "true" wholesalers. The authors of this book will teach you that real wholesalers rarely advertise online, and will show you how to go about locating legitimate wholesalers.

3. Many manufacturers will usually not sell directly to you. Shocked? I was too the first time I was turned down by a manufacturer who created the product I wanted to sell online. I was baffled: *Don't they want to make money?* But that is not how manufacturers usually think. This one tip alone could save you tons of time in researching.

4. You make your money when you buy your inventory, not when you sell. This one sometimes takes a bit to settle in, but it is the truth in all that is retail. The base cost of your inventory plays a significant role in the profitability of your business. Many eBay sellers are making middlemen (who are cloaking themselves with a "wholesale" name) rich by buying items at high unit costs, robbing themselves of profits.

5. You can't necessarily make money off of what you like. I hear many people teaching new sellers, "Sell what you know; sell what you are passionate about." I won't be the first one in this book to tell you that what you think you want to sell on eBay may not be what buyers want. The very best piece of advice I could ever give you is something I was told when I started my eBay adventure: "Sell what the buyers want." I realize this sounds simple, but you would be surprised at how many people do double the work necessary to sell online. Not only do they go through the learning curve of how to sell online, but also are in the unenviable position of convincing the buying public that they have to have this great new item. You don't have to know anything about what you are selling; you only have to know how to sell it. Listen to the people with the money—they will show you exactly what they want to buy!

6. You aren't born with "eBay Eyes" or, as co-author Lisa Suttora calls it, your Product Sourcing Mindset. When most of you walk into a store, you're looking for what you like—not what would sell. The true key to successful product sourcing is to gain inspiration from everything that is around you, and you need to train yourself to do this. This allows you to open up your mind to all possibilities, not just the ones you are comfortable with.

The authors of this book are going to expand upon these truths, and teach you so much more.

I met Lisa Suttora, owner of What Do I Sell (www.WhatDoISell.com) three years ago in one of my eBay University classes. In the tradition of the student surpassing the mentor, Lisa's company, WhatDoISell.com, has become a leader in product sourcing information. Her unique and creative approaches to product selection continually impress me. By teaching people how to focus on what the buyers want, she understands not only how to find legitimate product suppliers who sell products that will make you money online, but also knows how to promote and position those same items for the most amount of money.

I have never seen anyone take legitimate sourcing as seriously as Chris Malta, co-owner of WorldWide Brands (www.WorldWideBrands.com) does. I met Chris over a year ago and was instantly impressed with his passion for teaching people the "right" way to source goods for their business, in a way that would make them money. He truly desires to have entrepreneurs succeed. With so many companies out there who want to divert that success and take your money, Chris is truly a gem.

In reading this book, you will learn why it's better to sell in a niche and discover how to find your own. You'll use tools to find the products that buyers are demanding, and learn how to buy those products at the lowest possible price. You'll glean marketing tips and tricks to use with the products you source, and discover how to avoid the evil middlemen who are after your hard-earned money. You'll even get a script to handle that first phone call to the company from whom you're sourcing products.

You are about to read information that can change your business, and bottom line, from the best in the business. Now … what are *you* going to sell?

Janelle Elms
eBay University Instructor, best-selling author,
and corporate consultant
www.JanelleElms.com
Seattle, Washington

Acknowledgments

Special thanks to:

My co-author, Lisa Suttora, for her hard work and dedication to genuinely helping all those she comes in contact with.

Janelle Elms, for her selfless dedication to all those she works with and teaches.

eBay, Inc., for working so hard to provide platforms where experts in their fields can help to educate eBay users.

Editor Margie McAneny and the entire team at McGraw-Hill Publishing, for making this book such a wonderful thing to be a part of.

—Chris Malta

To my co-author, Chris Malta, for his dedication and passion to helping entrepreneurs find the true path to achieving their business dreams.

To Janelle Elms for her unwavering faith, vision, and friendship. And for giving wings to so many entrepreneurs so they can fly and reach the stars.

It truly has taken a village to write this book and for this I give my heartfelt thanks to Christiane, for her friendship and support and for being a second mom to my children. To Patty for happily inviting us into her home for frequent visits. To "playgroup," for watching the kids while I wrote on Friday evenings and for sharing in all the excitement with me. To John, for his friendship and support and for being a great dad. To Claudia, for our centering coffee meetings. To Martin, for keeping me grounded and being able to share in the vision. And to Denae, for her friendship throughout the years and for venturing into the entrepreneurial world with me.

Many thanks to Marjorie McAneny, acquisitions editor at McGraw-Hill, for her guidance in writing this book and wading through my many detailed e-mails. You made writing this book a lot of fun! To Agatha Kim for keeping things on schedule and to Claire Splan, project editor, for keeping things moving in the final stretch.

Thank you to eBay for providing a venue that allows so many people to become the master of their own destiny. To Rob Cowie, for making that initial phone call and for all the hours we have spent talking about creative product sourcing. And to the members of the community of What Do I Sell .com—your stories, dreams, visions, and goals inspire me every day to bring you the best and brightest ideas to help you achieve your dreams.

—Lisa Suttora

Introduction

If you are one of the millions of people who is considering selling merchandise online, one of the first questions you'll find yourself asking is "What should I sell?" And right on the heels of that comes the next question: "How do I find my suppliers?" These same questions hold true if you are already selling online, as the challenge of what to sell and how to locate the best suppliers will come up time and time again when expanding your product lines. Product sourcing, the skill of locating merchandise that your customers want to buy and suppliers who will offer you the best inventory opportunities, is a skill that ranks first and foremost in building a successful retail business. Without the right products and the suppliers to provide them, you will not be able to offer your customers the merchandise that they want to buy. And without in-demand merchandise, your business will suffer. Successful product sourcing is not a matter to be taken lightly.

WHY THIS BOOK IS DIFFERENT

This book is the first book entirely devoted to product sourcing for the eBiz owner. It is the first resource of its kind that will take you, step-by-step, through all the aspects of product sourcing, from finding the products that the buyers want, to creative product selection techniques, to determining if you have a potentially successful product on your hands. Additionally, you will learn tips for finding legitimate wholesale suppliers, including an in-depth explanation of how the wholesale industry works and strategies for building long-term product sourcing relationships.

What makes this book different is that the techniques, skills, and strategies that you will learn in this book are *professional* retail product sourcing strategies. These approaches and techniques are time-tested, proven classic retail product sourcing principles—principles that have been used for years by the world's most successful retailers, both online and offline. In fact, no matter what venue you want to build a retail business in, whether it be eBay, your own website, or even a physical brick-and-mortar store in your local area, this book is for you.

In the pages of this book, you will not find the get-rich quick schemes that proliferate in the online selling world. You won't find "shortcuts" that undermine your success, and you won't find promises of wealth building in two hours a day while wearing your pajamas. What you will find are techniques that, when applied, will allow you to build the business of your dreams and achieve success in the online retail world. This book represents years of collective product sourcing experience that will save you time and money in the learning process. Thomas Alva Edison once said, "Opportunity is missed by most because it is dressed in overalls and looks like work." The information in this book, combined with action, will allow you to find the opportunities that await you for a successful retail business.

WHO THIS BOOK IS FOR

This book is designed for the professionally minded seller—the eBiz owner who wants to source products that will enable him or her to build a consistent part-time or full-time income. Whether you are brand new to selling online or you want to take your existing business to the next level, the information in this book will allow you to advance your product sourcing skills to those of an expert. The better you become at product sourcing, the more profitable a business you will build. By learning the correct skills from the beginning, you put yourself and your business in a position to scale, or grow, from a small to mid-size operation to a large establishment if you so desire. If you have the intent to build a profitable online retail business the right way, this book is for you

> **Note:** Product sourcing is a skill that is learned and not one that you need to be born with. Even if you have never sourced products to sell retail before, by following the steps and techniques in this book you will learn how to master this expertise and excel at it.

HOW TO USE THIS BOOK

This book serves two purposes: first, as a source of education and training to provide you with the product sourcing skills you need to build a profitable and sustainable business. Second, use this manual as an ongoing resource to assist you as you move through the different stages of product sourcing for your business. There is a lot of information packed between the covers of this book. Read through it only once and you will find your head swimming with creative ideas, strategies, and plans. Keep it on your desk and use it as a reference manual and it will become your desktop product sourcing companion.

HOW THIS BOOK IS ORGANIZED

This book is organized into two different parts. The first part of the book, Chapters 1–8, focus on product selection. The second part of the book, Chapters 9–16, focus on how to locate and work with suppliers.

In Part I, we'll look at how to find the products that buyers want:

- **Chapter 1: Fundamentals of Product Selection** gives an overview of how to approach the question "What do I sell?" and lays the foundation for anyone who is trying to select products to sell for their retail business. Miss any of these steps and you'll find yourself floundering in your product sourcing endeavors.
- **Chapter 2: The Product Sourcing Mindset** teaches you to approach product sourcing in a way that will leave you in the enviable position of having more ideas for products to sell than time to sell them.
- **Chapter 3: The Product Sourcing Notebook** gives you an invaluable tool that many successful sellers have said they could not have built their business without.
- **Chapter 4: Idea Hotspots** shows you where a wealth of product selection ideas reside. Frequent Idea Hotspots and you will never find yourself wanting for ideas of profitable products to sell.
- **Chapter 5: How to Find and Identify a Niche Market** discusses exactly why finding a niche market to sell in is crucial to the success of your business.
- **Chapter 6: Evaluating Your Product Ideas** shows you how to determine if you have a potentially profitable product idea. And there is more to predicting a product's success than meets the eye.
- **Chapter 7: Creative Product Selection** gives you a variety of creative methods for assembling a product line that will outsell the competition. This chapter will show you how to build a dynamic, unique product line.
- **Chapter 8: Building Your Long-Term Business** explains that it's not just about building a successful business, it's about building a successful business that is sustainable over the long haul. Learn what you must do to run a profitable business long-term.

In Part II, we'll look at how to locate legitimate suppliers for your products:

- **Chapter 9: Getting Legal** explains that most online sellers don't realize that they cannot buy from a genuine wholesale product supplier without a legal business and a sales tax ID. This chapter will teach you why you need to form a legal business, and what steps you can take to do so.

- **Chapter 10: Why Wholesalers Exist, and Why You Should Use Them** explains how product supply is a process that moves through several stages, from manufacturing to wholesaling to retailing. Wholesaler suppliers are a service industry that manufacturers rely on to provide an established distribution network. Sellers need to understand that in the overwhelming majority of cases, they cannot shortcut this process and expect to go directly to a manufacturer.
- **Chapter 11: Middlemen, MLMs and Other Dangerous Things** explains why your product supply chain must be kept as short as possible. Any extra link in that chain that does not provide added value is known as a "middleman," and will seriously affect your profits in selling products online.
- **Chapter 12: How a Real Wholesaler Works** discusses how a factory-authorized wholesale supplier actually works, from an insider's view, allowing you to work with suppliers much more effectively. This chapter deals with how wholesalers become authorized by manufacturers, what their internal profit margins are, why they price their products the way they do, how their different delivery methods work, and more.
- **Chapter 13: Finding Real Wholesalers** points the way to wholesale suppliers for your business. Most Internet sellers believe that they can find genuine wholesale suppliers easily in search engines, through free or inexpensive lists, and more. This is definitely not the case, and this chapter explains why.
- **Chapter 14: Working with Real Wholesalers** shows you how to approach suppliers. Most genuine wholesale suppliers are hesitant to work with small, home-based businesses. The correct approach to these companies can make the difference between being accepted for a retail account, and being turned down.
- **Chapter 15: Other Product Sourcing Methods** discusses alternative product sources, such as importing, overstock purchasing, liquidation buying, etc.
- **Chapter 16: Building Product Sourcing Relationships** explains how to build your first relationship with a real wholesale supplier into a tool that can make it easier to gain new relationships with other suppliers in the future.

Product sourcing is an ongoing process. It is fun, creative, interesting, inspiring, and challenging. It is the fuel of your business. Master these skills and you will be able to repeat your success time and time again as you source new products and select new product lines. So let's get started. You are about to begin an exciting journey into the world of retail product sourcing.

PART I

THE PRODUCT SOURCING MINDSET: DECIDING WHAT TO SELL ONLINE

Chapter 1

Fundamentals of Product Selection

You've probably picked up this book because you are, or aspire to be, one of the millions of eBay sellers making a full- or part-time living online. Or maybe you have a Yahoo store, web site, or an existing brick and mortar storefront. Whatever retail venue you sell in, the question of "What should I sell?" is one you'll find yourself continually asking. In fact, one of the most frequently asked questions at eBay University, on eBay Radio, and on the Entrepreneur Magazine eBiz Radio Show is how to decide what kinds of products to sell and where to find suppliers. The amount of thought given to this question is not without merit. Deciding what to sell and finding the products that buyers want is the cornerstone of your success for one very important reason: your product line is the foundation of your business.

While marketing and customer service are very significant components to the ultimate profitability of your business, it's the products you choose to sell which set the stage for your business' growth. If you want to enhance your sales and increase your profits, you must learn to focus keenly on who your potential customers are, what they want to buy, and then translate that knowledge into selecting your products. Throughout this book, we're going to show you exactly how to do that. Without this knowledge, you can easily end up with shelves of inventory that *you* thought was great, but that the customers didn't want.

As an entrepreneur, you're most likely acting in several capacities for your business. Selecting your product line, selling and marketing your merchandise, even packaging and shipping are all "hats" that you may wear. But the latter three are dependent on the first. It all begins with solid retail product sourcing fundamentals. With the explosion of online retail businesses, there has been a profusion of bad information passed around about how to "make money," "sell hot products," and "find suppliers," all in two minutes with the push of a button. Unfortunately, many people take these tales of lore to heart, believing they will make them rich and teach them how to build a business. The reality of it is, if you want to build a *consistent* full-time or part-time income from a retail operation, you can't circumvent the fundamentals of product sourcing. Skipping over the groundwork only leads to a loss of time, money, and the potential for success. However, if you lay down your foundation properly, by learning how to choose the products that today's consumers want to buy, you will have a consistent edge on the competition. By the time you're through reading this book, you'll have a solid working knowledge of professional product and supplier sourcing. You'll know how to use the same strategies for product selection and supplier location that merchandise buyers for stores such as Nordstrom use. These same industry-insider strategies are also employed by those who purchase product lines for exclusive boutiques or the eclectic, wildly successful shop down the street.

Selecting products in order to build a successful store is not a matter of luck or guessing, but rather the use of a systematic technique to generate ideas for products to sell, and locating suppliers for those items. Whether you are a home-based business or have multiple warehouses, your product sourcing strategies will be based on the same intrinsic principles. Product sourcing is a skill that you will use over and over again in your capacity as a retail business owner. It's the very lifeblood of your organization. Whether you sell on eBay, have your own web site, or reach your customers through any number of popular online shopping venues, such as Yahoo or Overstock Auctions, developing your product sourcing skills will help you make wise choices, tap into the vast pool of products that buyers are looking for, and show you how not to just look for "a product to sell," but how to build a business as well.

Deciding what to sell and finding the products that buyers want is the cornerstone of your retail success for one very important reason: your product line is the foundation of your business.

Effective Product Sourcing—No Experience Necessary!

Product sourcing is a skill that anyone can learn. No matter what level of sales you've achieved, by applying the principles in this book, you will master the product sourcing techniques required to grow your business and increase your revenue. You do not need to be a born trendsetter, trend watcher, or even an avid shopper to learn to effectively source products. Some of the greatest retail businesses in the history of our country were started by people who at first new nothing about selecting products.

John W. Nordstrom left his home country of Sweden at 16 years old. He arrived in New York unable to speak a word of English and with only $5 in his pocket. After several years of laboring in the mining and logging camps, and then doing equally backbreaking work in the Klondike, John decided to go into business with a friend who owned a shoe repair shop. In 1901, the two opened their first shoe store in downtown Seattle. This was the start of what would become the retail legend, Nordstrom, Inc. Nordstrom's success was built by catering to the customer's needs, finding out what the buyers wanted. Product selection, in addition to value and service, was paramount in the growth of this mega-successful business. John Nordstrom's recipe for success is one that should be adopted by *all* retailers and is guaranteed to ensure *your* success. His philosophy was pure and simple: "If business isn't good, it's because you're not servicing right, or you don't have what the customer wants." It was this approach to retail that successfully launched the shoe store in 1901 and is the same philosophy that has built the business into one of today's premier retailers.

The Nordstrom approach to product selection has been equally as simple and successful. Focus on a niche and serve it well. John Nordstrom and his partner Carl Wallin believed that the best service you can give a customer is selling a quality product. From the very first shoes and boots they selected to launch the store, their eye was always on quality, locating merchandise that not everyone else was selling, and keeping very closely tuned to what the customer wanted. John Nordstrom also stayed very focused on building the store around a niche, and becoming the best retailer in that category. And where better to glean this information than by talking to the customers themselves. This laser-like attention to his business and his customer base gave him the information he needed about his buyers to even further build upon his success.

It wasn't until the 1960s that Nordstrom branched out into other product lines when the company bought Best Apparel. And even within their product line expansion, Nordstrom still remained focused on their new niche, providing the finest apparel, shoes, and accessories for the entire family. They are able to do this very successfully, not by offering people "merchandise," but by creating fashion departments that fit individuals' lifestyles.

While you may not have aspirations to be the next Nordstrom, this story is important because it illustrates several things. Retail success is not dependent on being born with a propensity for product selection, but rather on learning how to listen to your customer and respond by providing them with products that they want. When you focus on a niche market, you have the ability to better service that market. And finally, true retail success is not based on fad approaches. It is dependent on learning and implementing the classic and time-tested elements of product sourcing and customer service.

The Importance of Good Product Sourcing

No one goes into the process of product sourcing and inventory acquisition with the goal of ending up with a spare bedroom, garage, or warehouse of products that won't sell. But without good product sourcing skills, this is exactly what can happen. Whenever we get a call from a seller who has shelves of inventory that aren't moving, we usually find that something was amiss with their original product sourcing techniques. Oftentimes, hobbies, interests, personal biases, even the ease of locating inventory play into a seller's choice of product lines. Unfortunately, these preferences do not always reward the seller with what they want most: a profitable retail business.

Successful retailing can be summed up in one simple, but very powerful statement. *You must sell what sells.* While this sounds like an obvious statement, as you will see later in this chapter, it's very easy to get caught up in choosing products that don't have much of a chance of selling. In Chapter 1, we'll outline the fundamentals of good product sourcing and shatter the myths. We'll show you the principles of sourcing and the pitfalls to avoid. It pays to know these things. Literally. With good product sourcing, you'll be able to achieve higher sell-through rates on your products. A sell-through rate is the number of items you offer for sale versus the number of items sold. For example, if you have 100 products for sale and 50 of them sell, your inventory has a 50 percent sell-through rate. Your sell-through rate directly impacts your revenue. If things are selling well, you're usually making money. If things are not selling, most likely the profits are dismal. In-demand products will sell faster and for a higher profit margin. Slow sellers will languish in sales and tie up valuable inventory capital.

Some marketers will tell you that it doesn't matter what you sell—as long as you have good marketing. While it's true that an extremely savvy marketer probably could sell snow in Alaska, why go to all that trouble? There are millions of buyers out there, hungry to purchase the millions of products available for sale. Your job is to connect those buyers to products. Our job is to make your job easier. This book is designed to show you how to make the connection between the vast array of products to sell and the shoppers who will be happy to buy them from you! And it all starts with knowing what your buyers want.

How Can I Know What My Buyers Want?

A crystal ball? The psychic retailer's hotline? Luckily, none of these are required in order to learn what your customers want to buy. However, having an understanding of *why* people buy, and learning what's important to them, *is required* to create a successful retail business. When you first had thoughts of running a retail business, you may not have considered becoming an expert in the study of human nature. However, determining the market for goods or services is vital for an entrepreneur. No matter how good you think your idea is, if the customers don't want it, you won't sell it. Yet there are always other items, which you may consider ridiculous, that can lead to success. In the next chapter, we'll show you a very powerful strategy called the Product Sourcing Mindset. This approach to product sourcing will put you directly on the path to spot those products that consumers are clamoring for. Also, as you're about to see, understanding what is going on in the minds of your buyers is where all product sourcing starts.

Why People Buy

Before being able to identify what buyers want, you must first have a basic understanding of why people buy. People buy things for two reasons: to fulfill a want or a need. A customer may *need* a pair of shoes to cover their feet, but they *want* a pair of Nikes. Your child *needs* a toothbrush to clean their teeth, but they *want* the SpongeBob light-up spinning singing toothbrush to make the process all the more fun. When a customer buys from you, they are not simply purchasing an item. Most of their purchases have an underlying motivation, oftentimes a subconscious one. Products and services are usually purchased to either solve a problem, or bring pleasure to the buyer.

Consumers buy things to relieve stress, provide entertainment, save time and money, have fun, provide security, or improve the quality of their lives.

Recent studies show that in 2005 consumers are also buying experiences. No longer do they want to go to a plain old store to shop for running shoes; they want to purchase from a store that provides them with the experience of feeling like an in-shape (or soon to be in-shape), health-conscious, fitness-minded athlete. When a customer walks into REI, they instantly feel that they are part of the fitness lifestyle. Whether you're there to buy shoes for a triathlon, a canoe for a trip down the river, or skis to slalom down the snowy slopes, the moment you walk through those doors you just feel in better shape. Beautiful pictures of healthy outdoorsy people "just like you" are strategically placed throughout the store. You not only buy the products, you absorb the experience. When you look at the products you may sell as a vehicle to solve a customer's problem, bring them pleasure, or provide them with the experience they desire, you start to see potential inventory in a different light. How can your merchandise fulfill your buyer's fundamental desires? These all-important questions must be considered when building a product line. The answers will provide a framework for your sourcing decisions.

A hundred years ago, a typical consumer spent most of their money on fulfilling their needs and those of their family. It was only after all their basic needs for food, clothing, and housing were met that leftover money was spent on buying the things they wanted. Fast forward to now to witness the big change that's taken place. Percentage-wise, people are now spending more of their money on discretionary items. Such purchases are motivated by desire and emotion. It's because of this that understanding the way people think and feel about things will directly impact the products you choose to sell.

Let's look at the example of *Star Wars*. Millions of people love *Star Wars*. With each new movie that's released, millions and millions of dollars are spent on *Star Wars*–related products. Everything from toys to clothes to *Star Wars*–branded bags of M&Ms fly off the shelves as soon as they're available. Does anyone really need a bag of M&Ms with a picture of Darth Vader on it? No, but they want it. Why? Because people are passionate about *Star Wars*. In many cases, they will pay almost anything to get their favorite *Star Wars* item. Understanding that this is how millions of people *feel* about *Star Wars* will tell you why these products are in demand. Without the emotions of millions of buyers behind it, a Luke Skywalker bank would be just another container in which to toss your change.

It used to be in our society that products that catered to the wants of consumers were distinctly different than those designed to supply their needs. These days, the line is often blurred. Manufacturers now realize that the best way to sell a product that a person needs in order to live their life is to blend it with something they want. An alarm clock is a functional item and is very useful in helping you get up for work on time. A golf-themed alarm clock is also functional, but if you're an avid golfer, your "golf" alarm clock reminds you of your favorite hobby every day. It brings pleasure into your life. Given the choice between buying an item that is strictly functional and one that is practical but also brings pleasure, the consumer will choose the latter the majority of the time. If you understand what people want and desire to have in their lives, you'll be able to source the products that people are willing to spend money on time and time again.

What People Buy

In order to know what your buyers want, you must put yourself in the world in which your buyers live. Learn their buying habits. Become a student of what is going on in society. Watch for changes in trends, lifestyles, and demographics. In the next chapter, we'll show you a strategy that will allow you to do just that, *and* integrate this process into your daily activities.

Tracking the trends, needs, and desires of people for the purpose of selling products is nothing new. Even the first successful traveling merchants used this technique to source their products. These itinerant shopkeepers who, beginning in the early 1800s, migrated from town to town with a variety of goods, such as pots and pans, and the finest cloths, had learned to identify and tap into a societal trend, emerging market, or basic human need in order to successfully sell their wares.

Don't fool yourself into thinking that you can pick any random product and then do the hard sell to a consumer who has no interest in it. It generally won't work and unfortunately too many retailers make this mistake. Selling into a completely cold market rarely meets with success. But wait you say! New products are introduced to the marketplace every day. They can become a huge success. Were these products not introduced into a cold marketplace?

While it's true that new products are launched daily, they are not launched in a vacuum. The companies who create new products and services only do so (in the majority of cases) after researching the market they are entering into, finding a spark of interest, or capitalizing on a logical "next step" in the needs and wants of the consumers. In some cases, an opportunity to fuse two trends together and morph them into a new one can make a product rise to meteoric success.

Many years ago, it was only doctors and other on-call professionals who carried pagers. However, companies began recognizing the need for non-professionals to keep in touch with each other and began marketing pagers to the person next door. Suddenly, moms, dads, teens, and 'tweens were all carrying pagers. Pagers became a retail phenomenon. How did this happen? Did a company executive wake up one morning and say, "I think we'll start marketing pagers to moms and kids"? No. What they did do was look at the increasingly busy lifestyles that families were leading, *and* at the growing interest parents had in knowing the whereabouts of their children at all times. The need for this peace of mind and the desire to keep connected to their kids made parents realize that they both *needed* and *wanted* a pager for each member of their family.

The retailers who tapped into this trend early on also understood the trends behind these products. While other sellers looked at pagers as foreign objects and doubted if anyone would ever spend their money on one, those retailers who were looking at changes in trends were starting to see pieces of the puzzle emerge. The merchants who were students of society started to put together the parts of an equation that went something like this. Need (peace of mind) + Desire (stay connected) + Product (pager) = Sales. And lots of them!

Dissect the evolution of any hot-selling product and you'll find buyer emotion and desire involved. In other words, new products and services are designed to fulfill a very specific buyer wish. Conversely, if we evaluate new products that aren't selling well, you'll often find that no one ever stopped to figure out what the customers wanted to buy. In the following chapters, you'll learn how to educate yourself about your customers' buying habits. But first, let's get started cementing the foundation of your business by looking at the time-tested fundamentals for successfully choosing your inventory. Your methods for choosing the products that buyers want will be no different than those of the pioneer sellers. Yes, technology has changed, products have changed, and the vehicles you'll use to source them have changed, but the basic premise remains the same. And it's these same strategies that have made many retailers very, very successful.

People buy things for two reasons: to fulfill a **want** *or a* **need.** *If you understand what is in the hearts and minds of the consumer, you will be able to source the products that they are willing to spend money on.*

Tip: To immerse yourself in the world of your buyers:

- Learn consumers' buying habits
- Watch for changes in trends, lifestyles, and demographics
- Educate yourself about consumers' wants and needs—it will lead you directly to the kinds of products they will buy

Myths and Fundamentals of Good Product Selection

Good product selection is a combination of creativity, observation, research, and documentation. The more creative and open you are to the millions of products out there available to be marketed, the more likely you are to find the one that is going to fuel your business and send your sales skyrocketing. As you'll see later in this chapter, our Five-Step Product Selection System incorporates all of these.

Selecting products should not be thought of as a finite, one-time goal, but rather an ongoing process that you'll participate in over and over again through the life of your business. If you operate an online business, the following myths and fundamentals apply to you. If you've set up shop with a local storefront, they apply all the same. You wouldn't build your home on anything less than a solid foundation, and you should approach your business the same way. The following myths and fundamentals will set the framework for what you learn in this book. All the strategies and concepts in the next 12 chapters relate back to this core list. Our intent is that after you read through this book, you'll refer back to it time and time again as a useful reference. So let's get started exposing the myths of product sourcing and exploring the successful fundamentals which have stood the test of time.

Product Sourcing Myth #1: It's a One-Shot Deal (or Putting All Your Eggs into One Basket)

Oftentimes, a seller finds a hot product, strikes gold, and stops looking for their next success story. However, six months later, sales of that product have peaked and they have no new product lines staked out. Frequently, a new seller will start out thinking that once they identify a few good products, they can put product sourcing on the back burner. This belief is a business crusher. Having a consistent flow of new product ideas is critical to your success, because a profitable product can have either a long-term run or a very short-lived one. Often, you won't be able to predict the length of time a product will remain a strong seller, since there are many factors that can affect how long you can profitably sell an item. These include market demand, competition from other sellers, or newly released product versions that drive down demand for existing versions. Becoming complacent with your inventory leaves your sales vulnerable. If you're not consistently adding to your product line, looking for new products, and poised to enhance your existing product offerings, your business can stagnate and your profits will stall.

Product Sourcing Fundamental #1: You Must Always Be Looking

Frequently, sellers will wonder how another seller tapped into an emerging market so fast. The answer to that question is: because they were looking. In fact, most successful sellers always have at least three or more product ideas or product lines in the pipeline. When you're constantly on the lookout for new product ideas, trends, and changes in societal habits and preferences, your radar will start to pick up hundreds of different product selling possibilities daily. Information that one seller will miss because they are not constantly keeping their eyes open is the same information that another seller will see as an opportunity, pick it up and run with it … and make a fortune. Identifying which products you will offer to your customers is an ongoing journey—a journey that you undertake the day you make the decision to sell online or off. Throughout that journey you will see some great product ideas, some real duds, and everything in between.

Make selecting your products a part of your daily activities. If you're a solo entrepreneur, it's very easy to get caught up in the day-to-day operations of running your business and neglect the most important of tasks that will help you grow your enterprise. Fortunately, when done right, good product selection does not require a lot of time in your day. In Chapter 2, we'll show you a method which will enable you to easily and effortlessly always be looking.

Product Sourcing Myth #2: You Can Select Products in a Vacuum

A lot of people think that profitable sellers have a certain knack for just sitting down and coming up with product ideas. Many new online sellers have told us that they have been concerned because after a few hours of concentrating on the question of "what to sell," ideas just haven't materialized for them. Laboring under this misconception will only lead you to frustration. While there are sellers who have seemingly "fallen into" a profitable product line and there are those rare few who can sense an upcoming trend before the rest of the world does, most online sellers do not come upon their profit-generating product lines that easily. Successful retailers have achieved their sales performance through a process of trial and error. In Chapter 2, we'll show you the difference between sellers who turn their radar outward versus those who limit their vision.

Product Sourcing Fundamental #2: Live in the World in Which Your Buyers Live

As a retailer, you only need to look around to see who your customers are. It's when you open your eyes and ears and begin listening to your customers that they'll begin telling you exactly what they want to buy. You can learn what your customers want to buy in many places. In Chapter 4, we'll show you a variety of different Idea Hotspots where you can learn specifically what they're looking for. Tune into the world around you. Find out what people want in life and what people are spending their money on. In Chapter 2, you'll find out how easy and natural this is to do. You'll also see that the information you need to learn about what buyers want is right at your fingertips. An easy way to get started with this is to think back to the last several conversations you've had with friends, family, neighbors, and co-workers. Make a list of all the products, interests, and hobbies you discussed. From that list, what topics stand out in your mind as potential inventory? Hang on to that list, because in Chapter 6 we're going to show you how to evaluate those ideas!

A Dinner with Friends Spawns Profitable Product Ideas

One of the best-selling products that Lisa ever sold, came out of an idea she got at a dinner party with friends. A group of her friends were enjoying a tasty dinner when one husband mentioned that he was in the market for a particular bread machine as a birthday gift for his wife. All of a sudden there were four other people at the table talking about how they wanted that particular bread machine. The conversation branched off into other small kitchen appliances that were on the top of the list of the group, but Lisa forgot her meal temporarily, busily taking notes in her Product Sourcing Notebook about what she'd just heard.

Arriving home later that night, she spent several hours online research-ing the profit potential of some of the products her friends had dis-cussed. By Monday she had a list of five products with excellent selling potential—two that came directly out of the dinner conversation and three others that were offshoots of ideas they had talked about at din-ner. Had she not adhered to the principle that you live in the same world in which your buyers live, she wouldn't have recognized that a table full of friends who all wanted to buy the same product was a huge indicator of a product with profit potential. That's why sometimes all it takes is for you to look around you to see product-selling opportunities.

Product Sourcing Myth #3: Sell What You Love

Quite often, people are advised to sell what they love. And while some may find that their hobbies and passions spawn marketable products, selling what you love will only be profitable if there is a market demand for your product or a niche market. Determining whether or not your favorite hobby has associated products that are in demand by a hungry target market can be a great place to start. By doing the research as outlined in Chapter 6, you'll be able to make this assessment based on facts rather than emotions. If you love a product AND it sells, you have a great combination! Where you run into trouble is when you continue selling a product that you love, but that no one else does. If this is the case, move on quickly to the next opportunity.

Product Sourcing Fundamental #3: Sell What Sells

There must be market demand for your product. While "selling what sells" may seem like simplistic advice, it is one of the most critically important factors in choosing your products. Frequently, we see sellers struggling with a particular product or service. They're frustrated because their product isn't selling the way they hoped it would. After a quick check of their marketing and advertising practices, it's easy to see what the problem is—there isn't enough market demand for the product. At first glance, it seems like an easy problem to fix—don't sell that particular product. But problems arise when people are personally invested in selling a product for which there is no market demand. Keep in mind, no matter how much you like a product or think it has profit potential, you'll never be able to make any money unless you sell what sells.

Product Sourcing Myth #4: If You Don't Like It, No One Else Will

Right up there with selling what you love, having a personal interest in your product line can be one of the most limiting factors in your business. It is human nature for people to gravitate to selling products they like, allowing personal preferences to influence what you think people will buy. Unfortunately, this method of product sourcing will often lead you down the wrong path. Annie, an aspiring eBay Gold PowerSeller, struggled with this concept early on in building her business. "Every time I would source a product based on what I liked, I picked an item that wouldn't make any money," says Annie. "It got to the point where I started purposely considering potential products that I didn't like," she laughs. "As it turned out, many of *those* products *were* the ones that ended up being the real profit makers. Now that I have a considerable amount of product sourcing under my belt, I have the experience to choose products from both realms." Often, when we talk to sellers who are unable to find the right products to sell, it's because they're filtering their ideas for potential products based on what they like or don't like. When you can look past your personal preferences, you can begin to truly source the products that will sell to a wide variety of people.

Product Sourcing Fundamental #4: Value Is in the Eye of the Beholder

People will spend money on all sorts of things. When you judge a product based solely on whether or not *you* would part with your hard-earned money, you're guaranteed to pass over products that could be wildly profitable. Judging a product's potential should be based on objective research rather than personal preference. In his book *Bad Fads*, Mark Long looks at some of the most popular trends from the past 100 years. One only needs to think of the Chia Pet or Pet Rocks to understand how a product that you may not have a personal interest in can make big money. In Chapters 2 and 3, we'll show you a strategy you can use to look past that natural filter of personal preference and learn how to see every product you come across as a potential top seller online. When you practice your product sourcing strategies with an eye turned towards objectivity, you're able to expand the breadth of the products you would be interested in selling as well as tap into niche markets that you might otherwise ignore.

Product Sourcing Myth #5: Pick a Product and Hope It's a Hit

One of the worst approaches to product sourcing is to pick a product and then try and figure out who to sell it to. Unfortunately, this is a mistake that many newbies or even advanced sellers tend to make. This approach is practically guaranteed to leave you wondering "Why won't my products sell?" It's also the reason that, for some people, the word "sales" leaves a bad taste in their mouth. Ultimately, you cannot build a business by making people buy a product they don't want. While they may buy from you once, they will not be back for more. And picking a product to sell without having any understanding of who you're selling it to, and whether or not they want it, is a sure-fire way to end up with inventory you can't sell. Getting close to your potential customers, talking to them, and finding out what your target market wants makes your job of product sourcing much easier. Now, instead of trying to sell them a product they don't want, you're doing them a service by giving them exactly what they do want.

Product Sourcing Fundamental #5: Understand Your Target Market

To grow a product line into a consistent stream of revenue, you must understand who your target market is. Who are you selling to? What do they like? What do they spend money on? What related items might they want to buy—both today and tomorrow? Educating yourself on who will purchase your products is akin to giving yourself a window into the wallets of your buyers.

There are groups of buyers who are very willing to spend money *and* will spend more of it than other groups. As we discussed in the beginning of the chapter, people buy for two reasons: to fulfill a want or a need. When you start looking at all your potential products in that light, you begin to get a deeper understanding of whether or not your product has real profit potential. In general, buyers who are passionate about a hobby, product, or service are willing to spend money over and over again. We've all seen the golf enthusiasts, vintage car fanatics, or art aficionados who are willing to spend large amounts of money on a regular basis in order to own the items they love. However, buyers who purchase consumer goods are no exception to this rule—for example, pet lovers, parents who want the best products for their children, and health and fitness buffs who take their pursuit of a healthy lifestyle very seriously are all examples of consumers who are constantly on the lookout for new products to buy and who will become repeat buyers.

In looking for the products that buyers want, make sure that those buyers are also ready to spend their money and make a purchase. Chapter 6 of this book will give you strategies on how to discover key information for understanding your target market. Becoming well versed in this information will assist you in making smart inventory sourcing decisions. Additionally, knowing who your customers are will give you the ability to tailor your marketing efforts towards their interests and to expand your business to include more of the products that buyers want.

Educating yourself on who will purchase your products is akin to giving yourself a window into the wallets of your buyers.

Product Sourcing Myth #6: Sell What You Know

Many successful retailers started out selling products that they knew nothing about. When they first considered selling these items, they knew enough to have an understanding of how the product worked. Once they realized they had identified a profitable product line, *then* they began to get the education needed to become an expert in their niche. Janelle Elms, a lead instructor for eBay University, says, "You don't need to know anything about what you're selling initially, you just need to know how to sell it."

You can always find enough information about a potential product in order to start marketing it. Let's say, for example, you want to sell outdoor equipment, but you're a city girl through and through. First you can get some basic education on the niche market—you need to know enough about it to identify whether or not there is a demand for the products, and at what base costs you'll need to purchase your inventory. Additionally you'll want to investigate what styles and brands of products will sell.

Once you have that basic knowledge, you have enough information to source your products and do some sales tests to determine if this is a product line you would like to sell long term. There is a whole world out there filled with merchandise that sells like hotcakes. If you come across a product idea in an area that you know nothing about, don't rule it out as a possibility. Expand your horizons and you'll be amazed at the opportunities that await you!

Product Sourcing Fundamental #6: Learn About What You Sell

Once you've decided on a particular product to sell, it's now up to you to educate yourself on the product and product line. The most successful sellers are the ones who know their products inside and out. They know what version of the product is current, what new models or styles are under development, and what direction the product line is going in. This knowledge gives them the seller's advantage. And while you *can* sell an item successfully without knowing a thing about it, sooner or later that lack of knowledge will catch up with you. When customers ask you questions, want further information, or are looking for additional complementary products, it's up to you to provide those answers for them. Consider the difference between shopping in a store where the sales people have not been trained in anything more than how to ring up an item, versus shopping at a store like Nordstrom where the sales staff knows their product line inside and out and can provide you with relevant product information to help you make your purchase. Make it your business to know your business—it all starts with learning about the products you sell.

Product Sourcing Myth #7: One Size Fits All

A profitable product line is made up of an assortment of products selected for different reasons. Holding every product you consider selling up to the same standard for its profit margin, base cost, and sell-through rate (the percentage of products you sell) will skew your product sourcing decisions. Often, we're asked what profit margin one should look for when selecting inventory. Or whether or not a sell-through rate of "*x* percent" is an appropriate sales success rate. The answer is always: it depends. It depends on the specific product you're considering selling and how it fits into your product line. In Chapter 6, we'll show you a variety of different criteria you can use to select your products, which will clearly demonstrate why one size does not fit all.

Product Sourcing Fundamental #7: Select Your Products Based on Varied Criteria

When choosing products to sell, you'll use different criteria to select the products with which you'll build your inventory. You'll select some products because they'll be your "meat and potatoes" products. These items will be the staples of your business. Other merchandise will be chosen as cross-sell or up-sell products. And some goods will be necessary to stock only because they round out your product line. If you're an eBay seller, you may choose an item simply because its name contains highly searchable keywords that will bring traffic to your eBay store.

Some products will be long-term sellers, and as we talked about earlier, others you'll select only to make a short-term profit. These could be seasonal items, or merchandise that cashes in on a hot, but short-lived trend. In Chapter 6, we'll talk about the different criteria you can use to build a well-rounded product line, and in Chapter 7 we'll look at ways to be creative in your product selection.

Product Sourcing Myth #8: All the Good Products Are Already Taken

What first comes to mind when you think of a "good" product to sell online? Do you think first of mainstream, name-brand products? Do brands like Sony, Dell, or Ralph Lauren come to mind? Or maybe in-demand, glamorous lines like Prada or Rolex? Are people making good money online selling these kinds of products? Absolutely! But are well-known, famous-name items the only goods to sell online? Absolutely not! Let's look at the definition of a "good" product. A good product is one that there is a demand for and that people are willing to spend money on. It doesn't have to be a mainstream product, it doesn't have to be a name-brand product, and it doesn't even have to be a "hot" product (at least one you'll find on a product top ten list anywhere). In fact some of the best products to sell are those that are NOT commonplace, but which have a small and passionate following, who will spend ANY amount of money on their area of interest. In Chapter 5, we will explore how to find those niches with ravenous buyers, who are awaiting your latest merchandise offering.

Product Sourcing Fundamental #8: There Are Millions of Products to Sell

For every hot product being sold online right now, there are several more right behind them ready to take their place. New hobbies, interests, and niches emerge every day. As society changes, what we want to buy constantly changes and shifts. You can sell new products, revivals of old products, adaptations and upgrades to existing products, products that were "out" and are now coming back "in," new brands, styles, and versions of existing top sellers. Plus, for every oversaturated market online or off, there are just as many underserved markets waiting for sellers like you to come in and supply consumers with merchandise.

While selecting products to sell in a market that already has some existing activity is a good idea, selecting products and trying to break into a saturated market is a difficult road to travel. Unless you market your popular product in a different way, by providing added value to the product, or obtain your inventory at a much lower cost than your competitors, you're entering an arena where you'll be forced to go head-to-head with your competition and that usually results in one thing—price wars and prices spiraling down. When you go through this book, you'll constantly be learning new ways to find untapped fertile selling grounds. Don't follow the crowd—take a right, a left, a step forward or back, veer off the beaten path, and you'll be able to build your own market share in a niche, rather than competing with the rest for the same piece of the pie.

Product Sourcing Myth #9: Ready, Aim, Select

Start with the wrong expectations when selecting your products and you're sure to end up frustrated. If you've geared up to start your product search and don't find what you're looking for on the first, second, or third try, you may start to get the impression that there aren't any products out there that are right for your business. However, the reality of it is, you're very unlikely to find the right products the first time out. In fact, sometimes it can take a year or two to locate the products required to complete a solid product line. Expecting that you'll get it right the first time out of the gate not only puts undue pressure on you, it also sets up unrealistic expectations of what it takes to succeed.

Product Sourcing Fundamental #9: Product Sourcing Is a Numbers Game

So often, we see people with their mind set on selling one particular product. And if for some reason the idea for that particular product doesn't pan out, they find themselves at a loss for another idea. On average, you'll evaluate 30 products for every one product you decide to sell. Product sourcing, as with many things in life, is a numbers game. If you want a lot of great products to sell, you need to look at a lot of merchandise. Without this expectation, it's easy to get discouraged, if after researching four or five items, you haven't identified a profitable product. While this may seem like a lot of work, the good news is that with the strategies you'll learn in this book, you'll be able to quickly and easily identify, assemble, and sort out the products that have selling potential and those that don't. The more ideas you consider and the more product lines you look at, the more likely it is you'll find a product or a niche that will build a strong business.

Product Sourcing Myth #10: The Product's Not Selling? Keep on Trying

Are you married to your product line? So committed that you don't want to move away from it, even when your sales reports are telling you otherwise? Ask any long-term successful retailer about the key to their success and they will tell you that they have sustained their business growth by adapting the business to include what is in demand *now*. Expecting to remain profitable solely on the sales of a product line selected a year or more ago is a belief that will put your revenue stream in a dubious position. It all comes down to the law of supply and demand.

If the items you sell have never achieved a point of strong demand despite varied attempts at advertising and marketing, it's time to let go of that product line and move on. With so many products available to sell, continued commitment to a product that is not a money maker is not a good business decision. If your product has enjoyed financial success but interest in it is waning and all attempts to revive sales have failed, most likely your product has moved to the end of the product life cycle. Maybe supply is bountiful and demand is low. Or the product has just fallen out of fashion. If this is the case, proceed with selling the remainder of your inventory, at cost or at a loss, and free up your capital, your shelf space, and your mind and then go on to the next product opportunity.

If you're an online merchant, you have the advantage of being able to adapt to market changes quickly. If a product isn't selling well and you have two or three product ideas in the pipeline, with some potential suppliers identified you're positioned to order new inventory and introduce new merchandise to replace the nonperforming products. Ultimately, you may have the best marketing for a product and the best pricing. But if no one is buying that product, for the sake of your business you must withdraw your energies from selling that item and concentrate on better products.

Product Sourcing Fundamental #10: Abide by the Law of Supply and Demand

The law of supply and demand has been around for as long as man has been trading goods. When demand outpaces supply, prices go up. When supply outstrips demand, prices go down. In an oversupplied market, competition is tough and price wars ensue. Thus, it's much easier to sell a product successfully if you're not trying to break into an already saturated market.

Sound like an obvious thing? Well, it is until you look at the vast numbers of sellers who are ready to jump on the bandwagon of retailing an already wildly successful product. Consumer electronics is a great example. Many people want to start out, or branch out into, selling consumer electronics. True, they are glamorous to sell and there is a high demand for them. The problem lies in the supply and demand of these products. Online and offline, the marketplace is overflowing with consumer electronics. This presents some significant problems for a business person just starting out. Unless you have a huge credit line and the ability to buy electronics in bulk, in most cases you won't be able to obtain your inventory at a low enough base cost that you can make a profit. Additionally, you'll need to go head to head with other established sellers to make a dent in their market share. These obstacles are great, especially for the inexperienced seller. The law of supply and demand will prevail, however. The only way in is to offer a unique spin on your product or have a supply chain where you can source your inventory competitively. If you do have a special supplier, a value-added service, or any other special slant you can put on your electronics product (we'll talk about how to accomplish this in Chapter 7), then you have an opportunity to break into an overstocked market. But this tactic should be the exception, not the rule.

The opposite to oversupply in a saturated market is under-demand in a low-supply market. These are markets with little demand and few sellers. While you might think that selling in a product category that has NO competition would be the answer, this is not always the case. While you can cultivate sales in a brand new market, it's a hard sell if there is no pre-existing demand. Educating consumers on a product or service they have never heard of can be done, but it will take more time to become profitable. The best way to navigate the law of supply and demand for the majority of your products is to sell in a niche that has *some* interest or a growing interest. This way you're not the first to sell in an undiscovered, low-demand market, or the last to sell in one that is highly overexposed.

Product Sourcing Myth #11: There Is One Central Place You Can Go for Product Ideas

Have you ever wished there was one central place, one definitive source you could go to that would tell you *exactly* what to sell online? While we have all probably had that wish at one time or another in the course of our online careers, the truth is that even if such a product selection utopia did exist, it would not bode well for the online seller. Why? Because everyone would flock there in search of their product selection answers and the result would be a tremendous amount of competition for selling the same products.

While product hot lists, top ten lists, niche lists, and trend lists are all important tools in your seller's toolkit, none of these should be the definitive one-stop shop for product ideas. Can you get ideas from these kinds of places?

Absolutely! Should you stop there? Not at all! The reality of it is that there are as many ways to come up with product ideas as there are products available. And in Chapter 2, we'll tell you how to become a product sourcing detective and ferret out the ideas that other sellers don't dig for.

Ultimately, the more creative you can be, the more places you look, the more "out of the box" that you think, the less likely it is that you'll find someone else who has come up with the same product idea you have. In Chapter 4, we'll discuss a variety of different resources or Idea Hotspots that you can use to discover ideas for merchandise to carry. Give yourself the challenge of looking everywhere for potential product ideas. You'll see that some of your best inspirations come from the most unlikely places.

Product Sourcing Fundamental #11: Good Product Sourcing Is Not a Linear Process

Good product sourcing skills involve putting together the pieces of a puzzle to form a complete picture. Very rarely will you start at point A and stop at point B with a profitable product. A newspaper headline, fleeting thought, or story on the radio may spark an idea. What you do next with that information is where true product sourcing comes in. Most people will stop there. A thought come and gone, but not acted on. A true product sourcing pro will pay attention to that information, even if at the time it doesn't make much sense. The next step is where the magic happens. You start to relate morsels of information to one another. The newspaper headline about a new trend is affirmed by a human interest story in the local news. Then you start to hear some buzz about the same topic. Your puzzle is starting to take shape. Before you know it, what started as a seed of an idea has rounded out into a full-blown product-selling plan. In Chapter 2, we'll show you how to make those connections. How to associate the information from one product or product line and let the process trigger completely new ideas. With product sourcing, often the first product you evaluate isn't the one you end up choosing to sell.

Product Sourcing Myth #12: Product Sourcing Is a Piece of Cake

Assembling your product line is a very fun, creative, interesting task. But it isn't a sit back and take it easy, no-brainer thing to do. Finding products to sell online takes research, patience, thought, and effort. It's a business skill that must be learned. It doesn't matter if you're venturing into the world of retail, opening a computer-related business, or starting a construction company—you need to master the techniques that will allow you to become prosperous in your chosen field.

Whether you're a beginner or an established merchant, there's much to be gained from learning and practicing the product selection strategies in this book. If profitable product selection were as simple as 1-2-3, everyone would be able to do it without any training. The fact that you're reading this book shows that you have the desire and determination to learn how to do things right. Your dedication to educating yourself about product selection and putting into place the right techniques on a regular basis is what will allow you to become a master at this very important process in your business. And in this line of work, mastery equals profitability and a sustainable business.

Product Sourcing Fundamental #12: Successful Product Sourcing Requires Research, Research, Research

Online research, offline research—it's all a part of product selection. To locate the products that buyers want, you must do your research. Facts, not opinions, will confirm a product's profit potential. Researching involves using specific software tools to identify sell-through rates, average selling prices, the number of competitors, and marketing strategies. Without research, you're selecting your inventory in the dark. In Chapter 6, we'll look at exactly how to do this kind of research.

Research is often one of the most overlooked and underrated tasks as viewed by the online seller. There's no escaping that it requires time and the ability to analyze data. If you find you can't—or don't want to—spend the time to research what's selling in your target market, rather than skip this important process, find someone whom you can hire to assist you or do the work for you. However you accomplish it, don't skip this critical step.

Judging a product's potential should be based on objective research rather than personal preference.

Product Sourcing Myth #13: No Product Is an Island unto Itself

Do your products work together? When you select inventory, do you *only* evaluate each potential product individually or do you assess your merchandise as part of a larger product-sourcing picture? When determining how to spend your inventory capital, it's important to be aware of the fact that every product you choose to buy is a building block for your business. All your products tie together to form a branding—a presence that represents your organization in the minds of the consumer. Because of this, a product should not only be considered according to its own merit, but also be assessed in how it fits in with the other products that you carry, or plan to carry, in your store.

Product Sourcing Fundamental #13: See the Big Picture

When selecting products to sell, it's critical to look at how they fit into the big picture of your business. Is the merchandise you choose congruent with your long-term goals? On its own, a product might not seem like a wise sourcing choice. But when considered as a part of a larger selection of items, making the inventory purchase may make perfect sense. Jennifer, who owns a small online boutique, carries a wide variety of accessories to go with her unique, custom-designed clothing. While the accessories in general carry less of a profit margin, they are instrumental in helping customers visualize the "total look" they can achieve when purchasing one of Jennifer's hand-designed garments. This fact alone leads Jennifer to carry a wide variety of accessories in her store to round out her product line. When you're considering a particular inventory item, evaluate how it fits in with the other items you sell, and with your overall profit margin. Look at each individual item with the end result in mind.

Product Sourcing Myth #14: You Can Be Successful with Surface Sourcing

There is a difference between gathering a lot of ideas for products to sell and trying to sell a lot of different kinds of products all at once. The former gives you a rich, fertile field of ideas from which to draw on. The latter leaves you scattered and prone to "surface sourcing." Surface sourcing occurs when you start selecting a variety of merchandise to sell, and do not take the time to understand your target market, research how to price and position your products, or learn how to market them properly. Without these three components, even the best of products will have a hard time reaching maximum sales potential. Surface sourcing is similar to doing the spaghetti test—throwing products "against the wall" to see what sticks. Unfortunately, most of the products just "slide down the wall." If you have a wide variety of products you're interested in selling though, do yourself and your products justice by focusing on one or two at a time and not surface sourcing. Your end result will be a better selection of merchandise with a more likely chance of sales success.

Product Sourcing Fundamental #14: Variety Is Not Always the Spice of Life

While testing out a variety of different products is a great way to learn which items work best for your business and to help gather information before making bulk purchasing decisions (see the following box), spreading yourself too thin over the long haul can stretch your profits thin as well. Trying to run with too many ideas at once will only make you tired. Gather your group of ideas and then edit them. Use your Product Sourcing Notebook (as outlined in Chapter 3) as your repository, and then select a few items to sell and focus on making them profitable. It's easier to build a profitable product line one product at a time than to try and launch multiple products simultaneously. Think of product sourcing as a funnel. In the idea generation stage, the opening of the funnel is wide, for all the creative ideas to pour in. This funnel also allows you to keep three or four ideas in the pike as we discussed earlier. As you research and refine the concepts, the funnel gets narrower and fewer product ideas make it through. By the end of the process, the funnel is narrow and only the best and the brightest products remain. Those are the golden building blocks that will shape your business.

Think Niche

While there are successful merchants who started out selling a variety of things and have continued quite successfully in that mode, selecting a niche market or markets to sell in can provide an online business with several advantages over the "variety store" model. In fact, some of the most successful eBay PowerSellers are those who've discovered a niche and exploited it. Keep in mind that it's better to be a specialist about a few things than a generalist about many. In addition, selling in a niche market lets you focus your marketing efforts and concentrate your resources on capturing all the profits to be made from your niche, and allows you to delve deeply into a product line. As you'll learn in Chapter 5, if you have a good working knowledge about your particular product area, you'll also be able to buy inventory at better prices and find more sources to buy from. When you deal in a niche, you can position yourself as an expert, and from a customer's perspective this makes for a much more engaging buying experience.

Should You Commit to a New Product Line Right Away?

Before committing to a product line, it's in your best interest to "test market" a variety of different kinds of products. This applies both to new sellers or experienced sellers interested in expanding their product line. Testing out a variety of goods will give you a clear indication of what products are selling, and which ones work best for your business. Consider what happened to Christie, a new eBay seller pursuing a lifelong dream.

Christie had always dreamed of starting a small dress shop. But with rents in her local shopping district running so high, and no nest egg to purchase inventory, it was a dream she had put on indefinite hold. Then Christie found eBay. Christie soon discovered that she could use her keen shopper's eye for spotting bargains to pick up dresses at the local designer discount store and then resell them on eBay. After a few sales with tidy profits, Christie was hooked. A dress shop on eBay was the answer to her dreams. She immediately began contacting wholesalers, set up accounts, and ordered some inventory. But then reality set in. Selling dresses here and there had been fun, but the mechanics of selling clothing on a regular basis was a little more than Christie had bargained for. She soon realized that her eBay dress shop was not exactly the business of her dreams. Almost by accident, she found a supplier who had a great deal on high-end art supplies. She began selling those as a side venture, and found out that they were in high demand, easy to ship, and fun to sell. Christie knew it was time to make a product line switch. Fortunately, she hadn't invested a lot of money in her clothing inventory, so she was able to move to a new product line with relative ease. Other online sellers, however, haven't been as lucky as Christie and have ended up with storage rooms of merchandise that they could not sell. For this reason, it's always wise to do some sampling before you commit wholeheartedly to a product line. You'll gain valuable information and may discover a whole new profitable niche in the process.

You must engage in business activities that are consistently and regularly profitable, and product sourcing is at the top of that list.

The Three "D's" of Product Sourcing

In addition to the 14 fundamentals of product sourcing earlier mentioned, we've identified three "D's" of product sourcing: *Document* Product Ideas, *Diversify* Your Product Line, and build a *Direct* Supply of Inventory.

These product sourcing "diamonds" are additional fundamentals that will complete the framework of your product sourcing foundation.

Document Product Ideas

Innovative and creative product sourcing will leave you with an abundance of ideas. In Chapter 3, you'll learn how to use a Product Sourcing Notebook to document all the concepts you come across and catalog them for future use. Studies show that without a record of your ideas, 90 percent of them will be lost. Do you want to lose your most valuable thoughts? Forgetting your best product selection ideas is analogous to losing money, literally. Additionally, just because a product idea is not useful to you now, it doesn't mean it won't be in the future. You never know when a product idea you had six months ago will be exactly what you need to add into the mix right now. When you come across a good potential product idea, write it down!

Diversify Your Product Line

When evaluating a particular product line or niche, you want to take into consideration the diversity potential that this product line has. Does this product line have a mix of higher- and lower-priced products? What offshoots of this product line could you stock to reach a broader audience of buyers? While most people think it would be a dream to carry all hot sellers, in order to build a large customer base and consistent income you'll need to round out the top-selling commodities in your business with steady sellers that may not create as much cash flow but that are responsible for bringing people to your online store. In Chapter 8, you'll find all the ins and outs of creative product selection, as well as tips for diversifying your product line.

A Direct and Steady Supply of Inventory

In order to build a consistent retail income, you must have a direct and steady supply of inventory. This is a huge consideration when selecting products to sell online. While you can opt for a product to sell for a short-term run, you cannot build a business or a consistent income without product lines which offer a steady supply of goods. For example, for an eBay seller, one of the most common causes of peaks and valleys in income is an inconsistent number of listings. This can usually be traced back to low inventory levels, which tracks directly to a lack of steady suppliers. When you're sourcing your products, the optimal case is to have at least two suppliers for your products. If your products are hard to re-order, you need to think about this before you choose to sell them.

Repeatable Product Sourcing System Required

We've covered the fundamentals of product selection and looked at some widely held misconceptions about choosing your products. Now we're going to move on to the system that will tie it all together. In order for your sales and income to become consistent, your product selection techniques must be repeatable, regular, and reliable. The exclusive Five-Step Product Sourcing System is one that you'll be able to apply time and time again and produce guaranteed results. Systems save you time and money. With the Five-Step Product Selection System, you'll find that you're able to spot potential products faster and determine their profitability more quickly—and do so on a regular basis. As the great Roman emperor Marcus Aurelius once said, "Nothing has such power to broaden the mind as the ability to investigate systematically and truly all that comes under thy observation in life." By using the Five-Step Product Sourcing System shown next, you can broaden your product sourcing reach by leveraging the information you take in every day and turning it into usable product selection leads. This easy-to-follow system will work for any kind of product, any level seller, and any kind of business. In Chapters 1 through 8 of this book, we'll expand on the principles of the Five-Step Product Sourcing System. For now, take note of this as the road map for what you're about to discover throughout the rest of the book.

In order for your sales and income to become consistent,
your product selection techniques must be repeatable,
regular, and reliable.

The Five-Step Product Sourcing System

1. Brainstorm Product Ideas
   - Generate ideas for products on a consistent basis
2. Scan
   - Hundreds of products are seen every day
3. Document
   - You must keep a record of your ideas, or you risk losing them
4. Research
   - Online and with third-party tools
   - Assess demand and profit-margin potential
5. Creative Selection
   - Product-line staples and cross-selling opportunities
   - The reasons to select a particular product to sell will vary
   - Different products fulfill different purposes—don't evaluate all products using the same criteria

When you incorporate these five steps into your daily activities, automation of the system will set in, and the process of selecting products to sell online will become a pleasant and profitable habit.

The Five-Step Product Selection System serves some very important functions in your product selection endeavors. This system will assist you in

- **Systematizing your product sourcing**   Many online retailers often equate finding profitable products to sell to "looking for a needle in a haystack." Using a repeatable system will allow you to produce solid, consistent results and find more money making products.
- **Staying organized**   Without a system, you can literally have hundreds of thousands of dollar's worth of potential product ideas lying around your office but no way to catalog or utilize that information.
- **Building your own product sourcing library**   Once you put this system in place, you'll begin to build your own product sourcing reference library—one you'll refer to over and over again.
- **Fueling your creativity**   How does having more ideas for products to sell than time to sell them sound? Once you get into the rhythm of using this product sourcing system, you'll have an abundance of ideas for products to sell.

Summing Up

Now that we've covered the fundamentals of product sourcing and outlined the system of how to get the products that buyers want, we're ready to move on to Chapter 2 and find out exactly how to get into the Product Sourcing Mindset.

But before we do, here's a recap of some important elements of this chapter:

- Your product line is the foundation of your business. Selling strategies and marketing are important, but it all starts with your product line.
- Without good product-sourcing skills, you can end up with a lot of inventory you can't sell. Mastering the task of choosing your inventory will serve your business well over the long run.

- In order to know what your buyers want, you must put yourself in the world in which your buyers live. Become a student of what is going on in society around you.
- Don't sell only what you love or what you know. To build a business, you must sell what sells.
- Document your ideas; otherwise, 90 percent of them will never make it to the drawing board.
- Product selection is not cut and dry. This ongoing process is like putting together the pieces of a puzzle to form a complete picture.
- Research and testing is the only true way to know if your product has profit potential.
- All the good products are NOT already taken. There are as many products to sell as there are people to buy them.
- Think niche. It's better to be a specialist about a few things than it is a generalist about many things.
- In order for your sales and income to become consistent, your product selection techniques must be repeatable, regular, and reliable.

Chapter 2

The Product Sourcing Mindset

True product sourcing is not a task you can schedule in every Tuesday from 10:00 a.m. to 2:00 p.m. While there are certain aspects of your business which you can easily preplan and schedule time for, such as order fulfillment and shipping, product sourcing requires a much broader approach in order to locate the millions of products out there that buyers want to purchase. Being an entrepreneur is not a 9-to-5 job. To grow the business of your dreams, you won't be able to flip a switch in the morning to be tuned into product selection and flip it off before dinner. Nor would you want to.

While we're not advocating you work nonstop, when it comes to product selection, you must always be on the lookout. However, there is a way you can do this, without it feeling like you're working all the time. We call this living the Product Sourcing Mindset. The following can be used as a definition of a mindset: *A fixed mental attitude or disposition that predetermines a person's responses to, and interpretations of, situations.* When you're living the Product Sourcing Mindset, you'll be equipped with a new attitude and approach to product sourcing.

Oftentimes, sellers are advised to sit down at their desk or computer and create a plan for what they want to sell. The problem with this approach is that usually as soon as you sit down to develop your list, you draw a blank or find yourself with limited ideas about what to sell. The next logical step is for people to think harder and invent ideas regarding products to sell. Sadly, this approach can often leave a seller feeling frustrated and wondering whether or not they have the right stuff to make it in the world of retail sales. In fact, many sellers we've talked to have questioned their ability to run an eBay, Yahoo, or other retail business because of this very issue.

The problem, however, lies not in the person, but in the process used to generate ideas for products to sell. As you'll learn in this chapter, with the correct approach, rather than trying to pull product ideas out of thin air, you'll end up surrounded by an inexhaustible supply of sellable-product ideas. Thus, doing this will put you in a position to *choose* from a variety of product line opportunities. Louis Pasteur once said, "In the field of observation, chance favors the prepared mind." The Product Sourcing Mindset will leave you prepared at all times, for opportunities that others would only find by chance.

The Product Sourcing Mindset

The Product Sourcing Mindset is a vast, holistic approach to product sourcing. Unlike the method we just described, trying to drum up ideas for what to sell in a vacuum, the Product Sourcing Mindset lets you turn your attention outward and brings a fresh new dimension to your product sourcing activities. Being in the Product Sourcing Mindset enables you to open your field of vision, put up your antennae, and direct your awareness to the streams of profitable products that you come into contact with every day. When you're in the Product Sourcing Mindset, you see things differently. You look at every item or piece of information that you come across during the day as a potential product for you to sell.

With your product sourcing radar turned on, you are literally scanning information all day long, with the sole intent of tapping into concepts for potential products, product lines, and niche markets. For example, in the mindset, a trip to your local shopping mall to buy a pair of shoes now becomes an opportunity to scan for trends, see new products, or expand your knowledge of a niche market. For Chelsea, an avid shopper, this fresh approach changed her business. Up until learning how to use the Product Sourcing Mindset, Chelsea struggled with finding interesting new products to carry in her eBay store. She often found that her most frequent ideas for products were lackluster, or even worse—were already being sold by multitudes of other sellers. Chelsea was beginning to feel that you needed to be a born trendsetter or have a cutting-edge eye for product selection in order to find innovative, interesting merchandise. However, when we explained the process of the Product Sourcing Mindset to Chelsea, she began to understand that identifying in-demand product lines is a skill anyone can develop. Because Chelsea is an avid shopper, we taught her how to combine her frequent trips to the mall with scanning for any products, concepts, or ideas that caught her eye.

Using her Product Sourcing Notebook, which we will explain in Chapter 3, in conjunction with the Product Sourcing Mindset, Chelsea began developing lists and lists of ideas, concepts, and even specific product information for merchandise that she might like to carry in her store. Chelsea couldn't believe how easy the task of product sourcing had become. All of a sudden a familiar activity had been updated with a new direction. The result was an instant change in Chelsea's business, where she found herself in the enviable position of having more ideas regarding products to sell than she had time to sell them.

Tip: A visit to the mall or your favorite specialty store as an interested consumer can provide you with a wealth of information about what products are selling now. Find a knowledgeable salesperson and inquire about best-selling products in their line. Ask them, What styles are selling? What colors? A good salesperson will be able to tell you exactly what their customers are buying. This technique, combined with a relaxed, friendly approach and a consideration for the salesperson's time, can yield you invaluable market research data on what products are selling.

When you learn how to reinvent your product sourcing methods by employing the Product Sourcing Mindset, your eyes will suddenly open to a world of opportunities for marketable merchandise. You will improve the quality of your product sourcing ideas and greatly increase the quantity. Soon, you'll find yourself constantly surrounded with "factory-fresh" concepts and awake each day to anticipate new opportunities for you and your business. Utilizing this strategy will allow you to take your business to the next level.

Advantages of the Product Sourcing Mindset

With the Product Sourcing Mindset you'll break out of the mold and experience product sourcing in a whole new way. In this mindset, you will

- Integrate your product sourcing actions into your daily activities.
- Scan hundreds of ideas daily and be the first to pick up on new trends, emerging markets, and changes in buyers' habits.
- Make product sourcing an intuitive process. With regular use of the Product Sourcing Mindset, your product sourcing efforts become automatic.
- Find yourself infused with fresh, new energy that will translate into growth and profits for your business.

The Product Sourcing Mindset is an incubator for new approaches to the question of "What should I sell?"

Get into the Product Sourcing Mindset

Imagine how your business would be transformed if you had a constant stream of ideas for products to sell, starting from the time you got up in the morning until the time you went to bed at night? What could you achieve if you had marketable product ideas *coming to you* every day? Would you have more than enough ideas for products to sell? Often, just a small change in the way you think will pay you big dividends. And as you'll see, getting into the Product Sourcing Mindset is a fast and simple transformation. However, don't underestimate its power! This new perspective on product sourcing can mean unlimited income for your business.

To get into the Product Sourcing Mindset requires a simple shift in thinking, and "installing" what we call your product sourcing filter. Once your filter is installed, you are constantly scanning, oftentimes subconsciously, each piece of information that passes your way—looking at it not through regular eyes, but through the eyes of the Product Sourcing Mindset. With this filter installed, you'll continually ask yourself one question: Would this product, trend, or niche have selling potential?

Reading the newspaper is no longer just about keeping up on the current news, it is reading to spot trends, ideas, and information that can be translated directly into inventory for your online sales. Your favorite evening magazine show with its entertaining human interest narratives now has you riveted, not for the engaging story lines, but to learn what is going on in society—How are people spending their time? What are their interests? What are the latest trends? Where are they spending their money? Take a trip to the local mall. Listen carefully to your friends during dinner. All of these are opportunities for you to absorb what people are talking about, thinking about, and, most of all, spending their money on.

You can easily install your product sourcing filter by doing the following simple exercise. The method is a snap to apply. Imagine you have no preconceived ideas about any niche market in the world. Your mind is a blank slate, open to whatever information comes its way. Now, pick up your favorite consumer or hobby magazine, newspaper, or catalog. Make it whatever publication you have easily accessible in your home or office. You'll also need a piece of paper and a pen. Before you look at the magazine, you must mentally "install" your product sourcing filter. This means giving your mind the directive that every word, item, concept, or ad that catches your eye in the next 15 minutes will go through this filter and with each thought that crosses your mind, you will ask yourself, "Would this product, trend, niche have selling potential?" Now pick up your publication and start scanning. Remember, you're not reading in-depth, only identifying tidbits of information that catch your attention. Trust yourself and don't edit your thoughts. Write down things as you see them. You don't have to understand them or make sense of them right now, just take notice. Once you've scanned the entire newspaper or magazine, stop your search and take a look at your list. How many ideas for products do you have? How many new, fresh, creative concepts did you take note of?

For this book, Lisa did a sample test by scanning her local Sunday paper. By both scanning the articles and looking at the ads, this is the list she came up with:

1. Men's business attire back in style in corporate America.
2. Upcoming home and garden show.
3. Retailers ignore plus-size clothing market for teens.
4. *Charlie and the Chocolate Factory* movie opening.
5. More families looking for family entertainment, and toymakers are responding.
6. Kids now want to trick out (accessorize) their bikes.
7. Projected $500 million in sales from movie-themed toys.
8. Sega I-Dog, a robotic dog that can compose, play, and dance to music. Hot new product in Japan in April 2005.
9. Memory-making expands beyond scrapbooking. People of all ages now want to capture and preserve memories in unique ways.
10. Ad circular for camping products—new for 2005: backyard fire pits, water chairs, camp vacuums, and party coolers (decorative stand coolers).

This scan took Lisa just under 15 minutes. How many trends and ideas for products do you see in this list? At least hundreds of potential product ideas could be culled from this list alone! If you can come up with a great idea launch-pad like this by scanning for less than 15 minutes, imagine how many ideas you could discover by scanning every piece of information that you come into contact with for the entire day! The possibilities are endless.

While at first it may feel odd to look at every bit and piece of information that you take in each day as a lead for your next potential top seller, this habit is actually a very easy one to get into. As a child, you had an innate curiosity about the world around you. As an adult, you still have that same desire to absorb information, but now you have much more focus. And an even more important reason to take notice of the world around you is that you're building a profitable business! When you run every item through your filter by asking the question, Would this product, trend, niche, concept have selling potential?, you begin to turn your filter towards one thing: finding profitable products. This straightforward question can create extraordinary results because the human mind is designed to answer each and every question posed to it. By getting into the Product Sourcing Mindset and using your product sourcing filter, every time you scan for potential products you up the ante of finding the right product. The importance of being in the mindset all day long cannot be overstated, because you never know when you're going to come across a million-dollar idea.

Inspirations in Unusual Places

One of the consistent comments that we hear from sellers who have made the switch to the Product Sourcing Mindset is that they often find their product line or niche market ideas in the most unexpected of places. A trip to the airport gave one savvy eBay seller the lead she needed to find her next best-selling product. While walking through the airport, she noticed there were several parents who were pushing their tots in the same brand of stroller. Because she was in the Product Sourcing Mindset, her radar immediately picked up on the fact that she kept seeing this same stroller over and over again. She quickly pulled out her Product Sourcing Notebook (as we'll talk about later in the book), and made note of the brand name, style, and color of the popular stroller.

Upon her return home, she used that information to do her market demand research. Much to her delight, she found there was a strong demand for this stroller on eBay. Once she had established market demand, her next step was to find out more about the stroller. A quick trip to Google, followed by browsing some online parenting magazines, told her that this high-end stroller was in favor with new parents across the country. Recognizing this money-making opportunity, on Monday morning she contacted the manufacturer of the stroller to find the contact information for their regional wholesalers, a process you will learn more about in Chapter 13. This stroller went on to be one of her top sellers. A product that she knew nothing of initially, and therefore would never have thought of selling, became a break-out product for her, all because she took that first step of getting into the Product Sourcing Mindset.

See Things Differently

Why is it that two sellers can look at the same product or trend and one will see opportunity while the other one won't? Often, it's because the first person has trained themselves to look for opportunities in everything, while the other person is waiting for the obvious opportunity to present itself to them. It is the sellers who are looking for opportunities at every corner who find them. They are the ones who recognize markets that are underserved—markets that other sellers overlook because they are not the obvious "hot" ones. However, these underserved markets have buyers who are hungry for products and not enough sellers to supply them. There are literally thousands of niches right in front of us on a regular basis. And that is just the tip of the iceberg! But it is only when you learn to see everything in a different light, by getting into the Product Sourcing Mindset, that pots of gold start to emerge.

Meg and Josh, a husband and wife team who've been selling on eBay for three years, learned to see things differently, but it took almost missing the opportunity of a lifetime to see it. Josh's dad had owned a restaurant supply store for many years. Over the years, he'd collected a warehouse full of used equipment by getting deals that were either too good to pass up or freebies that people had wanted to unload. When Josh's dad decided to relocate the business, he was looking for a way to get rid of the equipment and not incur the cost of moving it all. At the time, Meg had some friends who'd been selling on eBay, and one of them had mentioned to her that she might want to check out the possibility of selling the used equipment on eBay. Meg didn't put much stock in the idea, but mentioned it to Josh who discounted it even further. To him, all that used equipment was nothing but junk. Almost on a whim, Meg decided to take a look on eBay and see if people even sold used restaurant equipment. What she found shocked her! Not only was used restaurant equipment selling on eBay, it was a hot-selling commodity. When she showed Josh the listings, his attitude did a 180-degree turn. All of a sudden this heap of stuff in his dad's warehouse didn't look so much like junk anymore. After doing some research on the equipment to understand the market, Meg and Josh began selling it piece by piece on eBay. It took several months, but when they were done, they had sold it all but one piece, and had amassed a significant sum, which Josh's dad later gifted to them as a down payment on their first house. From that point on, Meg and Josh have never looked at anything the same. Today, you can find them scouting deals in unusual places and always seeing things through their product sourcing filter. Frequently, the ability to recognize opportunity is the difference between success and failure. Sellers who are in the Product Sourcing Mindset are persistent in sharpening their skills of observation. They know that the best niche market is not always the most obvious one.

Why is it that seeing things differently works so well? Well, if you consider that the average person takes in 1,500 to 3,000 informational "messages" a day, just by virtue of getting up out of bed and making our way through life, we are presented daily with a huge amount of information. These messages can come from print publications, television, radio, billboards, trips to the store, conversations with friends and family, even something as simple as a glance at the person next to you to see what they are wearing, carrying, or doing. Received as just plain information, it comes and goes, never stopping long enough to warrant a blip on our radar screen. But to a person in the Product Sourcing Mindset, built into all of those messages that we take for granted is a potential product selling opportunity.

Let's look at an example of a recent trending article in a local newspaper. This half-page article outlined in detail a new trend among Americans—the desire to work with their hands. Increasingly, people want to do things for themselves, enjoy the process of creating or accomplishing something, and connect with other do-it-yourselfers. There are clubs, groups, and discussion forums springing up all around that support and cater to the up and coming do-it-yourselfers. The article went on to say that traditional pastimes like gardening, quilting, hand-painting walls, knitting, sewing, scrapbooking, home decorating, gourmet cooking, and one of the biggest do-it-yourself markets, home improvement, were coming back into favor with today's adult. All the things that we saw our parents do as kids, and that many of us haven't had time for in recent years, are experiencing a resurgence in popularity. Because of this interest, there are more companies, products, and individuals who are coming out with products to help people "do it yourself."

To the seller who does not see things differently, an article like this is just an interesting piece of trivia. Maybe something to comment on in a casual conversation with Uncle Jack at the next family barbeque. However, to the online seller who is in the Product Sourcing Mindset, this kind of article represents a potential million-dollar product idea. When Leonardo da Vinci needed to get his creative juices flowing, he sat and stared at clouds or rocks ... "If you look upon an old wall covered with dirt or the odd appearance of some streaked stones," he once wrote, "you may discover several things like landscapes, battles, clouds, uncommon attitudes, humorous faces, draperies, etc." Da Vinci heartily recommended this "new method" of invention as a practical technique for "opening the mind and putting it upon the scent of new thoughts." When you begin to see things differently, you're doing just that—opening your mind and allowing it to migrate naturally to the products and ideas upon which you will build your business.

Tip: To start training your mind to see things differently, you must do some different things every day. Try mixing up your routine a bit. If you drive to the Post Office the same way every day, try taking a new route.

If you have a favorite restaurant or movie theater that you go to each weekend, go to one across town near a shopping center that you've never been to. To see things differently, you need to break out of your daily routine. Give yourself the challenge to do one thing differently each day and watch the way you see things transform before your very eyes.

Find Products at 30,000 Feet

On land or in the air, there are always opportunities to scout for new ideas for products to sell. Returning from her speaking engagement at eBay Live 2005 on "How to Find the Products that Buyers Want," Lisa found information on two great niche markets while on the plane somewhere over southern Oregon.

Picking up the in-flight magazine, Lisa knew she held in her hand a literal catalog of merchandise. Flipping through pages of products, she came upon a section of the magazine that covered new trends. There were two articles that caught her eye. One was a story about a new kind of golf bag made especially for travelers. The story outlined in detail the reason behind the need for this product, who was buying it, the manufacturer, and how much it cost. The article even included contact information for the manufacturer. Not only did this article have a great idea for a product to investigate, it also sparked in Lisa a curiosity about what other golf-related items for travelers might be in demand. It's articles like this that give observant sellers the clues they need to pursue an emerging trend. Further research into travel items for golfers may turn up additional products, or it may steer you into another golf-related niche such as golf products specially designed for kids.

A second article in the in-flight magazine was a profile of a company that made organic pet food. The article gave a relatively in-depth analysis of the organic pet food industry and included some statistics that said that organic pet food sales for the first time outpaced sales of nonorganic pet food. There was also a notable mention about the burgeoning high-end pet product industry. This article fell right in line with other information that Lisa had gathered in the past six months about the high-end pet product niche and the move to organic pet food. This was another confirmation of a trend on the rise—further testimony to a potentially very profitable niche.

There were several other eBay sellers on the plane that day returning from eBay Live 2005. At the baggage claim, Lisa asked a few of them if they had found any ideas for new products to sell on the plane ride home. Most of them looked at her with a very quizzical look. None of them had spotted the trending information in the magazine. None of them had been looking. In the world of product sourcing, opportunity knocks 24/7. If you want to have an advantage over the competition, make sure you're ready to receive those opportunities when they're presented to you.

Become a Product Sourcing Detective

A good detective can solve any mystery. If you took any famous fictional detective and plopped them into the retail arena with the mission to source profitable products, their sage skills of deduction would have them ferreting out new and unique product lines in no time. Like a good suspense novel, the question of "What do I sell?" is a mystery waiting to be solved. And like your favorite mystery movie, half the fun of learning the answer is watching the process unfold while you're getting to the answer.

When evaluating ideas for products to sell, you'll very rarely get all the answers you want on the first try. One piece of information will lead to another one, one product often leads to another more profitable one. Like a good detective, you must take in the clues you get and use them as a pathway to arrive at your ultimate destination. In and of themselves, individual pieces of product sourcing data may not mean much, but when you put them together and connect the dots, all of a sudden you start to see a picture of a profitable product emerge. When you become a good detective, you gain the edge in solving product sourcing puzzles.

The first step in being a good product sourcing detective is being able to recognize bits and pieces of information as they come your way. Become a clue magnet of sorts. Not much gets by you! The next step is digesting that information, taking it in, and letting it percolate a while. Then taking it one step further and looking at how your clues can translate directly into a marketable product idea.

Three Detective Rules

The good product sourcing private-eye relies upon the following rules:

- Detective Rule #1: Look for clues and evidence. Product sourcing detectives are always on the watch for clues and evidence. A clue about a potential product to sell may be something as small as a snippet you read one day in a magazine discussing a particular trend or style. Evidence comes in when you begin to notice people wearing or using this product or you start to hear people talking about it.

- Detective Rule #2: Listen to your intuition. While clues and evidence give you a very good place to start, it's your intuition that kicks in and keeps you researching a product. Don't have good intuition, you say? Not a problem! Developing your product sourcing intuition will come naturally over time. After a certain point, you'll begin to tap into winning products and product lines more quickly and easily.

- Detective Rule #3: Know that you have a puzzle to solve. Don't expect that the answer to "What do I sell?" will always come quickly and easily. Granted, sometimes you'll get an inspired flash of brilliance and will be off researching and sourcing your product almost instantaneously. But if an idea is a "no-brainer," most likely thousands of other people have thought the same and you'll be dealing with a lot of competition. Relish the hunt, enjoy the process, and most of all, become comfortable with it. The more you do it, the better you'll get at it. Keep looking around you to see the opportunities coming your way.

How We Found the World of Footwear

A good product sourcing detective is, in a sense, an explorer: forging ahead in uncharted territories, not quite knowing what you're looking for, but determined to keep going until you find it. You never know where your direction may take you, which is exactly how Lisa found the "world of footwear." Her product sourcing journey into the world of footwear took just under 30 minutes. What started as a local search for a supplier in Lisa's hometown of Seattle took her "across the country" and back again to the biggest footwear trade show in the United States. Join us now, as we revisit the trip.

1. Lisa's journey into the footwear universe began unassumingly enough. She was looking for a name-brand shoe distributor in the Emerald City, Seattle, Washington.

2. Her first stop was to go to http://www.yellowpages.com and do a search in the SMARTpages yellow pages. Under Business Category, she typed in "wholesale". In the city field, she entered "seattle". See Figure 2-1. This brought up a list of all the wholesalers located in Seattle.

Note: When using http://www.yellowpages.com, you can also perform a search for suppliers by using the keywords "distributor" or "manufacturer".

3. She searched the list for the Shoes category and found six wholesalers and distributors in Seattle. Looking over the suppliers, she picked one at random.

4. The next stop was Google, where she did a search on the supplier's name. The Google search brought up the supplier's web site.

Tip: When searching for specific suppliers, always type the name in quotes—for example, "Lake Washington Shoe Company".

5. Perusing the supplier's web site, she didn't find the merchandise she was looking for, but she did see something that caught her eye. An icon that read WSA.

6. Curiosity was sparked in this super-sleuth's mind, and she clicked the WSA icon ... Jackpot! Lisa knew she was onto something big.

7. It was the web site for the largest footwear trade show in the U.S., the World Shoe Association at http://www.wsashow.com.

8. Digging further into this web site, Lisa found out when the next trade show was being held, who the show catered to, what the

requirements were to get into the show, and as if that weren't enough, Lisa found...

9. The list of show exhibitors at http://wsaspring.expoplanner.com/. This valuable list contained 1,600 exhibitors representing 6,000 brands of footwear worldwide and included the company name, address, phone number, e-mail address, web site URL, company profile, and the brands carried. This supplier list was a gold mine!

What started as a search for a local supplier opened the door to 1,600 new niche market vendors, centrally located all in one place. Lisa did a similar search for the American Apparel and Footwear Association web site at http://apparelandfootwear.org/index.cfm. Once there, she found a list of all the footwear industry trade shows scheduled for the entire year at http://apparelandfootwear.org/4col.cfm?pageID=153. The skills of the product sourcing private-eye paid off once again.

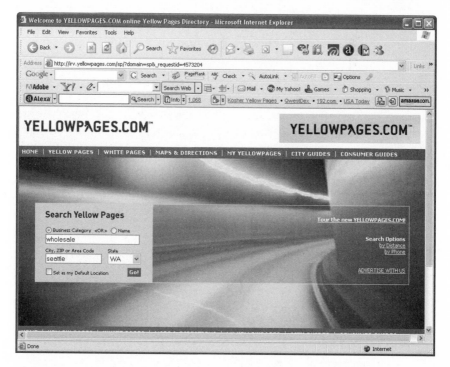

Figure 2-1 Yellowpages is a resource for finding wholesalers nationwide.

Brainstorm for Unlimited Ideas

Most of us have participated in a group brainstorming session. Ideas are bandied about by the group, while a scribe writes them on the board as quickly as possible. No idea is refused, evaluated, or censored. These flashes of brainwork can come from original ideas created by the participants or concepts pulled from a variety of places. Fortunately, brainstorming doesn't require a group. In fact, studies have shown that individual brainstorming can produce more highly creative results.

Brainstorming is a key component of the Product Sourcing Mindset. When you are in this mindset, you'll be instinctively brainstorming ideas all day, every day. Noteworthy thoughts will be noodling around in your mind. Or you may find yourself noticing and acknowledging interesting merchandise or markets around you. Brainstorming a collection of money-making ideas requires no money, time, or difficulty. But it gives you freedom, creativity, and a conducive environment in which to let the ideas flow. In a group brainstorming session, have you ever seen someone throw out what seemed like a completely crazy idea, only to find later that the suggestion was a runaway success? Often it is the idea that comes out of left field which is the one that will get you going. The one that will get your creative juices flowing. The one that will have you saying, "Ah, ha! I'm on to something here."

Tip: Successful product sourcing is a numbers game. The more ideas you consider, the more winners you'll find.

Frequently people will draw inward when put to the task of developing a product line for their store. We want to encourage you to look outward, to see that there are ideas all around you, ripe for the picking. Give yourself the challenge to see how many random ideas you can identify in one day. When you are brainstorming, the ideas don't have to make sense, they don't have to follow any logic, they don't even have to be related to any products you're currently selling or ever thought you'd sell. Engaging in this practice regularly helps you capture the spirit of innovation. Don't think of yourself as an idea person? Brainstorming will solve that! You're infinitely more creative when you brainstorm. Best of all, your future product idea may be as close as your next thought.

Note: Not only should you brainstorm for product ideas, you should also brainstorm ideas for your selling and marketing strategies as well as future plans for your business. The best way to grow a business is through constant brainstorming of new, invigorating ideas.

Brainstorming a collection of money-making ideas requires no money, time, or difficulty. Your future product idea may be as close as your next thought.

Guidelines for Fertile Brainstorming

When brainstorming, a constant flow of ideas is amazingly simple to achieve. By following these basic guidelines, you become a walking wellspring of creativity:

- Brainstorm all day long. After about 30 days of doing this, the process will become as natural for you as breathing.
- Scan and collect as many general or specific product ideas as you can, and amass a large ongoing list. In Chapter 3, we will introduce you to a tool that will allow you to organize and document all of this data so you can use it to the fullest extent.
- Do not eliminate any idea or thought that comes to you. Your job is to simply tune in to, recognize, and document any concept that catches your eye.
- Spark new ideas by getting stimuli from a variety of places. Don't limit yourself! In Chapter 4, we will talk about where to go to surround yourself with these ideas.
- Discard preconceived notions. When brainstorming, you are not yet at the place where you can be making decisions as to whether or not a product has profit potential. Only research and hard facts (discussed in Chapter 6) can truly eliminate an idea.
- Don't linger or analyze. Take note of the idea and move on to the next stimulus.

Tip: Brainstorming gives you a great advantage over trying to think up a profitable product idea in a vacuum. It has the ability to make you an idea magnet and allows even those who feel like they're at a loss for ideas to learn to think creatively.

Learn to Scan

Engaging in the Product Sourcing Mindset should not be a time-consuming process. Quite the contrary. It should be a spontaneous and effortless action. The way to achieve this is through scanning. Scanning involves looking at ideas quickly and systematically. Not stopping or pausing to analyze, judge, or prejudge. Scanning available products, ideas, and niches can, and should, be done in seconds. With your product sourcing filter installed, in the time it takes you to look at an item or concept, your mind will make a split-second decision as to whether or not to make note of it and pursue it further. Skimming and scanning is the quick acquisition of information about events, trends, and potential products. Scanning is an essential foundation for your own innovation process, as well as a means to help you win the product sourcing numbers game.

How Many Ideas a Day?

How many ideas have you had for new products today? One? Five? Twenty? Utilizing the Product Sourcing Mindset, you will have the ability to bring forth an unlimited number of product selling ideas daily. In order to generate momentum and keep the ideas flowing, you should document *at the very least* one new idea a day. That gives you seven ideas a week, or about thirty ideas a month. Why so many?

On average, you'll usually need to evaluate about 30 products for every *one* you choose to sell. In doing the math, it's easy to see that for every profitable product you want to identify, you'll need to view at least an idea a day. Keep in mind that while sometimes you will pick a winner on the fifth product you consider, other times it will take evaluating 30 products before finding one suitable for your store. If you find yourself starving for your next marketable product idea, stop and take a look at how many potential products you've considered this week. If it's less than seven, it's time to get going!

Mindset Key: Don't Censor Your Ideas

Often, people eliminate an idea that could be profitable before they even give it a chance. Like a tennis player batting away at balls, sellers often "bat away" some of the best ideas. When you're in the phase of idea generation, no censoring should take place. If an idea catches your attention, make note of it. At this stage of the game, it is not the time to rule out, shrug off, or discount any potential idea. Because the Product Sourcing Mindset is based upon creativity, if you are quashing ideas for products before you have done any research on their potential, it's very unlikely you'll find any true gems to sell. In Chapter 6, we'll talk about how to refine those ideas and mold them into tangible inventory. But for now, make it a given that every concept that catches your eye has its own merit.

Over the years, we've received e-mails from sellers at all levels asking us for ideas or leads on profitable product lines. At times, we've offered these sellers several potential product-line concepts. Once we extend the ideas, the scenario usually goes one of two ways. People embrace the concepts or they censor them. Carrie, Shawn, and Jeff had all requested help with product-line direction. At the time, however, they all had their blinders on and their minds blocked to new opportunities. For each idea we offered, we received replies in which it was clear they had prejudged the concepts that had been offered to them. Additionally, they had censored the ideas prior to doing any market research on the demand for the product lines we had suggested. Their comments ranged from "Oh, that won't sell" to "That's too hard/complicated/unusual/mundane/unprofitable for me to sell." Without any basis in fact, these three sellers censored ideas based on their own preferences. Samantha, on the other hand, welcomed all product sourcing input that we gave her. Instead of making proclamations, she asked questions. Rather than falling prey to preconceived notions, she turned to research to give her more information. Samantha's request for help had come right on the heels of the other three sellers' requests. Armed with the Product Sourcing Mindset, Samantha came right along behind them and built a profitable business from the exact same ideas that the others eschewed. Our guess is that Carrie, Shawn, and Jeff are still looking for products to sell, lamenting that all the good products are taken. Meanwhile, Samantha is enjoying continued success. Ruling out products upfront, based on presumptions, will dramatically reduce the amount of product sourcing opportunities available to you and prevent you from making a good business decision about what to sell.

Lack or Abundance

In Chapter 1, we talked about an important myth of product sourcing—the belief that all the good products are taken. Common wisdom holds that your beliefs determine your reality. Meaning, if you believe it to be true, your mind will find a way to support that belief and make it true. If you believe there is a lack of in-demand products to sell, that is exactly what you will find. Alternatively, if you believe there is an overflowing profusion of great product-line opportunities, you'll find them around every corner. Your attitude towards lack and abundance plays heavily in the Product Sourcing Mindset.

Even though there are literally millions of products in the world to sell, with new ones coming to the market every day, very often we hear people say there is nothing to sell. What is at the root of the difference between their perception and reality? The answer lies in part because many of us have been programmed since childhood to believe there are shortages and lack—not enough to go around. Whether its money, food, time, or products to sell, it all comes back to the same thought: there isn't enough of the "good stuff" to go around. This kind of thinking can greatly affect your approach to product sourcing. If you think there aren't enough great product ideas for everyone, you'll find yourself struggling with the question of "What do I sell?" If you tell yourself that there's an abundance of products out there, swirling around you every day, you'll find yourself bursting with ideas for products to sell. Ultimately, our success in business is, in many ways, a reflection of ourselves and how we approach things. If you find yourself with a tendency to approach things from a "lack" mentality, by adopting the Product Sourcing Mindset, learning to brainstorm, and banning the censors, you will be able to shift that paradigm in your mind to a place of abundance.

Tip: In order to approach product sourcing from a perspective of abundance, you need to be able to recognize when it occurs. Too many people "step over" their successes and ignore them, while keeping their eye on the next prize. Take a few minutes each day to celebrate your successes. Maybe you had a great conversation with a supplier, or negotiated a rock-bottom pricing deal on a Lot of merchandise. Or possibly you had outstanding sales that day. When you take the time to recognize the good that's coming to you and to your business, it changes the entire way you approach your product sourcing, and the way you run your business.

Surround Yourself with Ideas

A key component of being in the Product Sourcing Mindset is placing yourself in an idea-rich environment. Fortunately, you don't need to live in downtown Manhattan or some other hip and happening pop-culture mecca to do this. You can *create* the kind of environment that will be a conduit for a profusion of good ideas. In order to tap into the products that buyers want, you need to actively integrate some basic activities in with the Product Sourcing Mindset. Reading, talking to people, listening, and asking questions are all catalysts that will connect you with the voices of consumer desires. Turning your antennae outward is essential in building a vibrant, in-demand product line. If you get up every day, go straight to work, don't do any reading, don't take in what is going on in the world around you, and then come straight back to your desk to drum up product ideas, you'll be hard-pressed to come up with the merchandise that buyers want. By using the methods in this chapter, you'll be able to tap into your stream of consciousness.

Reading for Profit

If there is one "secret" we could share with you which would ensure your success in using the Product Sourcing Mindset, it is reading. Read everything. Read every day. Read a variety of periodicals. Read things you wouldn't normally read. Reading is the window to your product sourcing world. It is also the road that will lead you directly to finding out what buyers want to buy. You don't need to read articles, magazines, and supplier catalogs in-depth; scanning and skimming (as discussed earlier) will do the trick. For successful product sourcing, you must read a variety of publications every day. The only way to "cast your net" around the vast array of merchandising opportunities awaiting you is by reading widely.

The Art of Automation

There are only so many hours in a day to devote to your business activities. Without systems, you'd be hard-pressed to expand your business and your sales. McDonald's would never have grown to the behemoth company it is today without systems. They don't make the best hamburgers around, but they did figure out a way to systematize the delivery of burgers, fries, and shakes to their customers. This system allowed them to expand rapidly and focus on company growth.

The same applies to your business. You may have systems in place for ordering your inventory and shipping it after it's been sold, but you need to have a way to automate the selection and acquisition of inventory. The Product Sourcing Mindset will automate your product sourcing for you. It will bring efficiency to your business. Within a few weeks of using the Product Sourcing Mindset, you'll find that product selection becomes second nature. Best of all, after using this method, you'll feel like someone has taken off the blinders and, with the flip of a switch, tuned you into a new level of product awareness. The Product Sourcing Mindset can transform your business and give you the skills needed to develop a sustainable line of products for many years to come. And once automation sets in, you'll begin to build up momentum. Automating your product sourcing will save you time. And time equals money. The more automatic it becomes to source products, the more products you can investigate. The more items you consider, the more great ideas you'll find. And the more profitable ideas you have, the broader your merchandise line can be and the more products you'll sell.

The Product Sourcing Mindset can transform your business and give you the skills needed to develop a sustainable line of products for many years to come.

Summing Up

You've learned a very powerful method to propel you into the world of your customers and learn their buying habits, wants, and needs. In the next chapter, we'll show you what to *do* with all that information. Before we move on though, let's review the hallmarks of the Product Sourcing Mindset.

- Rather than trying to *pull* product ideas out of thin air, you must *surround* yourself with an inexhaustible supply of ideas for sellable products.
- Integrating your product sourcing tasks into your daily activities will help them become second nature to you.
- The person who trains themselves to look for opportunities in everything will find them. The person who is waiting for the obvious opportunity to present itself will miss the possibilities that come their way.
- Good product sourcing strategists have a bit of the private-eye in them. One idea leads to another, and one product leads to a more profitable one.
- Brainstorm ideas! Product sourcing is a numbers game. The more ideas you gather, the more product line winners you'll identify.
- When brainstorming, don't censor your ideas. Censoring up-front is one of the fastest ways to rule out a great idea.
- Ultimately, your attitude affects your product sourcing. If you approach the question of what to sell from a position of abundance, you'll find more than enough products to sell.
- The Product Sourcing Mindset allows you to intermingle your product selection activities in with your daily tasks.
- Reading "widely" is imperative for successful product sourcing. Reading is the window to your product sourcing world. Make it a requirement to read or scan a variety of things daily.

Chapter 3

The Product Sourcing Notebook

To successfully build a house, you need the right tools. The same applies with building your business. Without the correct tools, you can't build a good foundation for your business, nor can you make it grow. Disorganization, forgetting important data, and wasting precious time spent searching for important papers are all enemies of an entrepreneur's success. The same holds true for your product sourcing endeavors. Without a strategy to catalog your product sourcing information, you'll lose time and great product ideas will come ... and go ... before you have a chance to act on them. Studies show that without a record, 90 percent of your ideas will be lost by the time you're ready for them. 90 percent! This leaves you with trying to build a profitable business using only 10 percent of your product sourcing concepts. Not very good statistics, are they? In this chapter, we'll show you a valuable tool called the Product Sourcing Notebook, which will help you keep 100 percent of your ideas, and direct all 100 percent of them toward your profits.

Benefits of a Product Sourcing Notebook

Sellers lead busy lives and you can't leave your product sourcing to chance. Many people overestimate their memories and underestimate how busy they are. The Product Sourcing Notebook steps in to bridge that gap. In fact, this is one of *the* most important tools in your seller's toolkit. Your Product Sourcing Notebook is a physical notebook or, if you prefer, a PDA (Personal Digital Assistant) that you will use on a daily basis to document all your product sourcing ideas and potential supplier information. Successful sellers have told us that they could not have built their business without using a Product Sourcing Notebook of some sort. In fact, several sellers told us that it took losing the information on a few stellar ideas, and consequently a significant amount of money, before they really started taking the concept of the Product Sourcing Notebook seriously. Once they realized what it could do for them, it was never far from their side.

Using a Product Sourcing Notebook is critical to the success of your business because you simply can't remember every potential product idea that you come across each day. How many times have you read an article in the morning paper that got you thinking about a potential product, only to find by lunchtime you were already fuzzy on the details of what you read? Information you were sure you'd store in your "memory bank" about an interesting web site or the name of a manufacturer is now nowhere to be found. It's not surprising really. After all, how can you remember that great product idea when you had to immediately reach for a ringing telephone? And no wonder you forgot to follow up on that supplier, because two orders came in and you had to set aside that particular piece of paper. As entrepreneurs, we hop from one task to another, dozens of thoughts spinning in our minds. When a new thought occurs we frequently interrupt what we're working on and pursue it before it escapes us, or before we're called away again, that is. We're constantly juggling tasks and interrupting ourselves. Occasionally, we jot things down, but on scraps of paper, envelopes, napkins, and other odds and ends which get lost in the shuffle. To be effective, we must be organized, and this involves a system of recording that will eliminate the need to rely on our memory and prevent us from forgetting those product ideas and concepts that surround us. By using your Product Sourcing Notebook, the ideas you have today will be easily available when you're ready to use them two weeks from now.

Without a record, 90 percent of your ideas will be lost by the time you're ready for them. 90 percent! This leaves you with trying to build a profitable business using only 10 percent of your product sourcing concepts. Documenting your ideas in your Product Sourcing Notebook is vital to building your business.

Time to Write

"But wait!" you say, "I don't have time to write all these things down." Well, this is exactly why it's critical to have a Product Sourcing Notebook. We once heard a great saying: "The pencil remembers what the head forgets." By not putting the time in up-front to jot down your product sourcing notes, you'll end up spending time on the back-end trying to remember the idea, the details, or even worse, you won't even remember that you forgot something and it will be gone forever. In retail, ideas + products = revenue. If you do not take your product sourcing activities seriously enough to document the results, it will affect your bottom line. Why not use this inexpensive tool and get big results along the way?

Writing things down also brings clarity to your thinking process. Studies show that writing things down improves your efficiency, and is even good for your mental health. Another important feature of having a Product Sourcing Notebook is centralization. With your Product Sourcing Notebook, your ideas will be in one central repository, rather than spread all over on small pieces of paper in your wallet, on the back of your gas station receipt, or scrawled across the empty sack from last week's lunch. Centralization alone will save you time, money, and frustration.

With a Product Sourcing Notebook you have a living document of your ongoing product ideas, notes on niche markets, supplier leads, and contacts. You can track your ideas as they progress and refer back to your notebook on an ongoing basis. Most importantly, when you tap into the millions of potential products to sell, your Product Sourcing Notebook becomes your own product selection catalog. Eventually, you'll have multiple notebooks or a PDA full of ideas for products to sell. And as you assemble the information in your notebook, you'll be filled with ideas, creativity, and energy.

In Chapter 2, we explained how, with regular use of the Product Sourcing Mindset, automation sets in. The same holds true for the Product Sourcing Notebook. After using it for a short while, you'll wonder how you ever did business without it. And when used in conjunction with the Product Sourcing Mindset, the Product Sourcing Notebook will take your business to the next level.

"The pencil remembers what the head forgets."

—Anonymous

Choose Your Wonder Tool

In business, it's frequently the little things that make the biggest difference. Often, people overlook the basics in search of sophisticated techniques, software, and tools. Whoever said the secret of true greatness is simplicity was right. And the Product Sourcing Notebook is simplicity at its best. The shape, style, and design of your notebook is up to you. Lisa uses a 5" × 6" notebook. Some people prefer a PDA. For most people, an 8.5" × 11" binder is too cumbersome to do the trick. We recommend a smaller, more compact model. The only thing you need to keep in mind is that the notebook needs to be compact enough for you to carry *everywhere*.

A physical notebook gives you the advantage of tactilely experiencing the writing process, something that many experts say helps cement concepts in your mind more so than the process of digital logging. It is also a simpler process, as grabbing a notebook and pen and jotting down a few notes can be easily done anytime, anywhere. The disadvantage, of course, is that the information is analog rather than digital and will need to be transferred into a digital format at some point. We'll talk about how to do that later in this chapter. For those of you who have a PDA or want to start using one, there's only one important rule—back it up on a regular basis! We've never forgotten the story of one very successful eBay PowerSeller who had amassed over two years' worth of product sourcing data in his PDA. He used to call it his product sourcing bible. One day, something went bad in the unit and his data was unrecoverable. Sadly, he hadn't transferred the data from his PDA in many months. Months and months of work, and ideas from trips to two trade shows, went down the drain. Thankfully, he didn't lose all of it. A general rule for any electronic device that holds your business data, whether it's a PDA, computer, or cell phone, is to back it up! Only then can you be secure in the knowledge that the critical information you use to run your business will never be compromised. No matter what style of Product Sourcing Notebook you prefer, "hard copy" or digital, the most important thing to keep in mind about *your* Product Sourcing Notebook is that it is of a type that you both like and use.

Set Up Your Product Sourcing Notebook

In order to set up your Product Sourcing Notebook for maximum effectiveness, you'll want to organize it in a logical and useful fashion. This will allow you to quickly and easily access your notes, and make use of the data for full-scale results. To do this, there are ten specific types of information you'll want to document in your notebook. In the next section, we'll go into more depth about each of these ten categories, but first, let's outline the different sections you'll want to include:

- **Product Ideas**   Your product idea section will be your "jumping off" point. This section of your notebook that will drive all the other information you collect.
- **Descriptions**   Because you will come across multitudes of ideas as a result of being in the Product Sourcing Mindset, a brief but clear description of each product idea you come across will provide you with instant recall.
- **Prices**   No matter where you see an item, take the time to jot down the price associated with it, if available.
- **Model/Style Numbers**   A product's success can often be dependent on the model and style number of the item you sell. Don't skip this important detail.
- **Locations**   When you write down where you saw a particular product or idea, you'll have an instant "map" of it should you go back and need to research an idea further.
- **Trends**   Trending information is a big part of your product sourcing research and is invaluable in tying all the pieces together to make your ultimate product sourcing decisions.

- **Niche Markets/Profiles**   As with trending information, niche market details and profiles of target markets are a critical component in your product idea evaluations, providing you with direction and focus.
- **Supplier Information**   The companion section to your great ideas, supplier information is readily found in a variety of places. This part of your Product Sourcing Notebook will be the start of your own supplier rolodex.
- **Random Research Notes**   A repository for details that don't fall into any of the previous eight categories, making random research notes helps you chronicle the complete picture.
- **Follow-Up Notes**   In order to bring your product sourcing activities full-circle, creating a section for follow-up notes allows you to assess which ideas are worth pursuing and which can be put on the back burner.

In retail, ideas + products = revenue. If you don't take your product sourcing activities seriously enough to document the results, it will negatively affect your bottom-line profits.

Tip: Test different styles of Product Sourcing Notebooks to see which one works best for you. If you don't select one that's easy for you to use, it's very likely you won't use it. And without using your Product Sourcing Notebook, you're cheating yourself out of using all the great product sourcing ideas you get from using the Product Sourcing Mindset.

Good Data In = Good Results: Compile Your Product Sourcing Notebook

Your Product Sourcing Notebook is the place where you'll record daily all the ideas, products, markets, trends, and potential products there are to sell. Use it to make notes about all of your product selection ideas as well as any supplier sourcing information you come across. For example, if you're reading in a magazine about a new product, and something in the article catches your eye (as we discussed in Chapter 2), that information would go into your Product Sourcing Notebook. If you're scouring a trade show for new products, those notes go in your Product Sourcing Notebook. Out shopping at the mall? Not only will you find new ideas for products to sell, but you may also find the supplier's contact information for the product. If you have your Product Sourcing Notebook right there with you at the mall, you can write it all down and be primed and ready to call the supplier up on Monday and inquire about doing business with them.

As you start to add a variety of product names, niche market ideas, and supplier information, you'll see a picture start to unfold of what ideas to pursue first and which will be held for later investigation. Now let's look in more depth at the information that should go into your future Product Sourcing Notebook.

Product Ideas

A great idea can come from anywhere. It may be something that pops into your head unexpectedly, or it could be a concept you hear during the course of your day. Maybe your inspiration comes from a window display you see walking past your local store. Or it may be something as simple as connecting the dots between articles you've read recently. Keep in mind that you don't need to write volumes in your Product Sourcing Notebook, just enough information to highlight the key points you'll need in order to do further research.

Banking on Success

Kim, who sells teens and tweens clothing, had just read an article in a fashion industry trade magazine about the recent preppy revival, when her inspiration occurred. The article detailed how pullover sweaters, polo shirts with animal logos, and khakis were all the rage again. The new twist, the article said, is that the plaids are softer and the colors more muted this year. Kim made a note of this information in her Product Sourcing Notebook. A couple days later, going through the drive-up window at the bank, Kim noticed that the young college-aged teller working at the drive-up window was all decked out in her preppy best. Because Kim had just read the article a few days earlier, her "preppy radar" was turned on full blast. She noted the new preppy colors the girl was wearing as well as the way she had accessorized the outfit. At one point, Kim asked the teller about a very unique watch that matched her sweater perfectly. Turns out the watch was a brand new style that Kim had never heard of. After finishing her banking, Kim pulled into the parking lot and whipped out her Product Sourcing Notebook. Within moments, Kim made notes about the colors and accessories the fashionable teller had been wearing. Two weeks later, armed with the information in her Product Sourcing Notebook, Kim had done her market research on some preppy clothes and accessories and was ready to start calling suppliers. Because she had it all documented in her Product Sourcing Notebook, the turnaround time between the idea inspiration and idea implementation was very short.

Descriptions

Sometimes, when you see an item that interests you, you may not be able to get the brand name or specific style details right off the bat. Writing a brief description of the item in your Product Sourcing Notebook will give you enough information to go on so you can hit the search engines later and do a little detective work. In order to effectively research product information, you'll spend a considerable amount of time on your favorite search engine. Navigating the search engines is a skill that every good product sourcing detective needs to know. In the next chapter, we'll show you a variety of ways you can learn more about the potential of a product or idea by using a good search engine such as Google.

Tip: Target your searches and get more relevant search engine results by putting quotes around the words you're search for. For example, rather than searching for john deere lawn mower, by using quotation marks around "john deere lawn mower", you will be able to achieve more laser-targeted searches.

Prices

Try to identify some great product sourcing ideas every time you go shopping! But don't stop there. Make a note of the price the product is selling for at the local store. Even if you plan to sell a product online, and there may be a price variance, knowing price points out in the brick-'n-mortar marketplace is a good frame of reference. This will also help you when doing your pricing research since you'll be able to see what the local market price for your product is, as well as the national or global price points. When pricing your merchandise, the more information you have, the better. And the more you understand the prices in all marketplaces, the better sourcing decisions you'll make.

Model/Style Numbers

Panasonic model # KX-FPG376 is not something most of us would easily remember in a million years. However, this specific model and style information is something you'd need at your fingertips when you start researching the market demand for your products. Whenever you see, read about, or chat about a particular product of interest, be sure and get the model number and style name if possible. The retail success of a product not only rests on the brand name, but frequently on the exact model and style of the item. Cordless drills may have a strong market demand, but certain styles are out-of-this-world successful. Knowing the style or model # of the merchandise you plan to sell will allow you to compare apples with apples when researching the market demand for a product. Additionally, by using your Product Sourcing Notebook, you can gather as many model numbers as you want for future use.

Locations

"Now where did I see that again?" We hear this phrase time and time again with sellers who don't use a Product Sourcing Notebook. We talk to people who are trying to remember exactly where they saw an item or concept so they can go back and do more research, but are not able to remember exactly what newspaper, catalog, or consumer show they were at when they got their flash of brilliance. Talk about an exercise in frustration! Always write down where you saw your idea. If you saw it in a newspaper article you read at Starbucks, jot down the newspaper name and issue date. There's no time like the present to make note of where you found that potential money making idea.

Trends

As we discussed in Chapter 2, trending information is all around us. In fact you probably spotted ten new trends today without even realizing it! Tomorrow, with your Product Sourcing Notebook firmly in hand, and your product sourcing filter installed, you'll be ready for those trends to present themselves! Now you can document them and move on to something else, freeing up your mind. Recognizing and acting on a trend is a learned skill— and you don't need to be a born trend spotter to know how to do this. You do, however, need to be an avid note taker. When you begin documenting trends in your Product Sourcing Notebook, you'll begin to see some patterns emerge and be able to translate them into a profitable product.

Niche Markets

Like trends, niche markets are all around you, with more popping up every day. As you'll learn in Chapter 5, selling in a niche market is one of the best ways to ensure your success. Because of this, it's very important that you pay close attention to niche markets and document the ones that catch your eye. When you spot the subtle nuances of a niche, you've got to make some notes. For example, imagine one day you're driving down the street and spot a brand new store called The Organic Pet. You've never seen anything like this in your town before. At this point, you'll want to grab your Product Sourcing Notebook and jot down the name and address of the store, along with any other pertinent information. From there, you head home or go to your office and visit Google, researching the market for organic pet products. If you act on this information right away, you can be on the front of a sales curve before other sellers see the concept themselves. But if you don't write it down and act on it quickly, someone else might beat you to the punch.

Profiles of Target Markets

Who'd ever imagine learning about a target market at the dentist's office? Odd, yes, but that's exactly what happened to Brett and his wife, Cindi, an aspiring online entrepreneur. As Brett sat in the waiting room while Cindi was in with the dentist, he came across an article in *People* magazine regarding the high-end baby products market. It caught his attention immediately because Cindi was in the process of starting a web site that specialized in high-end infant and toddler clothing, furniture, and accessories. Brett read the article with interest since it was a fairly in-depth story on the niche, the target market, and featured products. Unfortunately, Brett didn't have Cindi's Product Sourcing Notebook, but as soon as she was out of the dentist's chair, he excitedly told her about the article. Cindi, who never went anywhere without her Product Sourcing Notebook, was able to make notes on all the important points in the article. Without her notebook, who knows what scrap of paper that information might have ended up on? You just never know when you're going to come across that nugget of gold. Be ready to grab it when you do!

Supplier Information

Whether sitting at your desk calling suppliers or writing down supplier contact information from a product box, by logging the details into your Product Sourcing Notebook, you can begin to build your own supplier file. Jordan, an eBay seller who was on the verge of making the leap from Silver Power-Seller to Gold PowerSeller, was driving through the industrial area in his city one Saturday afternoon when he stumbled upon a gold mine. He was going to visit a friend in a newly repurposed part of town when he came upon a little "manufacturer's hub" on a street he'd never been on before. Several manufacturers had relocated their businesses to the newly remodeled warehouse space. Jordan couldn't believe his eyes. "There were four or five companies lined up side by side that I never knew existed in the city. At the time I was new to the whole concept of a Product Sourcing Notebook, and I had a brand new one with me. I was writing down company names and addresses as fast as I could!" laughs Jordan. After making contacts with all of the companies, Jordan began doing business with one of them on a regular basis. The addition of their products to his product line allowed him to increase his revenue and expand his business to the next level of Gold PowerSeller. Additionally, a contact at another company provided him with the name of a distributor in the area, whom Jordan also began working with. He estimates that this latest supplier connection will allow him to reach the Platinum PowerSeller level within six months. As you can see, by writing the supplier information in your Product Sourcing Notebook, you begin to build your own database of suppliers—a database that is unique to you, based on your own research!

Random Research Notes

Bits and pieces of information are useless when they're floating around in your head or on Post-it notes that are falling off your desk. But in your Product Sourcing Notebook, they're no longer mental clutter, but rather stepping stones to your next successful product. If you have an idea that is "out in left field," write it down. One weekend athlete we know actually got one of his best ideas while in left field, waiting for a fly ball that never came. Fortunately, he had his Product Sourcing Notebook in his truck and was able to get his thoughts down on paper on the way to the post-game pizza bash. Remember, because you're scanning information when using the Product Sourcing Mindset, you'll have a lot of random thoughts to catalog. Make every thought count. Put them in your notebook.

Follow-Up Notes

You've gathered information, written it down, even done some research. What did you turn up? Set aside a few minutes and make some updates in your Product Sourcing Notebook. Lisa likes to use highlighter pens to highlight the ideas she wants to move forward with. Those later get transferred to an Excel spreadsheet which is used as a master file. Lisa also uses an up arrow or a down arrow next to each idea after she researches it. Hot product ideas get an up arrow, while duds get a down arrow. Items that require more research get a dash mark. These "icons" make important information easy to spot. Take a few minutes and give the thumbs up or a "needs more research" note in your Product Sourcing Notebook. Without follow-up notes, you run the risk of not remembering whether or not you looked into an idea further and what the outcome of that research was. Your Product Sourcing Notebook is a tool that should work *for* you. Think of it as a new employee, one who contributes daily to the bottom line.

Your Product Sourcing Notebook becomes your own product selection catalog. Eventually, you'll have multiple notebooks or a PDA full of ideas for products to sell. And as you assemble the information in your notebook, you'll be filled with ideas, creativity, and energy.

Success in the Midst of a Busy Day

A seller who was new to eBay credits her first successful product to having her Product Sourcing Notebook nearby at the right time. Attending an estate sale one Saturday, this observant mom noticed a group of brothers all absorbed in some sort of handheld device. Wondering what was keeping these boys so engrossed while their parents were browsing, she wandered over to the boys and casually inquired about their new toy. She learned from the group that they were all using a newly released handheld game player and that it was the hottest thing with kids these days. She talked to them a little more and found out the name of the product and a bit about the games and cords connecting the handheld players. Quickly leaving the estate sale, the minute she got to her car, she reached for her Product Sourcing Notebook. Jotting down notes, fast and furious, she was able to document the name of the portable game player, the titles of the games the boys were playing, and the description of the accessories she saw them using. Confident in knowing that she had written down all the pertinent information, she headed off to finish her Saturday errands. A trip to the grocery store, the library, and to pick up her oldest child at a friend's house took up the rest of the afternoon. It wasn't until everyone was in bed that night that she had a chance to pull out her Product Sourcing Notebook and review what she'd written earlier that day. "If I had waited until I got home that night to write all those ideas down, I guarantee I would not have remembered," she told us.

Organize Your Data

The way you organize the information in your Product Sourcing Notebook depends largely on the kind of notebook you choose. If you use a PDA to record all your sourcing notes, you have a variety of options in the way you can sort and categorize the data, depending on the model of PDA you own. Most basic PDAs handle standard personal information management (PIM) functions and run application software which will allow you to easily organize your product sourcing data.

If you're using spiral-bound notebooks, the process of organizing the data will be more manual. The easiest way we've found to document information in a spiral notebook is to create one page per item, thought, or category. Rather than cramming several noteworthy blurbs on one page, keep it to one piece of information per page. This gives you enough room to go back and make more notes as needed. Date each page with the month, day, and year so you can easily reference the timeframe in which you documented the information. This is the system that Lisa has used for several years. Additionally, sometimes Lisa will tab her hot information with small Post-it notes if there is something she wants to refer to right away.

Create a Master File

If you log your information in a Product Sourcing PDA, you'll want to upload the file from your PDA to your computer at least once a week. Because PDAs are designed to complement your PC, you'll want to work with the same information in both places. Synchronization software on a PDA works with companion software that you install on your PC. Check with the manufacturer of your PDA to determine which software programs work with your specific unit. The beauty of synchronization is that you always have a backup copy of your data, which can be a lifesaver if your PDA is broken or completely out of power.

Synchronize Data Between Your Computer and PDA

The following outlines how to synchronize data between your computer and PDA (also called syncing).

1. Connect your PDA to a PC with a cable or cradle/cable combination, normally through USB ports or serial ports located on the PDA and your PC. Some devices also support synchronization and data transfer through wireless connections such as Bluetooth.

2. Push the sync button (on the device or cradle) to start the synchronization process.

3. Wait as the process compares the files and information between the PDA and PC, and then copies the most current versions of the files to both the PDA and the PC.

If you use a spiral-bound notebook for your Product Sourcing Notebook, you will want to transfer that data to a central location on your computer. While there are several programs out there you can use to build a database of information such as FileMaker Pro 7, an easy way to organize your information is by keeping a master Microsoft Excel file. Most of us have Excel on our computers, and with this simple strategy you can use it to keep track of all your product sourcing data in one easy-to-access format.

Organize Data in an Excel File

Perform the following steps to organize your Excel file data.

1. Create a new file called Product Sourcing (or whatever you choose to name it).
2. Your file will have a number of worksheets, each with its own set of information.
3. Create a "shortcut" to your file and put it on your computer desktop for quick access to the file.
4. Create multiple new worksheets in your Excel file by going to the Insert menu and selecting Worksheet. This will give you several worksheets in your workbook.
5. Each worksheet should represent a single category of data. You can rename each worksheet using appropriate headings such as Product Ideas, Descriptions, Prices, Trends, Niche Markets, Supplier Information, and so on.
6. Within each worksheet, you can set up columns to track the specifics of your data.
7. You now have a master file of information that is current at all times.

If setting up and organizing your files seems like it takes a lot of time, keep in mind that searching your home, office, or computer for a critical product idea or supplier lead takes infinitely more time than centralizing your data. This is the only method that will allow you to build a custom-tailored library of potential products, concepts, and product sources with which to cultivate your business.

An up-to-date Product Sourcing Notebook is the only method that will allow you to build a custom-tailored library of potential products, concepts, and product sources with which to cultivate your business.

Embrace This New Habit

Remember the first time you attempted to ride your two-wheel bicycle with the training wheels off? Do you remember how awkward it felt at first? Even so, you kept on trying until you were able to glide smoothly up and down the sidewalk. What kept you going? Knowing that you would be able to ride through the neighborhood with your friends? Keeping up with your big brother or sister? Whatever your goals were, you were motivated to keep trying until you succeeded. Similar to your bicycle, your Product Sourcing Notebook is your vehicle to retail success. And while it may feel awkward to use at first, once you adopt this practice, it will become as second nature as riding a bicycle. Change is difficult for most people and new habits can sometimes be hard to form. Although you may have picked up this book looking for a fresh approach to product sourcing, learning about a new technique and actually *applying* it can be birds of a different feather. So when you are first starting out with your notebook, watch out for these gotchas.

When starting to use your Product Sourcing Notebook on a daily basis you may

- "Forget" to use it or put it somewhere where it's only sporadically used
- Find it isn't easily accessible
- Think you can't be bothered with going through the hassle of recording an idea which you are "sure" you'll remember

If this happens to you, don't worry about it! Just continue to reach for your Product Sourcing Notebook day after day. After the second week, it will become easier. And soon after that, it will become a habit. And good habits are hard to break!

Summing Up

Now that you're ready to transcribe all your valuable ideas, let's move on to Chapter 4 where we share the best places to go to get an abundance of product sourcing ideas for anything you want to sell. But before heading there, let's recap how to build your product sourcing library.

- Without a record, 90 percent of your ideas will be lost by the time you're ready for them. This leaves you with trying to build a profitable business using only 10 percent of your product sourcing concepts.
- Your Product Sourcing Notebook is a physical notebook or PDA (Personal Digital Assistant) that you use on a daily basis to document all your product sourcing ideas and potential supplier information.
- There's no need to write volumes in your Product Sourcing Notebook, just document enough information to highlight the key points you'll need in order to do further research.
- Studies show that writing things down improves your efficiency, clarity, and is even good for your mental health.
- If creating a Product Sourcing Notebook seems like a time-consuming task, consider how much *more* time you'll spend trying to remember or track down ideas you don't document—and how much money will be lost!
- After using your Product Sourcing Notebook for a few weeks, it will become second nature to you and you'll wonder how you ever ran your business without one.

Chapter 4

Idea Hotspots

Now that you're in the Product Sourcing Mindset, and have your Product Sourcing Notebook at the ready, you're primed to become an idea factory. All you have to do next is dive in and immerse yourself in an idea-rich environment from which you can pluck loads of creative, original, and blockbuster product ideas to sell. But wait? Where do you find this environment? Do you need to go to central New York and walk down the streets of Manhattan? Or move to southern California to be on the cutting edge? Well, you certainly could visit those places and find lots of good ideas, but fortunately, you don't have to. All you need to do is frequent some Idea Hotspots every day in order to create your own rich-idea environment.

Put simply, an Idea Hotspot is any fertile ground for product ideas. An offshoot of the term "idea hangouts," originally coined by infopreneur Jimmy D Brown, and "wi-fi hotspots," which allowed the world to plug in to the prolific realm of the Internet, the term "Idea Hotspots" truly embodies the spirit of creative product and supplier selection. Idea Hotspots are places that provide an unending source of new product ideas, market trends, developing niches, and product-line education. They can be physical locations, publications, or even people. Books, magazines, radio interviews, TV shows, shopping malls, stores, even your local coffee shops are all Idea Hotspots.

Best of all, you don't have to have special skills to tap into them, as one accomplished seller learned firsthand. Marguerite, an online retailer who initially dabbled in selling items both on Amazon and at her local flea market before settling on an eBay store, found out firsthand that frequenting Idea Hotspots offered an answer to her long-standing question of what to sell.

Marguerite describes herself as "one of those people who never used to know about trends, until after they happen." As she says, "By the time I found out about a trend, it was usually old news." In fact, when Marguerite first entertained the idea of forming a retail business, she struggled to come up with a list of creative ideas for her product line. "The worst part was," says Marguerite, "that I didn't think I was a creative 'idea' person." Or at least she didn't until she learned about Idea Hotspots. After she began frequenting

Idea Hotspots, Marguerite was able to make numerous lists of potential product-line ideas in her Product Sourcing Notebook. "What amazed me is that I realized that all I needed to do was hang out and become a sponge, and become aware of all the ideas that were surrounding me on a daily basis," muses Marguerite. "All of a sudden, surrounded by these idea-rich hotspots, I became a creative person by virtue of all the information flowing my way! And this made a very positive impact in my confidence level, being able to come up with great ideas for products to sell." Marguerite's favorite Idea Hotspots are magazines, trade publications, and consumer shows, all of which we'll explore later in this chapter. These days, Marguerite finds herself in the enviable position of having more ideas for products to sell than time to sell them. So much so that she's helped two of her friends launch their own eBay businesses with product ideas that Marguerite came across through her frequenting of Idea Hotspots.

Once you start frequenting the Idea Hotspots described in this chapter, you'll find yourself becoming a creative, idea-rich person, just as Marguerite did. Combine these hotspots with being in the Product Sourcing Mindset and you'll have a variety of resources you can count on to provide you with an abundance of product sourcing suggestions. Like a seed planted in rich soil, your business ideas will grow once you plant yourself in these Idea Hotspots.

Hanging Out with Ideas

There's a world of product sourcing ideas out there just waiting to be discovered. Information on trends, hobbies, lifestyle changes, adaptations of classic activities, new products, emerging markets, and technologies are all around us. Every piece of information you come in contact with is an opportunity for you to spin it into a sellable product for your business. As the old adage goes, birds of a feather flock together. And such is the case with product sourcing ideas. It's the words, phrases, thoughts, and stories that will lead you to your next profitable product. They congregate together, keeping company in many of the same gathering places, so all you have to do is show up and "visit" on a regular basis. In this chapter, we'll tell you about the best and brightest Idea Hotspots, which should allow you to surround yourself with concepts that can lead directly to products that buyers want. We'll also share with you some of our favorite, little-known idea coves that you'll want to drop by again and again.

Idea Hotspots are hubs of activity, a fresh renewable source of ideas. The places stay the same, but the information changes time and time again. Every time you return, you'll find something new. Idea Hotspots will generously bestow upon you more food for thought than you could ever imagine. And though you're about to learn of some time-tested proven Idea Hotspots, these are just the beginning! Once you recognize and understand the concept of

Idea Hotspots, you'll be able to seek out and find those special ones that really get your creative juices flowing. And the more time you spend at an Idea Hotspot, the more answers you'll have to the question: What should I sell?

Publications

In Chapter 2, we divulged one of our secrets to product sourcing success: daily reading. When it comes to lucrative product sourcing, reading is fundamental. The periodicals listed in the following sections should be required reading for every retailer. Within these categories are literally thousands of topics for you to choose from. These publications are where the ideas are, and where trending information lives. The writers, advertisers, and editors who contribute to these periodicals are experts in whatever industry or market they're writing about. And this is the very reason why these types of Idea Hotspots are a product sourcing lifeline.

When considering where to start or which publication to read first, there's no need to search around, trying to pick the right one for you. It's better just to start somewhere. Anywhere. As you work your way through the pages of the trade magazine, newsletter, or catalog you'll find yourself automatically drawn in the direction of where you should go next. If you already have some favorites, by all means keep reading those, but just as importantly, read publications that are new to you, and even ones you don't have any interest in. Remember, one of the key fundamentals of product sourcing success is that you don't need to have an interest in something for it to be a profitable idea.

Tip: When reading your product sourcing periodicals, use Post-It tabs to flag important pages and cross-reference the information in your Product Sourcing Notebook. Then devote a few shelves, or better yet, an entire bookcase to your product sourcing publications. You'll find that you can quickly and easily build a million-dollar library of product sourcing materials.

Trade Magazines and Newsletters

Trade publications are, hands down, one of the best sources of ideas for products to sell. If you want to source like a professional, understand trends like a professional, and market like a professional, you must live where the professionals do—and that's in the trade magazines. Trade publications are basically magazines, newsletters, and newspapers written especially for the "trade," a term used to describe professionals working in a particular industry. Every major industry has at least one trade publication. The style of publications vary—ranging from elaborate full-color magazines to brief but powerful plain-text e-mail newsletters. To stay current on what's happening in a variety of industries, we subscribe to several trade publications on a regular basis. Retail trade publications are not written for, or generally available to, the consumer. However, you do not need to be selling in the industry to have access to, or subscribe to, a particular publication. We'll discuss just where to find them in a moment. Suffice to say, trade publications will provide you with practically everything you need to know to sell in a niche.

A trade publication will provide you with:

- What customers in the marketplace are buying
- New industry trends
- Retailer sales and marketing techniques
- Advertisements from legitimate suppliers
- Trending information, including trend spotting and trend forecasting. Find out what products are projected to be hot 12 to 18 months down the road.
- New product introductions
- Editor's picks for up-and-coming best sellers
- Dates and locations of industry trade shows
- Industry-related web sites
- Customer service strategies
- Interviews with other retailers

Some examples of industries that have their own trade publications are children's wear and accessories, toys, cosmetics, footwear, gifts, sporting goods, hardware, and gardening products.

For example, *Gifts and Decorative Accessories Magazine* at www .giftsanddeccom/ is a leading trade publication covering the gifts and decorative accessories industry. When you subscribe to this magazine, every month you receive an issue that's jam-packed with product ideas, trends, and supplier information. *Gifts and Decorative Accessories Magazine* also prints lists of what products are popular, cited by region (North, South, East, West), as well as a list of the top five keyword searches on eBay for gifts and accessories items.

You can find a sampling of available trade magazines at www .diamondpublications.net. However, the best way to locate trade magazines for the industry you're interested in is by doing a Google search (or an Internet search using your favorite search engine). Let's use the example of a search for trade publications in the children's products industry. Perform the following steps:

1. Go to www.google.com.
2. In the search box, type in "children + trade magazine" or "children + trade publication" or "children + industry publication" (without using the quotation marks).

3. The search results returned by each of these searches offers you a variety of different trade publications, including *Baby Shop Magazine*, a magazine for independent retailers of juvenile products. This magazine contains a variety of articles on trending, the target market for the industry, and new products coming into the marketplace.

Note: A quick browse of the *Baby Shop Magazine* web site shows that you can receive a free subscription to this magazine. The web site also has a comprehensive list of suppliers for children's products.

Whatever industry you're interested in selling in, make sure you utilize trade publications. It may take some digging online to find them, but they're there, waiting and ready to help you with your product sourcing.

Consumer Magazines

Country Living, Organic Style, Parenting, Salt Water Fly Fishing—unlike trade publications, all these magazines are geared for the consumer. And these days there are magazine topics based on every subject. So why would you be interested in reading them for product sourcing? Because these magazines contain pages and pages of articles, advertisements, product reviews, and details on the niche they cover. Take the publication *Salt Water Fly Fishing*, for example. The publication describes itself as "a magazine dedicated to providing its readers with information, tips, and techniques about the growing sport of saltwater fly fishing. Its articles and columns reflect the philosophy of providing practical how-to articles on all aspects of saltwater fly fishing." So, if you're interested in building an eBay store or web site designed to sell saltwater fly fishing gear, this is the publication for you. Not only will you find out about the latest and greatest in products and trends, you'll learn from the articles what the problems, needs, and desires of saltwater fly fisherman are. This is how you start to get an insight into the minds of your potential target market.

Are you a car fanatic, a quilting maven, a train nut? Then you probably already subscribe to your favorite consumer magazine. But if you're not into a niche and know nothing about it, consumer magazines plunk you right down in the middle of the lifestyle. The following is another reason to pay close attention to the consumer magazines on the newsstands. If a publisher is going to invest money to create a monthly printed publication, it's because there is a niche, trend, or lifestyle change fueling demand for the magazine. And if there's enough demand to create a magazine, you can bet there are a plethora of products to go with that niche market.

To select a publication, go to your local Barnes and Noble bookstore or a full-service newsstand, and you'll see hundreds of publications—newspapers, magazines, special issues—displayed side by side for you to choose from. While you may not want to purchase every single issue that peaks your curiosity, you should still write down their names in your Product Sourcing Notebook.

Once you have a publication's information, you can then go back to your favorite search engine (we like Google) and research those titles online. A lot of print publications offer free access to some of their content online, which allows you to get a sampling of what they're all about. Once you've started reading these publications, you might want to subscribe to them on a regular basis.

Tip: Browse through any parenting magazine and you'll glean enough information to develop a complete product line for a baby/child-related store. In fact, most consumer magazines have a "What's New" product section—pages designed to introduce new products and tell you what items are hot. None better exemplifies this than the "O" list in *Oprah Magazine*. The "O" list is a compilation of Oprah's favorite merchandise. If a product is featured in the "O" list, it is hot across the globe. And while you may not be able to sell the exact same products mentioned in a review like the "O" list, you can use the information to forecast and spot trends.

Newspapers

If we told you that you could find the best scoop on products gaining in popularity, fresh ideas, niche markets, and emerging companies for about 50 cents a day, would you be surprised? You can find this information every time you pick up a newspaper. Newspapers are an ideal place to "hang out" in order to find pages and pages of information on trends in society—what's hot, what's not, what people are thinking about, how they're living their lives. Newspapers are also excellent places to find out about new products, up-and-coming companies, manufacturer profiles, company contact information, and more.

Every city has a paper that usually contains a Lifestyle section and a Business section. These are the sections to grab and read through (before reading the comics and the sports sections) when you're looking for products to sell. Newspaper articles often outline, in detail, information on market demographics and new product profiles with an explanation of underlying trends and lifestyle changes. They run stories on what products are in demand, what the future is for the market, who's buying the products, and how much money folks are spending on them. In fact, you can often find the name and contact information for the manufacturer of the merchandise referenced right in the article.

A recent article in a local paper outlined in detail the evolution of Hello Kitty, the playful Japanese character whose image adorns toys, clothing, accessories, and more. The article talked in-depth about what products were popular (profiled by age group), who was buying Hello Kitty products, and what they were buying. The article also discussed the direction of the product line and gave a list of the top ten Hello Kitty products. The writer even delved into the vintage Hello Kitty collectibles market. You couldn't have asked for a better product study to understand and source in this very successful niche. A newspaper a day get ideas underway.

Advertisements

Advertisements are all around us. Every day we come into contact with hundreds of print, TV, and radio ads. Some advertising, of course, has gotten a bad rap in our country. Junk mail, commercials, and newspaper fillers are often relegated to the trash or are TIVO'd away. To the average person, advertisements can be an annoyance. But to the retailer, advertisements are walking and talking idea-generation machines. When you're in the Product Sourcing Mindset, advertisements never land in the recycling bin until they've passed through your product sourcing filter. And those that have promise should go straight into a file marked "Product Leads"... scores of ads should be assembled there for future review, to apprise you of new products, illustrate variations of old products, and while you're at it, show you advertising techniques that can be used for your own retail advertising.

Katie used an ad she received in the mail as the foundation for building her new crafting store. One day, she received an 8.5×11 color brochure announcing that a major scrapbook show was coming to her city. Since scrapbooking was a part of her potential business model, she visited the web site URL for the Scrapbook Expo that was listed on the brochure: www .scrapbookexpo.com/index.html. She was immediately intrigued by what she saw. Here was an opportunity to learn about the scrapbooking industry from top manufacturers, see the products, and meet the exhibitors. At the Scrapbook Expo web site, she even found an offer to sign up for a free newsletter, and discovered a list with contact information for all of the vendors presenting at the show. Katie had recently learned about the new trend of "life caching," a trend so dubbed by the trend forecasting web site http://trendwatching.com. Katie knew that scrapbooking was a big part of this megatrend and decided that attending the scrapbooking show was a great opportunity to explore this product opportunity further. "If I still recycled ads without looking at them," says Katie, "I would've missed out on this great opportunity to learn more about this niche."

Ads sent to your home aren't the only good lead generators around—so are newspaper and magazine ads. Most major newspapers feature a Sunday ad section. Copious amounts of color flyers fill out the center of the paper, all with products jumping off the page. Want to get a snapshot of what's selling? Want a glimpse of what's hot and "in"? Looking to find out what colors and styles are coming back? Want to learn how to assemble a product line?

Just look through the ad circulars in the Sunday paper. If you're a retailer, ads are your friends, acting as free guides to the products that sell and the consumers who buy them.

Vendor Catalogs

Even though you may not have set up your first vendor account yet, you should at the very least be on the mailing lists for several suppliers. This is because, in addition to your Product Sourcing Notebook, supplier catalogs are literally another library of product selection ideas. Reviewing supplier catalogs is a critical link in finding products to sell and in locating merchandise that other sellers may not know about. Many sellers don't realize that vendors often manufacture and distribute multiple product lines *in addition* to the products you might be familiar with. Often, the only way you can find out about these products is by exploring the supplier catalog.

Your goal as a retailer should be to get on the mailing lists for multiple suppliers in multiple industries. Once you start getting regular mailings from these vendors, you'll in a sense be putting part of your product sourcing research on autopilot. This is because the vendors will start to send you new merchandise previews, special promotions, and inventory closeout catalogs without you having to request them. Some suppliers even have a "hot news" e-mail which they send out weekly. Because printed catalogs and web sites take a considerable amount of time to update, e-mail updates are the best way to learn about supplier information that's hot off the presses.

Supplier catalogs serve another purpose in that you'll have, right at your fingertips, suggestions for a variety of add-on products to complement your existing product line. When reviewing vendor catalogs, remember to keep an open mind and put the information through your product sourcing filter. After all, your next hot product might be buried in those pages. When ordering catalogs, be sure to consider suppliers that you're interested in as well as those you know nothing about. As with trade publications and consumer magazines, your eyes will be opened to profitable product lines you didn't even know existed.

Note: Most vendors will require a business license number in order to send you a wholesale catalog. Because their catalogs usually quote the wholesale pricing, they're not available to the general public. Make sure you have your business license in hand before contacting suppliers to request their catalogs, price lists, or to get on their mailing lists.

Consumer Catalogs

Similar to advertisements, many people view unsolicited catalogs as junk mail. A savvy product sourcing detective, however, views them as product cornucopias. In fact, we regularly sign up to receive as many catalog mailing lists as possible. Now while your postman probably won't appreciate the extra volume of mail delivered, hardly a day will go by that you don't receive a catalog spilling over with product ideas, new niches, and clues to what's hot. Thousands of catalogs are available to consumers today. So many, in fact, that there are actually directories of catalogs, such as the one at www .catalogs.com. Catalogs.com lists hundreds of free catalogs in all categories, everything from BMX cycling catalogs to catalogs dedicated to party supplies for the perfect bowling party. Another site, www.shopathome.com, offers a huge variety of catalogs along with a top-pick section. Even Google has gotten into the catalog indexing act at www.catalogs.google.com, a beta project that allows you to browse titles of thousands of catalogs, both old and new, online.

Why do you want to be on every mailing list there is? Because each catalog is a study in niche markets, emerging trends, and new products. Companies that produce catalogs spend millions of dollars collectively on researching their target markets, ferreting out new products, and figuring out the best way to present their merchandise. Then, they wrap all that knowledge up in a slick and glossy publication and mail it right to your door, usually for free. All you need to do is sit back and wait for your perfect product sourcing study manual to arrive. Use these catalogs as workbooks. Mark them up, make notes, and use them as idea springboards. Once you have a list of budding ideas in your Product Sourcing Notebook, you can begin to do your research on market demand, as outlined in Chapter 6. If you want to build a store or web site around a particular niche, associated catalogs also provide you with a perfect example of how to build a product line, and how to write good sales copy to sell those products.

Organizations

One personality trait that attracts many people to the idea of becoming an entrepreneur is the desire to be independent—the dream of striking out on your own and building your own empire. But it is that very path that can leave entrepreneurs feeling isolated and struggling to stay plugged in to what's going on in their field. To succeed in any business, you must have a good network of associates and contacts in your chosen industry. Professional and consumer organizations fill both the need for connections and for contacts. Additionally, organizations geared to your niche are vibrant and stimulating Idea Hotspots. As with trade and consumer publications, there are as many organizations as there are related products, interests, and niches. You can be involved as little or as much as you like. At the bare minimum, you can benefit from the information on their web sites or by signing up for a monthly newsletter. To fully immerse yourself, you can also attend associated trade and consumer shows, which we'll discuss in the next section. Whether you sell online or offline, the power of connecting with suppliers and other retailers through organizations is enormous and will help you to stay "in the know" about the products to sell and how to sell them.

Trade Organizations

Trade organizations, also known as professional associations, are a great way to gain knowledge of your industry, to network, and to generally keep on top of current news affecting your business. They're also excellent resources for connecting with suppliers, learning about new products, and being the first to forecast industry trends. Most every line of products has an associated trade organization. Some are very large with expansive web sites and associated resources. Others are small, but rich in benefits. No matter what the scope of the group, though, locating the trade organization for a particular industry is well worth your time.

The best place to start is with the trade organization web site. This will tell you what the organization has to offer, provide you with free articles and information about the industry, and let you know about upcoming events and trade shows. Keep in mind that you don't have to join the organization to start reaping the benefits. Even if you're just in the beginning stages of exploring a niche, by getting on the mailing list for an industry organization you'll start to get connected and begin to glean ideas on products and trends. Frequently, perusing a trade organization web site on a regular basis will also provide you with an ongoing stream of relevant product information.

The Home Sewing Association (HSA) is a trade organization that represents many different facets of home sewing. Any individual or company involved in promoting or servicing the home sewing industry is eligible for membership in HSA. This trade organization provides a forum for manufacturers, suppliers, retailers, educators, publishers, and other companies. The Home Sewing Association web site has trade show information, retailer resources, merchandising articles, cutting-edge innovations just hitting the market, and they cover national and global trends in sewing. Much of this information is available for free at their web site at www.sewing.org/.

The International Housewares Association at www.housewares.org/ bills its web site as "Your access point for the $265 billion global housewares industry." Sound like a place you want to be? Absolutely! At housewares.org, you can sign up for a free industry newsletter, search for manufacturer contact information (see Figure 4-1), and check out the New Product Showcase page (see Figure 4-2), all for free. This web site also provides you with a direct link to the information for the International Home and Housewares Show, a gathering of over 60,000 professionals who attend to sell, buy, and learn about the housewares industry.

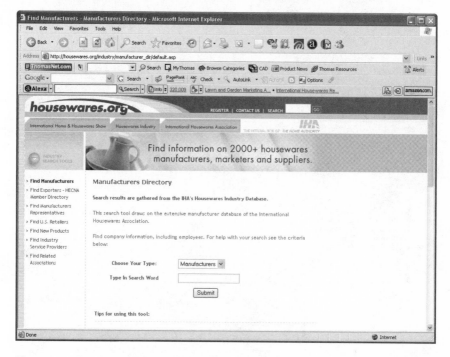

Figure 4-1   Search the Manufacturers Directory at housewares.org.

These two examples are just a sampling of the trade organizations available to you and the abundance of information that you can get from visiting their web sites. When you're ready, you can even become a member. The way to locate trade organizations for the industry you're interested in is by doing a Google search (or an Internet search using your favorite search engine). This search utilizes much the same process as that used for finding trade publications, except it incorporates different keywords. Let's use a search for trade organizations in the sporting goods industry as an example. Perform the following steps:

1. Go to www.google.com.
2. In the Search box, type in "sporting goods + trade organization" or "sporting goods + trade association" (without using the quotation marks).
3. The search returns a variety of results, including the web site for the Sporting Goods Manufacturers Association at www.sgma.com.

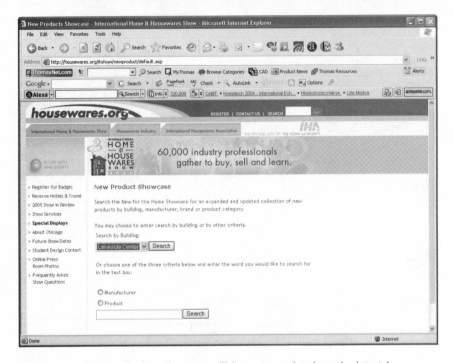

Figure 4-2 The New Product Showcase will keep you updated on the latest housewares products.

Note: This trade association, while rather expensive to join up-front, offers you the opportunity to join several free e-mail lists that provide information to you on different areas of the sporting goods industry, including apparel, footwear, and equipment. The Sporting Goods Manufacturers Association is also the owner of the largest sporting goods trade show in the country—the Super Show at www.thesupershow.com. Finds like this will utilize your product sourcing detective skills! Remember, one piece of information leads to another, one puzzle piece leads to another puzzle piece, until you've formed a complete picture.

Consumer Organizations

Like trade organizations, consumer organizations are geared towards bringing together groups of people with common interests. While you may think that a trade organization would be of more benefit to your business than a consumer organization, keep in mind that as a retailer you want to be close to your customer in order to find out what they want to buy. And where are your potential customers? Hanging out with consumer organizations.

A consumer organization can take many shapes or forms. It could be a web site, a national convention, or a local chapter of a larger entity.

For example, the American Quilter's Society at www.americanquilter .com/ is an organization dedicated to the growth of the American quilting community. Their web site provides a list of quilting shows, quilting publications, and in-demand quilting products. Anyone who sells in this popular craft category will tell you that quilters are passionate about their craft, and that they're always on the lookout for new, creative materials with which to further their art. As a retailer, where will you make the connections to these products? At a consumer organization like the American Quilter's Society.

People with common interests love to have a sense of community and so you'll want to tap into that community to find out what products and services they're looking for. Groups and clubs exist for every kind of interest and hobby, and by doing some research on Google—using the specific keywords for product, product line, or niche market—you can find a variety of consumer groups that will give you a window into the world of consumers. Also, keep your eyes and ears open for groups in your area that you can participate in. For example, if you're a retailer in the Pacific Northwest interested in selling outdoor recreational products, you'll find a variety of local groups and events that center around every sport imaginable. Pick a few that interest you and get on their mailing lists. Connect with people who use outdoor recreational products on a daily basis to find out exactly which products your global buyers might be interested in buying.

Tip: No matter where you live, each area of the country specializes in certain niches, markets, and products. What are the "natural resources" in your city or state? There are items that you'll only find in the Pacific Northwest that have a strong demand from buyers on the East Coast. A product that is plentiful in Maine and local to its source could be something that Californians are clamoring for. Ask yourself: What's special about the place where I live? What products are manufactured only in my area? This can be great way to tap into a market that other sellers don't have access to.

Yahoo Groups

Yahoo groups are a great way to find out what buyers of your potential products are looking for. Why? Because Yahoo groups allow you to get in and mix closely with your target market. If you want to know exactly what customers of a particular niche are talking about, thinking about, and buying, join the major Yahoo groups. You can find the Yahoo Groups directory at www.groups.yahoo.com. The groups are sorted by category, and from there are split into subcategories (see Figure 4-3). If you sell recreation and sporting goods, there are over 88,000 Yahoo groups for you to peruse through, and under that umbrella, hundreds of specific categories.

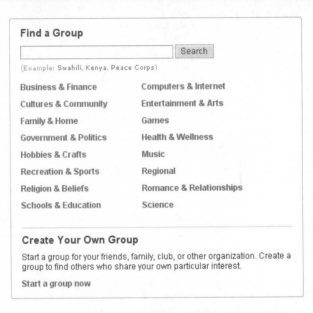

Find a Group

	Search

(Example: Swahili, Kenya, Peace Corps)

Business & Finance	Computers & Internet
Cultures & Community	Entertainment & Arts
Family & Home	Games
Government & Politics	Health & Wellness
Hobbies & Crafts	Music
Recreation & Sports	Regional
Religion & Beliefs	Romance & Relationships
Schools & Education	Science

Create Your Own Group

Start a group for your friends, family, club, or other organization. Create a group to find others who share your own particular interest.

Start a group now

Figure 4-3   Yahoo Groups are a great way to tap into what is happening in a niche market.

When you join a Yahoo group you should be listening for particular industry-related pieces of information. What topics are hot? What problems do members of the group have? What products and services are of interest to them? This is often where trends start. Not from the top down, dictated by major manufacturers, but on the streets, sparked by the interests of a few trend-setting people. It is then that the manufacturers respond with new products. If you're selling in the health and fitness categories, joining Yahoo groups related to health and fitness will tune you in to the products people are using, what they like about them, and what they wish they could buy. When people are passionate about a subject, they're always happy to share information and recommend products and services they enjoy.

Another great source for discussion groups can be found in the Community section of eBay at http://pages.ebay.com/community/boards/index.html. eBay's Discussion Groups are segmented by category and are a great place to find out what buyers are looking for, and what other sellers are talking about.

Companies spend millions of dollars annually surveying focus groups to find out what's in the minds of potential customers. You can quickly do your own "focus group surveys" by becoming a part of a discussion group and simply listening to and asking what people online have to say about a particular area of interest.

Tip: When you join a discussion group, your primary goal should be to become a member of the community, in order to be able to listen and learn. Joining a Yahoo group with the intent of prying information out of its members will get you nowhere fast. Start with being a "lurker," a person who reads the posts. If you have something to contribute, share your knowledge and expertise. Getting product sourcing ideas from a discussion group is a process of give and take. The more you get to know people, the more you'll tap into their needs and desires.

Shows

There's not a week that goes by without some merchandise show taking place. In the past several years, there's been a profusion of new shows for both consumers and professionals as both kinds of groups clamor for a place to meet to find out about new products, to network, and to participate in educational seminars. With a plethora of products and suppliers on site, along with brochures and catalogs free for the taking, what better place is there for your product sourcing endeavors!

Trade Shows

With over 4,000 trade shows being held across the U.S. each year, it's not a question of *if* you should attend one, but a question of which one and when. No matter what niche market you sell in, there's bound to be a trade show you should attend. A trade show is a large exhibit designed to bring together suppliers and retailers. Exhibitors in a specific industry can showcase and demonstrate their new products and services, while retailers can make those all-important supplier connections, touch and feel the products, and participate in educational seminars provided at the show. Trade shows are not open to the public and have specific attendance requirements (see the sidebar on the next page). They host hundreds or sometimes thousands of vendors and showcase literally tens of thousands of products. These industry shows are one of the best product sourcing venues available. Additionally, most trade shows offer networking events where you can meet with other professionals in the industry. Keep in mind, too, that trade shows are not only held nationally, but globally as well.

A small sampling of trade shows includes the following:

- The Housewares Show in Chicago at www.housewares.org/ihshow/about.asp
- The National Hardware Show at www.nationalhardwareshow.com
- The California Gift Show at www.californiagiftshow.com

Tip: For a list of all trade shows being held in the U.S., go to www .tradeshowweek.com. Trade Show Week allows you to search for upcoming trade shows by industry, location, month held, year held, show name, and keyword.

Additionally, Trade Show Week has a free online newsletter to keep you updated on all the latest news in the trade show industry. Attending trade shows and knowing how to navigate them and work successfully with vendors is an important skill to learn. For strategies and tips on attending trade shows, go to www.whatdoisell.com/tradeshowtips.

To locate trade shows, in addition to using the web site earlier referenced, you can perform an Internet search by doing the following:

1. Go to www.google.com.
2. In the Search box, type in the keywords for the industry + trade show—for example, "apparel + trade show" (without using the quotation marks).
3. The search then returns a variety of results for trade shows related to the apparel industry.

Tip: When attending trade shows, pick up as many catalogs and brochures as you can. You never know when a product you're not interested in today might be the perfect item for your store tomorrow. Additionally, pay close attention to the information at the trade show web site. Most trade shows will have an exhibitor list, complete with contact information for each exhibitor. If you're interested in doing business with a particular supplier, you might not need to look any further than the trade show web site to find out exactly how to contact them.

Requirements for Attending Trade Shows

Since trade shows are only open to professional retailers, it's of the utmost importance that you have all your legal paperwork in order before registering for the show. Some shows will have slightly different requirements than others, so you'll want to check the web site for that individual show to see what's needed for you to register. The following are the general requirements for attending a trade show:

- A business license. Also called your UBI# or Tax ID#.
- Professionally printed business cards. (No inkjet printer cards please!)
- A business checking account with your business name printed on it.

- Photo ID.
- Wholesale receipts. Some shows require that you provide them with $2,000 of wholesale receipts for relevant merchandise purchased in the past 12 months. If you're a new business owner and haven't yet started selecting your inventory, that requirement will be waived. However, to attend the show the following year, you'll have needed to make that purchase amount.
- A resale certificate. Print out and bring with you several copies of a resale certificate. This is required oftentimes by vendors if you place orders at the show. Resale certificates vary for each state. You can locate resale certificates at your state's Department of Revenue web site.

For more information on trade show requirements, visit www.whatdoisell .com/tradeshow.

Expand Your Product Sourcing Horizons

eBay is a great place to generate ideas for products to sell, no matter what your actual selling venue is. With millions of products and thousands of categories (52,000 at last count) browsing eBay categories will give you a mind-boggling assortment of ideas for products to sell and niche markets to explore. By going to eBay's All Categories page, you'll find a list of all the categories of products sold on eBay. This is a great place to start your product idea generating journey, but don't stop there!

Get your product sourcing detective magnifying glass out, and after you click those top level categories, drill down to the subcategories:

1. Go to the eBay All Category list at http://listings.ebay.com/_WO QQfclZ3QQfcoZ1QQloctZShowCatIdsQQsocmdZListingCategoryList.

2. Find the category you're interested in. Here, we'll pick Home and Garden.

3. Click the link at the bottom of the category listings. In our example, it says "See all Home & Garden categories." See Figure 4-4.

4. This will bring you to a full page list of hundreds of subcategories that can spawn thousands of ideas for products to sell. See Figure 4-5.

Consumer Shows

Consumer shows are another place to find hundreds of product ideas. They're also a way to entrench yourself in the best and brightest of a niche market. A consumer show is, in essence, a trade show for retail customers, meaning it's a public show serving specific industries or interests. Consumer shows span the range of everything from home shows to car shows, sportsman shows, RV and camping shows, computer and technology shows, craft shows, bridal shows, pet shows, and many others, both large and small. Currently, there are more than 1,500 consumer shows throughout the United States.

Home & Garden (#11700)
   Bath (#20438)
   Bedding (#20444)
   Building & Hardware (#3187)
   Dining & Bar (#71236)
   Electrical & Solar (#20595)
   Food & Wine (#14308)
   Furniture (#3197)
   Gardening & Plants (#2032)
   Heating, Cooling & Air (#41986)
   Home Decor (#10033)
   Home Security (#41968)
   Kitchen (#20625)
   Lamps, Lighting, Ceiling Fans (#20697)
   Major Appliances (#20710)
   Outdoor Power Equipment (#29518)
   Patio & Grilling (#20716)
   Pet Supplies (#1281)
   Plumbing & Fixtures (#20601)
   Pools & Spas (#20727)
   Rugs & Carpets (#20584)
   Tools (#631)
   Vacuum Cleaners & Housekeeping (#299)
   Window Treatments (#63514)
   Wholesale Lots (#31605)
   See all Home & Garden categories...

Figure 4-4   The "See all..." link at the bottom of each category section will take you to a long list of subcategories.

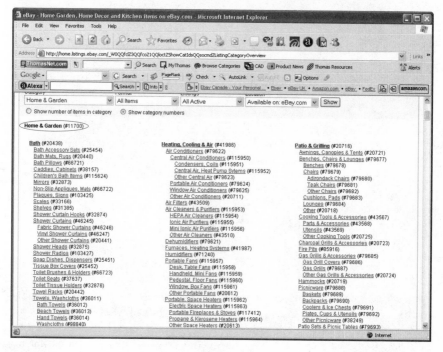

Figure 4-5 Browsing product subcategories on eBay is a great way to springboard product sourcing ideas.

While you can't buy wholesale at these shows, you can benefit from seeing a diverse product mix, gain product and brand awareness, and perform research and product testing. In addition to seeing the products in person, you can make numerous lists of potential top sellers in your Product Sourcing Notebook. Another advantage of attending consumer shows is that you can talk with the exhibitors one-on-one about their products and learn more information about a particular product line, usually getting manufacturer and distributor contact information along the way. Generally, the people who staff booths at consumer shows are very knowledgeable. Spend some time talking to the representatives and you'll walk away with enough information about their wares to know if it's something you might want to sell in your store. Consumer shows are another place to stock up on brochures and catalogs. You never know what you'll find in the manufacturer's literature that might lead you to your next great product idea.

Some of the largest consumer shows in the country are

- The Eastern Sports and Outdoors Show at www.sport.reedexpo.com/ eastern/eshome.htm
- The Seattle Home Show at www.seattlehomeshow.com

- The Pennsylvania RV and Camping Show at www.prvca.org/largestrvshow.html
- The Super Pet Expo at www.superpetexpo.com

To locate consumer shows, do an Internet search by performing the following steps:

1. Go to www.google.com.
2. Do a search on the keywords *year + industry show*—for example, "2005 + womens show" (without the quotation marks).
3. The search results will give you listings for all consumer women's shows being held in 2005.
4. The National Association of Consumer Shows at www.publicshows.com/displaycommon.cfm?an=1&subarticlenbr=5 also has a list of NACS consumer shows throughout the U.S.

General

Idea Hotspots come in all shapes, sizes, and forms, as you're probably starting to notice. Now that you have an understanding of what an Idea Hotspot is, you can begin making a list of your own special hotbeds of creativity. The following sections describe a few more of our favorite Idea Hotspots that we thought you should know about.

Bookstores

Can you generate product ideas by spending an afternoon at your favorite bookstore? Absolutely! One must only go to the bigger bookstores, like Barnes and Nobles or Borders, to be able to create an instant list of timely topics that have associated products with them. Surrounded by thousands of titles and subjects, you'll find a bounty of ideas within reach. Or you can go to a virtual bookstore like Amazon.com and browse for books on the niche you want to sell within.

Thinking about selling in the organic gardening market? Hop on over to Amazon.com and do a search for organic gardening. Not only will you find a list of books and magazines on the subject, if you look at the book listing itself and scroll down the page to Product Details, you can see the Amazon sales rank for the book. This number tells you how popular the book is. If your subject is a topic with a number of books that have a high Amazon sales rank, you can be pretty certain you have a hot target market out there looking for products.

When you're at the bookstore, don't forget to make use of the knowledgeable sales staff. If you're interested in selling in the decorative home accessories market, ask the sales clerk what the best-selling design books are.

This can be a boon for your product sourcing efforts. By knowing what books consumers are buying, you'll have an idea of what kinds of products the buyers who are reading these books will be looking for.

Current Events/Pop Culture

Try this test. Get a daily paper, look at the top stories, and then go to eBay to see if there are related products being sold. For better, or sometimes worse, there very likely are. Current events and pop culture happenings spawn product sales. People in the news, breaking stories, the good, the bad, and the ugly all have within them marketable products. Entrepreneurs through time have capitalized on product sales based on current events. We see this happening all the time when a particular sports team makes it to the World Series or the Super Bowl. For a short period of time, sales of related products go crazy, and then taper off. Sometimes all it takes is a newsworthy event about a public figure to spur a feeding frenzy of sales.

Other times, an international event, such as the war in Iraq, spawns not only a short-term fad, but a trend in sales. When the U.S. Defense Intelligence Agency issued playing cards to American soldiers with a photograph of a "most wanted" Iraqi on the face of each card, the decks became hot collectibles on eBay. Soon after, a commercial card printing company issued copies of the decks and sold untold thousands. After that, everyone wanted a piece of the pie, and now you can find a variety of political parody trading cards available. While the original defense agency playing cards may have started a fad, the war itself opened the doors to a trend: an overall resurgence of interest in war-related merchandise. History buffs, both young and old, are now snapping up new war-related items and vintage collectibles. Even toy makers got into the act and responded to this burgeoning interest with the reintroduction of GI Joe and WW2-related merchandise that hadn't been seen in stores for years.

Whether you act fast on a fad, or position your business to take advantage of an emerging trend, keeping track of what's going on with current events and pop culture will lead you in a variety of new product sourcing directions.

The Entertainment Industry

If it's "happening" in the entertainment world, there's usually a product, trend, or fad associated with it. People love to immerse themselves in what they see on the screen: big screen or small. Thus, the entertainment industry has spun off more trends, fads, and products than practically any other industry. In fact, these days the products generated by movies often make more money than the movies themselves. It used to be that entertainment was a commodity for entertainment's sake. Nowadays, movies and TV shows are designed to sell associated products. DVDs, CDs, books, clothing, toys, furniture, dolls, games, food, and the like are all positioned to be spin-offs of popular films and television shows. The entertainment industry represents a huge selling opportunity for retailers. Cult shows and mainstream movies all have products associated with them, and both kids and adults are snapping up the goods.

People have a fondness for, and attachment to, the TV and movie characters they grew up with. They also have money in their pocket to surround themselves with memorabilia from their favorite shows. When you connect the dots between those desires and the products available to sell, you end up with a one-way ticket to profits. Want to find out what's trendy? Keep your finger on the pulse of the entertainment industry. Reading the entertainment newspapers, magazines, and, yes, watching entertainment shows will help you become an expert in the field of related products.

You can find this information online also in the following entertainment hotspots:

- To find out what's popular in the entertainment industry, do a daily or weekly watch of the Lycos Top 50 at http://50.lycos.com/.
- This web site, http://movieweb.com/movies/releases/month.php, will tell you exactly what movies are being released for the entire upcoming year! Take a look at just some of the movies soon to be released. See any potential blockbuster hits on the list that might have million-dollar product lines associated with them? You bet!

Profits from *Star Wars* products over the course of the films' history are now in the *billions* on dollars. Retailers have made a lot of money selling *Star Wars*–related products. So tap into what's hot in the entertainment world, find out what people are searching for currently on the Web, and develop a huge list of potential product ideas. The entertainment industry is an ever-green, ever-changing niche. You can follow this one on an ongoing basis and always come up with new ideas for products to sell!

Shopping Malls and Retail Stores

Generating product ideas requires movement—getting out there in everyday life to see what products are being bought and sold and observing what products people are using. Shopping malls and retail stores are your marketplace for product sourcing ideas, and act as springboards for offshoots, combinations, and variations of products sold locally. When is the last time you went to the mall or a local store on an inventory sourcing expedition? If it wasn't this month, you're missing out! All major retailers do this. A big story broke in the news the other day about a Wal-Mart employee who was seen in his blue Wal-Mart uniform browsing the shelves of a Target store. He was scouting out their products and prices. In the industry, it's called shopping the competition. And whether you're Wal-Mart or an independent retailer, this process can provide you with very valuable information.

When you shop the competition, you're looking to see what the stores sell. What's being prominently displayed? What colors are new? What styles are hot? If you head to a specialty store, you can do in-depth research on the kinds of goods being offered to consumers. Keep in mind, you're not doing this to copy directly what another store is doing. You're spending time in these Idea Hotspots because you want to find out what is happening *now* and then translate it to what products or services you can specialize in, or offer alternatives to, *in the future*, in your own business.

When you go into a store, always check the displays. It's there you'll see the new colors and styles. When you go to a major retailer like Target, check the "end-caps." These are the displays at the ends of the aisles that face outwards and are usually where they stock the newest merchandise. As with all other Idea Hotspots, spend time in places that you don't usually frequent, too. If you're a sporting gear nut, head to a map and globe store instead. Get a fresh perspective. If you don't shop for yourself in high-end apparel stores, take an afternoon and go to the swanky downtown shops trolling for ideas. Try to go to at least one new (to you) retail store a week and make a list of ten potential product selling ideas. Not only will you have fun, but you'll be surprised at how many fresh merchandise ideas you come up with.

Trend Web Sites, Trend Spotters, and Trend Forecasters

Trend web sites are a great way to keep your finger on the pulse of what buyers want. Pick a niche and find the most popular related web sites, and within those sites you'll find articles about trends, changes, and what's hot in that area. Web sites that are an authority on a subject are great places to hang out and get specific information on what's happening in the marketplace. There are even unique web sites dedicated to trending information. For instance, www.trendwatching.com places trend spotters across the globe who report back on the latest trends. Trendwatching.com is designed for anyone who wants information on consumer trends and hands-on examples of new business ideas that will be making an impact in the near future. At Trendwatching.com, you can sign up for a free e-mail newsletter to keep you updated on current trends.

The media also loves to run stories on trends. A quick Google search of the keywords *industry* + trends (for example, "toy + trends"—without the quotation marks) will turn up a number of articles written on trends in the toy industry. Articles such as "Top Five Trends from Toy Fair 2005" and "Five Trends in Baby Toys" will tell you where product line direction is headed and what you should add to your inventory.

One of the most overlooked Idea Hotspots is people. We all know people who are constantly abuzz with talk of the latest and greatest gadgets, gizmos, or happening things to do. These trend-spotting folks are great Idea Hotspots. Ideas all start with people. How many trend spotters and trend forecasters do you know? Who do you know that always has the latest style shoes *before* they're cool, or who was into belly dancing before it became mainstream? These folks are trend forecasters—people who have that innate ability to know what will be popular before the rest of us do. And while you don't have to be a trend forecaster yourself, if helps to hang around people who are. Think of your current circle of friends, family, or business associates. Are there any trend forecasters in the bunch? If so, make a point of hanging out with them and asking them questions. They'll be flattered and happy to share what they know—and you'll have an insider's track into best-selling products that are still on the horizon.

Your Product Sourcing Network

Who makes up your product sourcing network? "My product sourcing network?" you may ask. "I don't even have one!" Well, every retailer needs a product sourcing network—a formal or informal group of people who act as your eyes and ears in the world, keeping track of all the product sourcing ideas *they* come across. When it comes to product sourcing, ten eyes are better than two, meaning if you have four other people out there keeping their eyes and ears open to new product ideas, your results will be multiplied. You don't need to hire a network of people or even make it a formal arrangement. Just enlist a few friends or associates to turn on their radar, give them a Product Sourcing Notebook, and keep in touch with them to see what they encounter in their travels.

The more people you can pull into your product sourcing network, the more ideas you can tap into. What passions or hobbies do your friends or colleagues have? Ian, an entrepreneur, who two years ago ventured into the world of online retail, has a friend who is an avid consumer technology fan. His buddy knows about new products before they even hit the stores. "Talking to him is always a great source of inspiration," says Ian, "and one of the primary ways I find out what is happening in the consumer technology arena." Once a month, Ian and his friend grab a burger and fries and spend a lunch hour talking over consumer technology, ideas which Ian continually transfers into profitable inventory purchases.

Search Term Suggestion Tools

If you want to know what products buyers are looking for, an important place to hang out is with Internet Search Term Suggestion tools. Search Term Suggestion tools are free powerful tools that tell you exactly what people are searching for on the Internet. Why is this important to your product sourcing endeavors? Because if you have a behind-the-scenes glimpse at what people are looking for on the Internet, you have some very strong clues as to products that people might want to buy.

The Overture Keyword Selector tool at http://inventory.overture.com/d/searchinventory/suggestion/ is one of the best Search Term Suggestion tools you can use. Let's say, for example, that you're interested in selling lamps, but you want to find out what style of lamp is popular and in demand. Using the Overture Keyword Selector tool, type in the keyword **lamp**. At the time of this writing, the search results told us that 138,696 people searched for the term *lamp* in the month of September 2005. (Overture provides search results for the month prior to the search.) See Figure 4-6. Good information to know, but here's where it really gets interesting. The search returns *all* associated keywords that were searched for *with* the word *lamp*. As you can see in Figure 4-6, every *kind* of lamp that people searched for is listed: floor lamps,

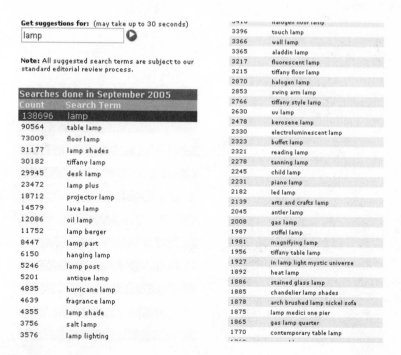

Figure 4-6 The Overture Keyword Selector tool can tell you exactly the kinds of products that buyers are looking for.

tiffany lamps, lava lamps, piano lamps, antique lamps, solar lamps, hurricane lamps, chandelier lamps, and more. Now all of a sudden you have hundreds of ideas for potential styles of lamps to sell! As if that wasn't enough, next to each keyword listing is the number of times a search was performed. So you can easily see that more people searched for tiffany lamps last month than desk lamps. This particular search returned over 250+ different entries for the word *lamp*! How's that for an Idea Hotspot? Before you started the search, you only knew you wanted to sell lamps. Now you know 250+ variations of lamps to sell and you know how many people are looking for them!

In addition to Overture's tool, Google provides a free Search Term Suggestion tool at https://adwords.google.com/select/KeywordSandbox. This keyword tool also gives you a list of terms most popularly searched for on the Internet. It does not give you the number of people searching for a particular term, but it does give you additional keywords to consider. Keep in mind that Google and Overture are completely different search engines, and different people search on one or the other. Therefore, the results you get with each report will be slightly different. Because of this, it's important to use both tools.

eBay also provides its own keyword report at www.buy.ebay.com, which gives you a list of highly popular terms that people search for on eBay. You can either browse these lists alphabetically or search by keyword. eBay's keyword searches are free for anyone to use.

Tip: eBay Pulse, at www.pulse.ebay.com, provides a daily snapshot of current trends on eBay, popular keyword searches, hot picks for products, eBay stores, and more. eBay Pulse is a great Idea Hotspot and you should frequent it on a regular basis.

eBay Seller Central

eBay has its own Idea Hotspot that's open to the public called eBay's Seller Central at http://pages.ebay.com/sellercentral/. Seller Central is a hub for finding out what products are hot on eBay as well as a place to learn about category-specific trending information. In the Category Tips section at http://pages.ebay.com/sellercentral/sellbycategory.html, you can discover what's in demand in a particular category, learn tips and tricks for selling in that category, and find links to category-specific discussion groups. The eBay Hot Items Report at http://pages.ebay.com/sellercentral/whatshot.html is organized by category with merchandise sorted by levels of Hot, Very Hot, and Super Hot. While the Hot Items Report provides a great entry into the world of in-demand items on eBay, don't stop at the top level! Use this as a jumping-off point for ideas. Too many people take this report at face value and consider only selling the merchandise on the list. To successfully find profitable products and niche markets, you should dig deeper. Combine the Hot Items Report with the Search Term Suggestion tools that you learned about earlier to refine your product sourcing ideas and chip away at the information like a jeweler cutting a diamond in the rough. It is then that your product sourcing ideas will begin to sparkle.

Summing Up

Thank you for coming with us to visit some of our favorite Idea Hotspots! There are many more enriching places to hang out at that we didn't have room to mention in this chapter, so if you'd like to find out about more great Idea Hotspots, visit www.whatdoisell.com/hotspots. Next, we'll move on to finding out how to carve out a niche for yourself among all the millions of products out there. But before we do, let's review some of the most important Idea Hotspots in this chapter:

- An Idea Hotspots is a fertile ground for product ideas.
- Frequent Idea Hotspots every day and you can *create* your own rich product sourcing environment.
- When it comes to lucrative product sourcing, reading is fundamental. Publications are where the ideas are, and where trending information lives.
- Both professional and consumer organizations geared to your niche are vibrant and stimulating Idea Hotspots.
- Discussion groups allow you to mix closely with your target market and glean knowledge that will enhance your product sourcing efforts.
- Trade shows offer a plethora of products and suppliers onsite, along with brochures and catalogs free for the taking. What better place for your product sourcing endeavors!
- The entertainment industry has spun off more trends, fads, and products than practically any other industry.
- Trend web sites are a great way to keep your finger on the pulse of what buyers want. Pick a niche and find the most popular related web sites, and within those sites you'll find articles about trends, changes, and what's hot in that area.
- Shopping malls and retail stores are your marketplace for product sourcing ideas and act as springboards for ideas regarding offshoots, combinations, and variations of products sold locally.
- If you want to know what products buyers are looking for, use the Internet Search Term Suggestion tools.

Chapter 5

How to Find and Identify a Niche Market

A re you a jack of all trades, master of none? Then it's time to find a niche! Selling in a niche market can give you greater power, profitability, and precision—the three "P's." And all of these can lead to a very strong and sustainable business. Finding a niche in which you can build your own market-share and attract and maintain a strong base of customers is one of the best ways for an entrepreneur to carve out a lucrative piece of the pie. And selling in a niche market can also be one of the fastest paths to success, with the least resistance.

The concept of selling in a niche market isn't new. Niche selling has been around for as many years as there have been retail stores. One must only reflect back on the phenomenal success of the Kirby vacuum cleaner company who 90+ years ago started selling *only* vacuum cleaners and *only* door to door. The top three specialty retailers in 2004—Best Buy, The Gap, and Staples—have all prospered by focusing on niche markets. And while variety store–model retailers, such as Wal-Mart and Target, do perform very well, their success is based on a system of volume and price. If you're just starting your retail business or are in the process of building up to a larger business, volume and price are a hard platform to compete on. So what is a niche and how does one go about finding a profitable one?

What Is a Niche?

A niche is a profitable segment of a larger market. When you sell in a niche, you're focusing on supplying products and services exclusively to that market. Rather than trying to be all things to all people, a niche seller strives to be a unique retailer to a narrow segment of the market. For example, women's apparel is a profitable market, while women's plus-size apparel is a niche. When you sell in a niche market, you can strongly identify the specific needs of the market. And those needs can be translated directly into products. In short, a niche is a small, distinguishable market that can be uniquely served by retailers, such as yourself, who provide products, services, and information.

Another critical component to niche selling is that your target market must be willing to spend money. Webster's New Millennium Dictionary of English defines a niche market as *a specialized and profitable part of a commercial market; a narrowly targeted market*. The keyword here is *profitable*. If your target market isn't willing to spend money on the product or services that support their interests, then you don't have a niche. You may have a small market, at best. Niche market buyers are hungry. They're ravenous for the products that will meet their needs. They have money to spend and they're willing to spend it—on whatever you can offer them that will further entrench them into the niche. A niche market has sustainable demand and potential growth for related products.

Often, people confuse a niche market with a small market. A small market has limited demand and limited growth for products. It's a market where people are either unwilling to spend a lot of money on the products, or where there's limited interest or demand for such products. If you sell a piece of farm equipment that's only used by a very limited number of people in three states, you have a small market. If you sell a specialty tool designed to perform a very specific task for people in 22 different countries, you have a niche. Small markets in and of themselves aren't bad; however, if you're dealing in a small market, you must realize that your sales and revenue potential will be somewhat limited. Sometimes, what starts out as a small market can grow into a niche, but in order for it to do that, it must possess some of the niche characteristics we'll discuss later in this chapter.

Another hallmark of a niche market is that your customers have similar needs and desires. Pull a random sampling of buyers in a niche market and you'll find some very strong commonalities among all of them. What they want, what they need, and why they want it, all arise from similar base values. If you sell in the organic food products niche market, you'll find that the majority of your customers have a concern for their health—not wanting to eat pesticide-laden or "lab-made" foods, they have a desire to conserve the earth's resources and want to know what it is exactly that they're putting in their bodies. This group of people is easy to select products for. Compare this to purchasing grocery inventory for a supermarket where your customer base is all over the board and it's hard to know who they are or what they want, and you can start to see why selling in a niche can be a much more attractive prospect.

When looking to identify niche markets to sell in, keep in mind the following very specific characteristics:

- A niche market should translate directly to tangible products or services. If you can't associate a number of products with a niche interest, then you won't have anything to offer your customers.
- Buyers must be willing to spend their dollars. Unless people are willing to make purchases on a regular basis, you don't have a sustainable *market* for your product. When selling in a niche market, you must first establish market demand.

- A niche market has steady interest *and* the potential for growth.
- There must be room for product expansion. A niche must have enough facets to have the potential for inventing new products and services that will cater to the needs of that niche. Although new products may branch out from the original product line, or become a hybrid and spawn related products, the end result is that they still cater to the needs of the target market. And as the needs of that target market grow, the opportunities in the niche grow.
- A niche has to be approached from a unique angle. Often, all it takes is a new angle on an old product or consumer need to springboard into a profitable niche. Thinking outside of the box is paramount when selling in a niche.
- A niche market capitalizes on a specialized product in an existing larger product line. Such a market isn't an unknown market. It morphs out of an industry with existing demand. While you can build an unknown product line into a niche, the time from market to profitability will usually be much longer.
- A niche is repeatable. Once you learn to identify and build sales in a niche market, you can use that same process to develop other successful niches.
- Niche sellers listen to their customers very closely. They're in touch and in tune with the pulse of what's happening in their customers' minds *and* hearts.
- A niche market seller focuses on satisfying the emotional needs of the consumer in addition to selling product features.
- A niche seller goes deep and narrow in their product line rather than broad and shallow. If you sell pet supplies in a variety store, you may sell only one or two brands of dog collars. If you sell pet supplies in a niche store, you might carry several brands of collars, as well as several styles.
- Niche markets emerge frequently as a result of new trends or changes in lifestyle. When you source products for your niche market, you'll concentrate on taking part of an existing market, putting it under a microscope, and locating the "gems" that retailers in the larger market have overlooked. Businesses selling in a broad marketplace often don't have the time or inclination to cater to a niche. That isn't their focus. But for a smaller retailer, it's a match made in heaven. Within every large market, there are underserved segments: *groups of buyers who are literally being ignored.* The niche seller who designs a business to serve those customers well will find a loyal group of buyers who'll shop with them time and time again.

In the women's apparel industry, the plus-size clothing niche has been hot and profitable for the past several years. But within that market, there's another niche of buyers who have been—and for the most part still are being—disregarded: the plus-size teen and young 20s group. It's only since these buyers have lately become very vocal about the lack of clothing choices that manufacturers and retailers have finally started to sit up and take notice.

Tip: The most successful niche retailers are those who become a specialist in a market. A business that becomes a respected authority and the "go-to" place for consumers with a common interest can gain the competitive edge quickly and retain customers on a long-term basis. Because of this, niche marketing demands a very different approach to the mass marketing of goods and services. Niche market advertising should be extremely refined in order to touch the "hot buttons" of the target group. What do they care about most? It's that area which you need to address.

Within every large market, there are underserved segments: **groups of buyers who are literally being ignored.** *The niche seller who designs a business to serve those customers well will find a loyal group of buyers who'll shop with them time and time again.*

Is It a Niche or a Fad?

Frequently, people confuse a niche with a fad. While selling products in either arena can be very profitable, you need to make sure you know what you're dealing with before building your business around it. While a niche enables you to build a long-term sustainable business based on a closely knit spectrum of related products and common interests, a fad gives you the ability to make a lot of money in a short amount of time. A fad is a product that starts with the glow of an ember and is then fueled by the fan of popularity until it bursts into a full-blown roaring fire. At the peak of the blaze, there's a massive buying frenzy—one that can make the primary suppliers millions of dollars. Shortly after the fire reaches critical mass, however, the fad starts to burn out, often quickly. The faster and stronger a fad comes on, the quicker it will burn out. If you're selling at the beginning of that fad, you can make a fortune. However, once a fad burns out, it becomes a commodity. Prices spiral downward and stay there until the fad is revised some years later or morphs into a new fad. Very often you'll see fads come and go in a particular niche. Don't miss opportunities to capitalize on those, but don't expect to build a long-term business on them either.

One of the most unbelievable yet profitable fads that ever existed is that of the Pet Rock. In 1975, an enterprising gentleman by the name of Gary Dahl began to package rocks and sell them as the perfect pet. The fad came on fast and furious, although the heat of it lasted about six months. The sellers who got in on this fad in the beginning were laughing all the way to the rock garden. Before the flame on this fad burned out, five million Pet Rocks were sold. You couldn't build a niche using the Pet Rocks market, but from that fad you could have made enough profit to reinvest in a new niche.

Niche Buying from the Customer's Perspective

Buyers are drawn to niche stores for two very important reasons: lack of time and choice overload. With scores of new products entering the marketplace each day, and more and more options of brands and products to choose from, buyers are feeling overwhelmed in a big way. When a customer buys from a store that focuses on a niche, some of the shopping has already been done for them. The retailer has preselected products that they know are of interest to their target market, they have done the work of locating an extensive selection of products, and with their merchandising, they're presenting the products in a manner that makes sense and appeals to the buyer. One very successful niche store, www.jugglenow.com, has done just that. Jim, an avid juggler of 25 years, began Juggle Now as a way to reach out to other jugglers and jugglers-to-be. He started with just one product and some expert information on juggling. Today, he carries over 100 products and maintains a focus on variety, quality, and customer service. Jim's customers love that they can go to Juggle Now for the "best of the best" in selection and value when it comes to juggling equipment and information. When you sell in a niche, you're providing a service for your customers before they ever make that purchase. Juliette, a frequent shopper of specialty stores, says it best, "When I shop at a store that specializes in my favorite products, I get to see a lot of merchandise that I wouldn't see in other stores and that I wouldn't find any other place. Sometimes, it makes me feel like I have my own personal shopper."

Niche stores also provide another very important benefit for buyers in that they offer a buying experience that in and of itself makes shoppers feel more connected. Recent studies have shown that today's consumers are trending towards experience buying. Hot Topic at www.hottopic.com began providing customers with experience buying when they opened their first store in the mall. Hot Topic specializes in apparel, accessories, gifts, and music for teenagers. When you walk into Hot Topic, the first thing you feel is the energy—energy from the music being played in the store, energy from the niche merchandise, energy from the people who work there. All of this is what makes Hot Topic different. Hot Topic's merchandise reflects a variety of music-related lifestyles, which include street wear, retro-influenced lounge, punk, club, and gothic. Add to that the wide selection of unique gifts and unusual accessories and you've got a niche store like no other in the mall.

When a customer shops for an item, it's not just about acquiring the goods, it's about making their purchase from a store that supports their values and lifestyle. We'll talk more about experience selling a bit later in this chapter. Ultimately, if a niche store supports a buyer's values, interests, and motivations, the buyer is very likely to support the niche store.

The Benefits of Niche Selling

If you're just starting out with your business or are in the process of expanding, selling in a niche can be the fastest way to success. When you sell in a niche, you're able to focus your energy, working capital, advertising, and customer service rather than dividing your efforts among several different types of product lines and customers. This allows you to be a more effective, efficient, and profitable retailer. One mistake many sellers make is to proceed without a clearly defined product or a sharply defined target market. These businesses are trying to be everything to everyone, and in doing so they water down their appeal and their profits. Even businesses that expand too quickly from their core product or service can experience the same negative effect.

When you sell in a niche, you can

- **Focus your product sourcing efforts.** A niche seller can concentrate their efforts on locating suppliers within a specific industry and building relationships with those suppliers. One of the keys to successful product sourcing is making contacts, and the more vendors you work with in a specified market, the greater your ability to find out about other vendors through word of mouth. Amelia, a seller who specializes in selling exotic and hard-to-find textiles, found that when she started focusing her product sourcing efforts in one industry, she was able to make supplier connections at lightning speed. Before focusing in on the textiles niche, Amelia was trying to source products for two other unrelated niches. "I felt like I was spinning my wheels and not getting anywhere," she recalls. "Once I identified the niche that I wanted to focus on and really made an effort to make contacts within that arena, I found myself a part of the supply chain network that enabled me to source my inventory." If you sell in the variety model, you'll need to establish supplier connections in every corner. With niche selling, you can leverage your product sourcing activities and use one supplier to network into another.

- **React quickly.** When sourcing products in a niche, you have the ability to make fast, effective product sourcing decisions that other bigger broader retailers can't. If sales start to pick up in one area, you can quickly build up your inventory. Steve ran a successful eBay business selling ski equipment for three years. At a certain point, he noticed that demand for the traditional ski equipment he carried had tapered off a bit, while sales of a few new "extreme snow sports" products he was trying out had picked up considerably. Because he was already selling in a niche, Steve was able to quickly identify an emerging offshoot of his existing product line. Some research with his existing customer base and a few phone calls to existing suppliers told Steve that the popularity of extreme snow sports was on the rise. He was able to quickly order more extreme snow sport industry items and get them listed on eBay right at the peak of the season. If he hadn't been so focused on both his customers and his niche, Steve wouldn't have been able to identify the growing trend so quickly. When selling in a specialized market, if you see a part of your niche morphing into something else, you can quickly react and source out the products to fill that need.
- **Focus your education.** When building any retail business, you need to educate yourself about your target customers. Niche selling allows you to focus your attention on the industry magazines, trade shows, and contacts specific to that niche. When you delve deeply into your niche network, you'll be the first to learn about new products, new suppliers, and new ideas. Compare this to selling a wide variety of merchandise and trying to keep up on several different industries at once. At a certain point, this becomes virtually impossible to do. Without focusing your attention, you can become surface-educated, at best, on the products you sell. However, as a niche seller, you're so entrenched in the marketplace, you move from fishing for information to being an industry insider.
- **Acquire customers more easily.** By virtue of selling in a niche, it's much easier to define what your customer wants and focus on their needs. Once you do that, the customers will start coming to you. Why? Because you provide them with exactly what they told you they wanted. Terence has built a strong repeat clientele who shop at his web site frequently. He also converts visitors into buyers with relative ease. Terence has done this by specializing in educational toys for children from birth to five years old. By focusing on products, services, and information that are in demand by a specific group of people, Terence has also been able to learn what their wants and needs are. This has put him in the enviable position of giving his customers more of what they want and they in turn return time and time again to shop.

- **Streamline your marketing energies.** Niche sellers have a huge advantage over the variety-store model when it comes to marketing and advertising their products. Advertising to the variety-store crowd is very difficult because each of your potential customers is different. How can you advertise if you don't know who you're advertising to? Bethany sells products online that are designed for senior living. Her clothing, gadgets, and accessories are all tailored for the needs of the 65+ crowd. Her advertising is geared the same way. Bethany uses specific colors in her ads that will be well-received by seniors. She used photos of people who are in her target market, as well as words and phrases that are familiar to the group she is selling to. Bethany also understands the problems and desires of her target market, allowing her to craft her advertising messages so she speaks directly to them. Imagine if she created an advertising image that was more appropriate to the early-20s set. Her sales message wouldn't be geared to a niche, but would instead be spread across the board. There's no doubt that Bethany's advertising method wouldn't be as effective. Niche market advertising can be so tightly tuned that you can "laser beam" all of your marketing efforts to create maximum results by advertising right down to the very last character of your audience.

- **Maximize your marketing dollars.** For every dollar you spend on marketing and advertising, you need to measure your return on investment (ROI). When you know who your customer is, and you know what they want to buy, you'll know exactly where to spend your marketing budget for the best ROI. For example, if you sell fishing products and accessories, your marketing dollars should be spent in arenas that attract your target market. Fishing magazines, pay-per-click advertising with targeted keywords, or using eBay's e-mail marketing to advertise your products to your mailing list are all venues where you can achieve a maximum return on your advertising dollar. Conversely, let's say you sell a little bit of everything. Who do you advertise to? Where do you advertise to get the most for your advertising dollar? While generic advertising can be done, specific niche advertising is more cost effective and will ultimately connect you with a group of buyers looking to buy exactly the products you're selling.

- **Plan and focus better.** As an entrepreneur, you must juggle many balls in order to run your business. Add to that multiple product lines across multiple marketplaces and some of those balls are bound to start dropping. When your business is focused on a niche, it's much easier to plan and strategize. In addition, it's easier to hire staff for a niche business because the requirements for the position are so much more easily defined. A seller who specializes in racing bikes, parts, and accessories, for example, can easily get a handle on inventory forecasting, attend cycling trade shows, and review related supplier catalogs. While people often think that focusing on a niche market will limit their options, the reverse is actually true. Planning and focusing bring you in touch with the products and the customers, which will ultimately lead you to higher sales and profits.

- **Differentiate more easily.** In a niche market, you can add layers or benefits and advantages to your products and services which will help you create a blockade to keep out the competition. The more uniquely you serve your market, the harder it will be for your competition to copy you. A great example of this is Jayna, a European eBay seller who specializes in selling high-end yarn designed for knitting and crocheting. Jayna knows her product and she knows where to locate the best of the best when it comes to yarn. What sets her listings above the rest of the pack is her hand-designed, exclusive patterns and instructional materials. Jayna has effectively created a barrier to her competition since no one else can easily duplicate the creative patterns and detailed instructions she offers.

- **Control your expansion and growth.** With a niche store, you have more control over the growth of your business, because you have more control of the business in general. Since a niche seller is in sync with their customers, they're better poised to make a good business decision about when to add a product and what products to add. Excess inventory, cost overruns, and poor buying decisions can all come as a result of a business whose expansion and growth are out of control. This is often a direct result of losing contact with the needs and wants of your customer base. When you sell in a niche, you have the ability to keep a better handle on what's working in your business and what isn't, and then make the appropriate changes.

- **Generate higher profit margins.** Generally, the more specialized your product line is, the higher profits you can command. For example, the seller who offers an exclusive baby stroller such as the hot Bugaboo stroller from the Netherlands (retailing for $729) or Maclaren's high-quality line strollers will operate with higher profit margins than those who sell a stroller that can be found in every "big box" store in the city, such as Target and Wal-Mart. When selling goods that are generally available as commodities, you're more vulnerable to price wars. Additionally, if your niche shop is unique and adds value, such as including specialized diaper bags, purses, and stroller baskets to go with your high-end strollers, you can charge more overall for your products and services.

- **Lower the cost of your goods.** Niche selling allows you to build relationships with your suppliers, which over time can lead to better pricing and a lower cost of goods. If you do business with a supplier on a regular basis, they may be motivated to work with you on price negotiations, including special deals like free shipping, and let you in on inventory specials before other retailers do. In some cases, you may find that selling in a niche leads you to order smaller quantities of inventory up front, which in turn can lead to higher base costs. However, this additional expense can often be balanced on the back-end by what you're able to charge for your products—because you're providing a more valuable service, a wider selection, and a better buying experience for your buyer.

- **Repeat the process in other areas.** Probably the best part about selling in a niche is that if you can build one successful niche, you can repeat the process and build another. Once you understand how to build a niche successfully, even though the products and the market may be different, the process remains the same. When you gain the expertise to build a successful niche, you can do it over and over again and build multiple streams of income. eBay PowerSeller Zoe honed her niche-building skills on eBay when she created an eBay store designed to cater to saltwater aquarium enthusiasts. The skills she acquired when building this niche—doing product research, locating trade publications and industry shows, and networking with industry suppliers—were all transferable to building her new niche store designed around ergonomically-correct office equipment. Although the product lines were completely different, the process for building the niche remained the same.

Desks and Chairs Spawn Multiple Niches

To many sellers, desks and chairs may seem like just your garden-variety office equipment, but to a niche seller, these time-tested products represent the potential to sell profitably in several different niche markets. In addition to corporate offices that need to be outfitted to a T, home-based entrepreneurs want to work in style and comfort as well. With the huge increase in the number of new home-based businesses being started every year, along with employees who've begun telecommuting, a brand new, and very lucrative, niche has opened up in supplying the home-based entrepreneur with high-quality office equipment. Gone are the days where working from a spare bedroom or a corner of the garage was satisfactory. People want office environments that they can feel comfortable in, and work productively in. This has kindled a huge demand for office products designed for the home-based business person.

Children are also sparking another new "office" trend. Even though kids' "office equipment" is used for homework, style and comfort is in no less demand by the younger set. Desks, storage units, task lighting, wall units, shelving, and more—all designed especially for kids—are hot sellers in this new niche. In fact, the very successful Pottery Barn Kids catalog devotes a large part of their pages to these products. Not only do these products appeal to parents' and kids' aesthetic sensibilities, they also touch on parents' desire for happier, more enriched children. A recent Pottery Barn catalog highlighted this by explaining the benefits of shelving and storage to potential buyers when it said, "Parents can encourage imaginative explorations by providing children with a warm, comfortable space that's generously outfitted with age-appropriate art supplies and simple, flexible storage with open shelves and a range of containers."

Niche Spotting

You've already taken a huge step towards finding your niche with everything you've learned in this book up to this point. You're in the Product Sourcing Mindset, you've got your Product Sourcing Notebook by your side, and you're spending time each day in multiple Idea Hotspots. Now it's time to adjust the dial ever so slightly and turn your radar toward looking for some specific characteristics of niche markets or up-and-coming niche markets.

- **Underserved niches** New niche markets crop up every day. Every time you hear about a new trend, take some time then and there to research whether or not there are any online retailers who've stepped in to fill this need.

- **Inadequately served niches** A lot of niche markets are being served by retailers, but not very well. Sometimes you only need to look as far as your latest shopping experience. Julie Aigner-Clark stumbled on a niche idea when she was looking for videos to entertain and educate her baby. Finding nothing age-appropriate on the market, she began creating them herself. The result was Baby Einstein, a company adored by moms and tots alike that spawned a huge niche in children's educational videos.

- **Partially served niches** Women's plus-size clothing is a niche that's fairly well served, but not completely so. As we discussed earlier in this chapter, the market segment for teens' and 20s' plus-size clothing still holds a lot of opportunity since it's part of a market that isn't being served.

- **Refreshed niches** Everything old is new again—only this time with a twist. A niche market with a new twist is sometimes the fastest to be accepted by consumers. We see this all the time with fashion. Styles touted as "new" are really remakes of styles that were popular and successful years ago. Look for ideas that can be updated and made more relevant to today's consumer. The portable media device trend got its start with Sony Walkmans, pagers, and cell phones. Several years and styles later, portable media devices are on a convergence path. Cameras, cell phones, music players, and PDAs are all being melded into one device. These are the products of the future and have spawned a newly refreshed niche. Occurrences like this happen every day, so make it a point to keep an eye out for a new twist on an old product.

- **Adapted niches** If it works in California, it may very well work on the East Coast. Several years ago, a trend started in California of remodeling your home and adding in brand new hardwood floors. Suddenly, wood tones and natural tones were in. Retailers in California were selling these floors right and left, and alert retailers in New York who spotted this trend early on were the first to adapt it to East Coast buyers.

- **Combined niches** Some of the hottest niche markets have come out of two or more combined niches. For several years, the cell phone market has been a hot niche market. The same holds true for the digital camera. A convergence of these two niches now brings us the camera cell phone—and a brand new hot niche is born.

- **Redirected niches** Sometimes all a niche needs is a new direction for it to take off on its own. If you see a lucrative niche, stop and think about what variations and changes could be made to it to form a new niche. The number of female soccer players, both youth and adult, has been on the rise for years. It was only recently that retailers recognized the fact that this niche market wanted to play soccer in clothes that were geared towards them. Modifications were made to the soccer basics and a new niche was born. Today, sales of girls soccer clothes are growing at an accelerated pace.

- **Newly created niches** While a niche must have an existing demand or a trend fueling it, being the first to create a niche store to serve that market can put your business in the position of being the first to capitalize on this demand for products or services.

To find out more about how to spot a niche, go to www.whatdoisell .com/niche.

A Niche Reborn

A few years ago, the game of poker was not something many people talked about. In fact, prior to 2003, there was virtually no public interest in the game of poker. Sure, there were still those die-hard poker players who'd never lost their love for the game. But for most of mainstream America, poker was out of fashion. Sales of poker-related items were relegated to a small but passionate niche market. In March 2003, however, all that changed. Filmmaker Steve Lipscomb filmed and aired 13 major poker tournaments from around the country on the Travel Channel. As a direct result, people began watching poker on television and practicing poker online. Shortly thereafter, casinos nationwide experienced a resurgence of excitement regarding poker rooms. Suddenly, interest arose among people of all ages to learn and play the game.

A niche was reborn. A market that didn't exist in 2002 was, by 2003, starting to take shape. Instantly, poker-related items became a hot ticket. In the beginning, virtually no sellers of poker products existed. Today, the sale of poker-related merchandise is a multimillion dollar business—an immense change that unfolded in less than two years. This niche market came on fast and strong. Those sellers who had their eyes and ears open, listening and watching for trends, were the first to bring poker merchandise to the mainstream consumer. And the niche was very profitable, with these sellers essentially dealing themselves a Royal Flush (the best possible hand in poker). Some of the early poker merchants took their earnings and moved on, while others are still selling today, having built a long-term sustainable business around poker. Because they know that poker won't maintain this peak frenzy forever, however, these savvy sellers still have their eyes open, watching for the next trend.

Turning Trends into Niches

Niche markets frequently stem from trends and/or lifestyle changes. And new trends develop every day. Becoming a trend spotter or trend forecaster allows you to watch for trends as they emerge, and then determine whether or not there's a product line that goes with them. Trends are sparked by many things, and changes in consumer buying habits, their preferences, needs, and demographics are all factors in sculpting the next trend.

In the mid-1980s, baby boomers helped create a demand for golf-related products in the United States that was perhaps unparalleled in the game's history. The baby boomers, many of whom took up golf in their 20s and 30s, became part of a niche market primed and ready to spend money on their favorite sport. As a result, golf-product retailers have done very well over the past 20 years. Profitability in that niche market will continue, but now it's due to a new and different trend. The first wave of 78 million baby boomers is now moving through their 50s, and research shows that golfers not only play more as they get older, but that their overall spending on golf-related products also increases. Therefore, this shift in age for the baby boomers should spark another surge in both rounds played *and* spending. Currently, even though they represent only about 25 percent of the total U.S. golfer population, senior golfers (age 50 and above) account for close to 53 percent of all spending on golf. Following on the heels of this transition are the "echo boomers," the sons and daughters of the original boomers, who grew up watching their parents play golf, and now may likely take up the sport themselves. Most of the 72 million young adults who comprise this group will be well into their 20s and 30s by the year 2015, which is the time of life when the vast majority of people take up golf. Consequently, there's reason to believe that the projected surge in sales of golf-related items could last for at least 15 more years.

Another new trend, which has started off more slowly but that's gaining momentum, is that of men's skincare. Men of all ages have a growing desire to look their best, and this means taking care of their skin. It used to be that men's skincare products were used primarily by actors, models, or those in front of a camera, but these days, dads, brothers, and Uncle Bills are all getting into the act. Men's skincare is going mainstream. Men are becoming more concerned about their appearance and this is driving up sales of male skincare products and sparking the development of a whole new niche market. In 2004, department store sales of men's skincare products jumped 13 percent, more than twice the total overall growth in the women's skincare market.

One niche-market entrepreneur jumped into the men's skincare market early on and has seen a phenomenal growth in his business. Tom Granese launched Regimens at www.regimens.com, an online store that sells high-end grooming products for men. The response was overwhelming. He very successfully tapped into a growing trend and turned it into a niche business. Less than two years later, Tom opened his first storefront in Dallas with a projected $210,000 in first-year in-store sales.

To learn about the latest retail trends and hot niches, go to www .whatdoisell.com/trends.

Trend Spotting

So how do you spot these trends or trends-turned-niches, and translate them into profitable products? By simply employing all the methods you've learned so far in Chapters 1 through 4 of this book! Finding out about new trends all comes back to being in the Product Sourcing Mindset, carrying your Product Sourcing Notebook with you, and spending time daily in the Idea Hotspots we talked about in Chapter 4.

Once you become an idea sponge, as you'll be when you're in the Product Sourcing Mindset, there are just a few pointers you need to be on the lookout for when it comes to trends.

- Trends are a reflection of how people feel and how they think, which then translates into what they buy and do.
- Trend indicators will start to show up in a variety of places. If you find yourself noticing articles in different publications about changes in society, that's a sure indication that a trend is brewing.
- Trends don't pop up out of nowhere. There are signs along the way. As a savvy seller in the Product Sourcing Mindset, you'll be tuned into these little flags, which other people will most likely miss.
- Trends, like niches, have an identifiable group of people behind them with a definable set of needs. There's always a set of reasons behind a growing trend. A fad, on the other hand, does not need justification and often strikes it hot for no apparent reason.
- Trends are sustaining but changing. A trend builds for a specific reason, and then may morph itself into something different along the way. Twenty years ago, Sony introduced the first Walkman and sparked a trend towards listening to high-quality, portable, personal music. Today that trend still exists, but with the introduction of MP3 players, the direction of the portable music trend has changed.

Tip: As a trend spotter, you're looking for signs of existing trends that can be translated into niche market products. But you can also approach the quest to find your niche as a trend forecaster—one who analyzes existing trends in society and then figures out what the next one will be. A trend forecaster will often put together the pieces of the puzzle before anyone else does. Trend forecasters are often described as being on the cutting edge. However, these prognosticators of the future are not making a wild guess at what will be the next trend. They spend time acquiring an understanding of where consumers have been, where they are now, and how things are changing in society, and then use that information to foresee the next trend.

Lifestyle Changes

Sometimes trends become so sweeping that they evolve into completely new lifestyles in our society. Before the advent of the personal computer, you wouldn't have found any niche retailers selling computer software, peripherals, and computer-related books. But home-based computer use, which started out as a small trend, has now mushroomed into a requisite lifestyle for millions of Americans. With it has come literally hundreds of niche markets in which products can be sold. Will this trend ever reverse itself? Most likely, no. Will we ever go back to not having computers in our homes? Highly doubtful. The computer has sparked a lifestyle change, and with it, new niche markets that are here to stay.

Experience Selling

Can you sell a feeling? A growing trend in sales and marketing not only proves you can, but you should. "Experience" selling has been gaining momentum the past few years. And according to recent consumer studies, this is what customers are clamoring for. When they go on a quest to locate the merchandise of their desire, how they feel in the store where they make their purchase is as important as the purchase itself. Experience shopping lets buyers connect with their emotions more intensely than ever before. For years, the old advertising adage has always been "Don't sell the steak, sell the sizzle." Experience selling takes this strategy to a whole new level. Studies show that shoppers who "experience" a product or service will buy more of the product, buy it more frequently and often at higher prices. And even though, at the most fundamental level, you're buying a "thing," in the bigger picture you're buying the way that "thing" makes you feel.

Experience selling is a tall order for a variety or big box store that's long on cost savings but short on "experience." However, for the niche seller, it's a strategy that's right up your alley. So what does experience shopping mean and how will that help you source products to find your niche? Experience shopping means you're not only selling a product or a brand name, you're helping your buyers connect to the image and values identified with the group of people who use these products. For example, does buying a very expensive baby play gym with all the bells and whistles of a Lexus make you a better parent? No! However, parents who seek out these kinds of products often feel, at least subconsciously, that providing their beautiful babies with the ultimate in luxury products makes them better parents and will make their babies smarter, happier, feel more nurtured, and ultimately more successful in life. If you sell a product like this, you're selling an experience. Gee, and here you thought you were just selling an expensive play mat in bright colors!

When Walt Disney first envisioned Disneyland, he never thought of it as a place for people to go and buy ride tickets and eat cotton candy. He dreamed of it as being an experience—*Experiencing the Magic Kingdom*. And consumers go there in the millions every year to do just that. Another leader in the genre of experience selling is Starbucks. Starbucks doesn't just sell coffee, it sells the way you feel when you spend time in your local Starbucks—hip, smooth, successful, a part of the in-crowd. Starbucks has done with their coffee shops what you need to do with your store—turn it into a destination. A place to go because it makes you feel good. Starbucks not only caters to a niche market of consumers who want a place to go to drink coffee, they cater to consumers' desires for an experience *while* they're doing it.

Niketown is another example of a store that caters to the experience. For sports fans young and old, Niketown offers a place to connect with the feelings evoked by seeing pictures of their favorite athletes hanging on the wall, as well as being able to touch, feel, and buy the products that their sports heroes wear and endorse. At Niketown, you get a sports-related experience you can't get anywhere else.

Whatever niche market you choose to sell in, you must fulfill your buyers' need for experience with the product and services you offer. If you operate in the gourmet cooking niche, all the products and services you sell must have one goal—to make the customer feel like the gourmet chef they desire to be. When you sell the "sizzle" or the experience, you'll have customers flocking to you for more, time and time again.

Are You Insperienced?

In 2002, Whirlpool opened its doors to one of the most revolutionary niche selling "stores" of our time. In reality, Whirlpool's Insperience Studio® isn't really a store, it's an experiential studio, designed to allow potential customers to experience Whirlpool's products before they buy them. Given the new consumer climate of wanting experience shopping over the old-school style of pick it out, pay for it, and leave, Whirlpool has embraced this need and taken it one step further.

Whirlpool recognized what was missing in the customer home appliance buying process early on. When shopping for appliances, customers would go into the store and see a "sea of white"—rows upon rows of white boxes that all looked the same—and would consequently get confused as to where to start, because everything looked alike. After talking to many home-appliance shoppers, Whirlpool came up with a way to differentiate their appliance buying experience from their competition's—and thus Insperience was born. Whirlpool's Insperience Studio, located in Atlanta, invites shoppers to "bring their chores with them." Some potential customers do their laundry there, while others try baking bread or cookies: Visitors are welcome to fry eggs on a high-BTU Whirlpool range or see for themselves if a KitchenAid convection oven can make fast food of a raw chicken. One man brought in a bag of trash to crunch in the compactor. In fact, they can do just about anything they want there—except buy the appliances they test. For that, they're referred to an appliance store. While Whirlpool's Insperience store may be on the leading edge of experience shopping, it clearly demonstrates that anything you can do as a retailer to engage your customer and help them connect emotionally to your products will help them make the decision to buy from you all that much easier.

Subniches and Microniches

Within a niche you'll also find highly profitable subniches and microniches. These narrowly defined and refined segments of a larger niche are in essence a niche within a niche. And while they are smaller segments of a market, they still cater to a definable group of customers with common needs and interests. A retailer who operates a pet supply store sells in a niche, while a seller who deals only in dog supplies sells in a subniche. And the very targeted shop owner who sells only pet products for black labs sells in a microniche. As with niche markets, subniches and microniches can be very lucrative, and oftentimes have less competition from other sellers. When you're looking at niche markets to sell in, keep peeling away the layers of the niche to see if there's another profitable niche underneath that's underserved and needs to be addressed with your products and services.

Experience selling takes niche selling to a whole new level. Studies show that shoppers who "experience" a product or service will buy more of the product, buy it more frequently, and often at higher prices.

Summing Up

Now that you know why niche selling is such a strong formula for success, you're ready to jump right in and spot the next trend. But how do you know if it will be a profitable one? In the next chapter, we'll look at the bottom-line numbers and the "X" factors that will tell you if a product or niche market has profit potential. First, however, let's review some key points from this chapter about niche selling:

- A niche is a profitable segment of a larger market. When you sell in a niche, you're focusing on supplying products and services exclusively to that market.
- While a niche enables you to build a long-term sustainable business based on a closely knit spectrum of related products and common interests, a fad gives you the ability to make a lot of money in a short amount of time.
- Buyers are drawn to niche stores for two very important reasons—lack of time and choice overload.
- When you sell in a niche, you're able to focus your energy, working capital, advertising, and customer service efforts, rather than dividing your labors among several different types of product lines.
- Niche markets frequently stem from trends and/or lifestyle changes, with new trends developing every day.
- Trend indicators will start to show up in a variety of places. If you find yourself noticing articles about changes in society, that's a sure indication that a trend is brewing.
- "Experience" selling has been gaining momentum the past few years. According to recent consumer studies, this type of sales environment is what customers have been clamoring for.
- Within a niche, you'll also find highly profitable subniches and microniches. These narrowly defined and refined segments of a larger niche are, in essence, a niche within a niche.

Chapter 6

Evaluating Your Product Ideas

So you've been busy soaking up ideas and making long lists of potential products to sell in your Product Sourcing Notebook. You think you have some winners on the list and are excited about picking a few ideas and starting to build a product line. But how do you know which items to proceed with? And which ones are potential profit machines?

Frequently, people ask us if we think a particular product will be a best seller. While it's possible for us to give an opinion based upon our experience in this field, our answer to that question is always, "You'll have to do your research." For every product you consider selling, you must do some quantitative market research and have a product evaluation strategy. While you may have a preliminary idea of whether or not a product will sell well, your ultimate decision to sell a product must always be substantiated by looking at the numbers. This data includes evaluating the number of customers looking to buy a particular product, how well a product is already selling, and how many suppliers of the product exist. Understanding the market demand for a product will determine whether you should proceed, and how to go about it. With a product evaluation system, you can look at the statistics of sell-through rates, consumer buying patterns, and the competition, not to mention a host of other variables which will help you decide whether or not to invest your working capital in a particular line of products.

In this chapter, we'll outline a product evaluation strategy you can apply not only to individual products, but to any concept or niche market idea you come across. You'll learn the skills and strategies for looking at the measurable factors of successful sellers, and also discover how to evaluate the X factor of a product. Successful product evaluation takes into consideration the "science" (the numbers in black and white) and the "art" (the X factor of a product) and combines those factors together so you can form a complete picture of a product's potential for profitability. This system takes out the guesswork and, once learned, is a repeatable process that will allow you to source successful products time and time again.

The Big Picture

As with generating ideas for products to sell, product evaluation cannot be done in a vacuum. To accurately determine if a product has profit potential, you must look at several factors, those that are part of the big picture and those that lie in the minutest of details. Understanding from a big picture standpoint whether or not an item should be part of your inventory involves understanding the market demand for the product, discerning what stage of its life cycle the product is in, and, most importantly, knowing how a particular product fits into your overall business model. It's only after you've looked at those factors that you can drill down to the level of specific evaluation criteria which will give you the final pieces of the product evaluation puzzle.

Market Demand

No matter how you slice it, the only way to make money in retail is by selling products that people want to buy. Understanding how many people want to purchase a product (known as *market demand*) is a skill that every retailer must learn. Crack that code and you'll find yourself able to repeatedly select merchandise that buyers are clamoring for.

Simply put, market demand is the amount of a product that a group of consumers want to purchase at a given price, balanced with the supply of that product. When there's high demand for a product and low supply, a strong market demand will result. When there's low demand and an overabundant supply, a weak market demand will be present. If supply is held constant and demand remains strong, a strong market demand will also occur. To determine market demand for your product, there are some very specific metrics you'll want to know, which we'll discuss later in this chapter in the section "Evaluating Product Demand: Science, Art, and More." But before we get there we need to look at the overall picture for evaluating your products.

Product Cycles

Every product goes through different market demand stages. These stages (or cycles) are referred to as a product life cycle and are a critical factor in determining whether or not an item will have a strong market demand. If you begin selling an item in the early stages of the product life cycle, you have an opportunity to maximize your selling price, as well as to allow room for product line growth and extend the length of sales. Come in towards the tail end of a product life cycle and you're now dealing with the issues of oversupply and decreasing prices.

A product life cycle has five distinct phases and one optional one:

1. **Development**   In this stage, a product is not readily available in the marketplace or the product has not yet been introduced. If you're creating your own product or sourcing merchandise from a company that's introducing a new concept to consumers, it's important to understand whether or not there's a pent-up demand for the item in the marketplace. Items that have a hungry target market that's ready and waiting for a product (like the Apple iPod mini, for example) will result in sales that take off like a rocket the minute the item is introduced into the marketplace. Conversely, merchandise that requires education of the consumer *to establish a need or want in their minds* will require more time to realize a profit. Several years ago, Compaq and Fisher-Price teamed up to create a line of software and toy computer controllers called Wonder Tools. The gadgets looked great, but the marketing challenge of getting parents to understand how these toys worked and what benefit they would provide to their children was an uphill battle and the products never took off as expected. The introduction of the Wonder Tools, however, paved the way for other products, such as the LeapPad by LeapFrog, that came along later and were huge successes in the marketplace.

2. **Introduction**   The success of a product that's introduced to the market-place relies heavily on two things: pent-up demand and advertising. As discussed earlier, pent-up demand for a product can result in your inventory being sold out the moment the item hits the shelves (or the virtual shelves if you're an online retailer). The introduction of a successful product with pent-up demand is the stage in which you'll see products selling on venues such as eBay for astronomical prices that are way over the manufacturer's suggested retail price. When Nintendo introduced its new Nintendo DS handheld game player in 2004 there was massive pent-up demand among consumers. Buzz created by Nintendo, the media, and owners of other Nintendo products all contributed to the DS's anticipated arrival. When the product hit the shelves, they were snapped up, and hungry buyers were left wanting more. However, the reverse is also true in that introduction of a product with little demand will result in products going unsold or selling below base cost. Awareness of a product is critical in driving sales right out of the gate. If you're considering marketing a brand-new product that has little brand awareness or is an entirely new concept, the need for advertising and product publicity, either by you, the manufacturer, or other retailers, will be key in generating sales.

3. **Growth**   In this phase, product awareness is building and demand is strong. It's in the growth stage that you begin to realize the most consistent revenue from your products. The do-it-yourself home improvement products industry has seen strong and steady growth over the past several years. As more and more Americans have a desire to remodel and expand their homes, many are becoming do-it-yourselfers, both for the enjoyment of the work involved and because it keeps costs down. This has resulted in a steady growth in products geared to this market. As a seller, when you're in the growth phase of a product line, you can carefully add more depth of inventory to your stock, and with careful sales tracking, know that you won't end up with excess inventory on the shelves. During the growth phase, demand still outpaces supply and therefore prices remain steady.

4. **Maturity**   As a product matures in the cycle, sales are still strong but the relationship between supply and demand soon begins a subtle shift. In the maturity phase, supply and demand remain in balance, and retailers haven't yet begun to try and attract more sales by discounting prices. The length of the maturity phase directly relates to how flooded the market becomes with supply. If a manufacturer releases products to the retail sector in a controlled fashion, the maturity phase can last for a considerable time. However, if a manufacturer overproduces products and consequently floods the marketplace, or miscalculates and introduces a newer version of the product too quickly, the maturity phase will soon end and the scales of market demand will be tipped.

5. **Decline**   In the decline phase, manufacturers are selling their products into the retail channel at a significant discount, often at a loss. In the decline phase, a product has become a commodity, the customer's sale often going to the seller with the lowest price. It's in this phase that you have an opportunity to pick up inventory at a greatly reduced base cost. Liquidation suppliers, close-out and overstock dealers, and wholesalers all sell products in the decline phase at rock-bottom prices. You can also buy products in the decline phase from a brick-n'-mortar retailer by shopping the clearance sales and discounted racks. However, when considering selling merchandise in the decline phase, you also need to take into consideration that you'll be selling your merchandise at lower prices and lower profit margins. There's still a considerable amount of money to be made, however, in merchandise that's being sold in the decline phase, especially if the product is being sold in a niche market.

6. **Extension**   In some cases, products go into an extension phase. In this phase, manufacturers and retailers employ different strategies such as special packages and promotions to try and delay the decline stage of the product life cycle. For example, as the popularity of the Nintendo Gameboy Advance SP began to mature, retailers began bundling games

with the Gameboy Advance SP systems in order to generate more interest and new sales. Nintendo also introduced some specific product bundles and exclusive "limited edition" colors of the Gameboy SP. The result was an increase in sales and an extended interest in the product while Nintendo readied the SP's successor: the Nintendo DS. As a seller, you have a lot of opportunity to be creative with your techniques in order to promote an extension phase for your products. In Chapter 7, we'll show you some strategies for creative product selection that can also apply directly to creating an extension phase.

Sourcing products in any of these six phases can allow you to make a profit. The key is in identifying which stage a product is in, and not convincing yourself that a product is in the growth stage when it's really in the decline stage. Doing your research on the product itself, as you're about to learn, will give you a view into the big picture you need, in order to know exactly what stage of a product you're buying into.

Market demand is the amount of a product that a group of consumers want to purchase at a given price, balanced with the supply of that product.

Profit Margin

Often, retail success stories focus on impressive gross sales numbers. If you sell on eBay, you may have a desire to be a Platinum PowerSeller (sales of $25,000+ per month) or a Titanium PowerSeller (sales of $150,000+ per month). While these are certainly very worthy goals, they do not take into consideration one very important thing: profit margin. While selling $150,000 worth of products a month sounds like a money-making venture, it won't be if your costs are $160,000 per month. Sadly, there are many retailers who sell a tremendous amount of goods, but operate on such a slim profit margin that they're either not making any money at all or, even worse, losing money.

$Profit Margin$ = gross sale price – costs (cost of goods and fixed expenses)

If your base cost for your product is too high, and the expenses to sell your product are excessive (labor, advertising, fees, web site hosting, and so on), you won't be able to make a sufficient profit on your products. Your profit margin will depend largely on your ability to source products at reasonable wholesale prices, and your ability to control the costs of doing business. Additionally, your profit margin will be directly increased by good product marketing. To learn how to market your products for maximum profit margin, the book *The 7 Essential Steps to Successful eBay Marketing;*

Creative Strategies to Boost Profits Now by Janelle Elms, Phil Dunn, and Amy Balsbaugh will show you exactly how to get the edge on the competition and boost profit margins in the process.

How Much Is Enough?

Determining an acceptable profit margin per product is something that only you as a retailer can decide. Frequently, people are advised that they should take no less than 100 percent, 250 percent, or 400 percent profit on a product. In reality, there are no cold, hard, and fast numbers that apply across the board to every product and every business.

Certain product lines—electronics, for example—come with a built-in profit margin range. In the case of electronics retailers, even very large companies are working on a very slim profit margin, often about 10 percent. They make their money on volume and add-on products and services. If you're a small retailer attempting to sell electronics on a 10-percent profit margin without being able to do the sales volume of a Best Buy or offer the add-on products and services, you'll be operating in the red before too long.

Conversely, expecting that every product you sell will carry with it a 100-percent profit margin isn't realistic. Profit margins vary based on market demand and product life cycle as well as your ability to sell and market your products. A store that sells high-end luxury products in a hot niche will be able to elicit a much higher profit margin than a store that deals primarily in lower-price commodities with a customer base focused primarily on price.

When asking yourself how much of a profit margin is acceptable for you, keep in mind the following five points:

1. Not every product will be a candidate for keystoning, a retail term that connotes selling a product at a price that's double the wholesale cost. For example, if you purchase a table at $100 base cost, and sell it for $200, you're keystoning the price. If you're selling it for a "triple key" price, the retail price is triple your costs. Even though you won't be able to command these markups on every product, you must have a base of products in your business which are at keystone and, ideally, triple-key pricing, to build up your profit margins.
2. Some products you'll sell based on volume, others you'll sell based on profit. There's nothing wrong with accepting a lower profit margin on a product that you sell a lot of. Especially if it's an item that's quick to package and easy to ship. What is important is that you have a *mix* of products that contribute to your profit margin based on volume and a higher margin.
3. Profit margins will change with market fluctuations and product life cycles. Just because you're selling a product at a 150-percent profit margin today, doesn't mean you'll continue at that profit margin 6 months

from now. Tracking your margins, which we'll talk about next, is critical so you're not lulled into a false sense of profitability.

4. It's your overall profit margin that's important. A high-end luxury watch may command a profit margin of 1000 percent, but if you only sell one every three months, that won't generate enough income to build a business with. Add to the mix a watch with a 200-percent markup that you sell on a daily basis and you now start to build a business model with a margin and a volume to generate significant revenue.

5. Testing and tracking are also key. Unless you test different ways to market your product, you'll never know whether or not you can increase your profit margins. And until you track those results, you won't be able to identify trends and spot the inventory winners and losers in your store.

Costs

Oftentimes sellers focus on retail sales prices, while virtually ignoring the costs of doing business on the back end. In retail, there's one overriding principle that applies across the board, no matter what products you deal in. You make your money when you buy, not when you sell. What this means is that the price you pay for your inventory has a direct result on your profit margins. You can market your products in a way that will garner higher sales prices than the norm, but it's not a model you want to institute across the board.

The same comes into play with the costs of doing business. If you're too freely spending money on marketing, advertising, shipping materials, office supplies, selling fees, and all the expenses that are part of the cost of doing business, you'll cut away at your profit margins until there's nothing left to pay yourself a salary with. Thus, costs are just as important as sales in making a strong profit margin.

When selecting your inventory, there's one overriding principle to keep in mind: You make your money when you buy, not when you sell.

What Kind of Products Do You Want to Sell?

Before you start evaluating specific products, you need to have an idea of what *kind* of products you want to sell. This especially comes into play if you're operating a home-based business. Do you want to sell small items that are easy to ship or are you open to selling big-ticket items that are large in size? What kind of inventory are you set up to receive and sell right now? In order to help you focus on the specific products you want to sell, you need to narrow down your requirements for the type of products first.

Tip: When evaluating the kinds of products you want to sell, don't limit yourself to only sourcing within your current business situation. It's important to take a broader view and consider the option of business expansion, asking yourself if it's time to take the next step. Too often, sellers limit their inventory possibilities based on storage space, funding, shipping capabilities, and so on. Being able to expand your vision and see the long-term potential of your business is key to the growth of your sales and revenue. This may mean finding a warehouse or storage facility to house your inventory, bringing in employees to list, wrap, and ship the merchandise, or exploring alternative funding sources to provide for inventory expansion.

The following is a checklist to take you through the process of deciding what kind of products to sell:

- Do you want to sell a variety of different items or develop a niche line of products?
- How much space do you have to store your inventory?
- How much money do you have to purchase inventory?
- What size items are you set up to ship?
- Will you ship to the U.S. only or internationally?
- Are you able to receive shipments via big trucks, or is your location conducive only to delivery by smaller shippers?
- Do you want to deal with only small shipments of merchandise or are you open (and have the space) to deal with large pallets of merchandise?
- Do you want to have your merchandise drop-shipped?
- Do you have your photography system geared to take pictures of a variety of item sizes or do you have limitations on the size and type of items you can photograph?
- Do you have an idea of where you can find shipping materials for a variety of product sizes?

Your answers to these questions will be a key factor in selecting products from the list in your Product Sourcing Notebook. Kenny had originally envisioned building his business around selling large, high-end, custom-made aquariums. While the demand was there and the profits were good, Kenny soon realized that packaging and shipping these heavy bulky items was more than he'd bargained for. Space for inventory was also an issue as Kenny was running his business out of his home. Kenny decided to put that part of his business on hold and concentrate on selling smaller aquariums and accessories. Recently, Kenny branched out into selling a few exotic fish as well. As his business grows and moves out of his home to a warehouse, Kenny has plans to bring back his line of large, custom-made aquariums. In hindsight, Kenny realized that if he had taken into consideration all the factors just listed, he never would have opted to start his business based around a large, bulky product.

Going through this product checklist could have saved Kenny a lot of time and effort. Your answers to these questions, too, will be a key factor in determining what items you want to sell and what vendors you'll be working with.

To get your free product evaluation checklist, go to www.whatdoisell .com/checklist.

Tracking

"How is this product doing?" If you can't answer that question immediately, it's time to drop everything and head quickly to purchase the latest copy of Microsoft Excel or QuickBooks. At any given point, you should have a snapshot of how your products are selling. Are they hitting the profit margins and selling briskly, or are sales slow and profits slim? This knowledge will go a long way in helping you determine if other merchandise you're considering selling has profit potential.

Annika, who sells children's toys on eBay, was able to make some important changes to her product line by tracking and assessing her product sales. When she purchased a small quantity of high-quality wooden toys to test in her eBay store, she wasn't sure how they would do. It soon became apparent that the customers who were visiting her store for brightly colored plastic toys equipped with batteries were now hungry for the back-to-basics wooden toys of the past. Annika was able to quickly assess the market demand of this new product line and check it against the numbers because she tracked all her costs and sales revenue in Excel and QuickBooks. Without this information, she may have missed the emergence of the opportunity to move into an entire new product line.

One enterprising company, Mpire, Inc. at www.mpire.com, includes financial tracking as part of their eBay listing tool. Dave Cotter, the CEO and President of Seattle-based Mpire, says: "We realized early on that in order for eBayers to successfully source products, they needed to be able to track their profit margins so as to be able to better source inventory. This ability allows sellers to quickly evaluate whether or not a product is profitable and determine if it should continue to be a part of their product line—information which directly translates into increased revenues."

Evaluating Product Demand:
Science, Art, and More

Frank Lloyd Wright once said: "Get in the habit of analysis—analysis will in time enable synthesis to become your habit of mind." Applied to product sourcing, this means that once you're in the habit of analyzing all the separate elements that go into a product's profitability quotient, you'll be able to easily see the combination of factors that exemplify a profitable product.

In this section, we'll look at the "art" and "science" of product sourcing, since blending both approaches will give you the information you need to make good product sourcing decisions. Additionally, we'll suggest some tools that will make the entire evaluation process go faster and more efficiently. Ultimately, product evaluation is where the rubber hits the road, and where the product winners are separated from the losers and the wanna-bes. Once you've mastered these steps, you'll be in a position to select profitable products time and time again.

Science: Where to Look

If you're not a numbers person by nature, hold on, because you're about to become one! In business, number crunchers sometimes get a bad rap. Bean counters, penny pinchers, and in some cases, Scrooge himself, are all monikers assigned to the folks who keep their eye on the bottom line. Oftentimes, there can be a conflict between the visionary in the company, with dreams of grand inventory plans, and the accountant, who foresees a bad business decision in the making. This dynamic can get all the more interesting when you're both the visionary and the financial officer for your business. Fortunately, with each personality looking over your shoulder you'll be equipped to make creative, yet solid, inventory purchasing decisions.

The science of product evaluation is all about knowing exactly what's happening with pricing and sales volume in the marketplace you sell in. Understanding this information will lead you directly to assessing the market demand for your product and determining its profit potential. Whether you sell on eBay, Yahoo, your own web site, or out of a brick-n'-mortar store, the first place to look at sales volume and pricing is in your own marketplace. Think of it this way, if you're planning on opening a store in your local shopping mall, the first thing you'd do before ever looking for space or signing a lease is to go to the mall and see who else is selling there. What kind of stores make up the mall demographics? What products are they selling? How are the prices? What is the tone of the mall? High-end, mid-price, close-out, or liquidation? If you have plans to open a high-end specialty store, you wouldn't want to locate that store in a mall that caters to the close-out directed shopper.

The same applies to evaluating a product. Pick a product or a concept from the list in your Product Sourcing Notebook, and then head to your shopping mall to start your research. If you plan to sell your item on eBay, your first stop to see if a product would be profitable is eBay. If you plan to sell this item from your Yahoo store, you'll want to start your research on Yahoo. The most successful sellers are those who spend a considerable amount of time shopping the competition and researching what's selling in their chosen sales venue. If you don't have the time or inclination to do this kind of research, then it's important to find someone who can assist you with this task. By skipping over it or doing it haphazardly, you're in effect sourcing products in the dark with no assurance that they'll sell for a profit or sell at all. After you've done your research in your shopping venue, expand your horizons and look at some other sales arenas just to get a frame of reference. You never know—during this process you may find an additional venue in which to sell your products.

Tip: In the final analysis, researching a potential product's profitability must be done in the venue in which it will be sold. The same crystal vase will sell for a different price in your local store than it will on eBay. The price you can command for a titanium racing bike in your Yahoo store will be different than the sales price on your web site. While you should look at other sales venues as a *part* of your research, profitability rests in the arena the product will be sold in.

Science: What to Look For

You know where to go to do your research, but what do you look for? Fortunately, there's a checklist you can use to evaluate every potential product you're considering.

The following is a checklist to take you through the process of deciding what kind of products to sell. At the end of this chapter, we'll tell you about some tools that will help you calculate some of these numbers quickly and effectively.

The Product Profitability Checklist

1. What is the product's sell-through rate? The sell-through rate is the number of items sold versus the number of items available for sale. On eBay, the sell-through rate would be the number of items sold divided by the number of items listed.

Note: Sell through = number of items sold ÷ the number of items listed. For example, a 50-percent sell-through rate = 50 clocks sold ÷ 100 clocks listed.

2. What is the current selling price of the item?
3. What is the average selling price of the item? You can find this information by using the tools described in the next section.

4. How many items are up for sale? Is there a glut of merchandise available for purchase or is there room in the marketplace for another product offering (yours)?

5. For eBay sellers—How many listings closed in the past two weeks? How many new listings are running for your product right now? Is supply holding steady or dwindling? Has another seller recently flooded the market with products?

6. Where is this product in the product life cycle? Are you evaluating a brand new product with strong growth or liquidation merchandise at the end of the cycle?

7. How many other sellers are selling this item? Are you competing against hundreds of other web sites or just a handful of sellers on eBay?

8. Does any one seller have market share? If a particular seller sells to a majority share of the market, it can be very difficult to break into selling in that market without a way to differentiate yourself and your product from the market leader.

9. How much will it cost to ship this product? You'll need to know the approximate weight in order to calculate shipping costs. You'll also want to look at what other sellers are charging for shipping and make sure you can ship at a competitive rate.

10. Will special packing supplies be required to pack and ship this product? Shipping materials can play a large part in whether a product will provide a reasonable profit margin. Heavy, fragile, or odd-shaped items can all make you incur added expenses for shipping materials. This consideration must be factored in when determining whether or not a product has profit possibilities.

11. Once you've put your potential product through the first ten steps on the checklist, calculated the numbers, and concluded that you have a successful idea, the next step is to contact your supplier and determine what the base cost will be for purchasing the product wholesale.

12. You now have the science portion of product selection almost complete. From here you can take the average selling price of the item, subtract the costs, and the resulting number will be your profit margin. If this number works for your business, you're halfway there—halfway because you still need to proceed with the art of product selection.

Art: Evaluating the X Factor of a Product

While the numbers you gleaned in your research during product evaluation give you an excellent start in deciding whether or not a product has profit potential, they don't tell the whole story. Every successful seller will tell you that there's more to generating sales and profit than focusing on market demand and seller competition alone. While strong market demand, high prices, and few competing sellers offer an excellent prognosis for your chosen product, there are other things to consider when evaluating a product for its profit potential. This is called the X factor of your product—and it's the art of product selection.

Part of the art of product sourcing involves the creativity *you* bring to your selling and marketing strategies, along with your customer service. However, the reasons you select a product along with the characteristics of the product itself can turn an otherwise ho-hum item into a top seller.

As you continue your evaluation of a potential product, you'll want to review it against the following questions to decide if there's an X factor present which will make your product a definite yes ... or maybe a no:

1. Is the product you're evaluating seasonal? If so, are you coming in at the beginning or end of the season? Maybe you're considering selling a line of Christmas ornaments or want to branch out into outdoor holiday home décor. If you're thinking about buying your inventory as the end of the season approaches, you must take into consideration that the sales prices of your seasonal items will start to decrease. For example, in late December, interest will generally begin to wane in Christmas décor. If you're planning to recoup your inventory investment right away, you'll need to establish whether or not you can sell enough of your product before the current season ends. If not, you'll need to determine if this is a product you want to source when wholesale prices are the lowest and save the inventory for next season.

2. Is the product trendy or a fad? If you're buying on the front of the wave, you'll be able to capitalize on growing consumer interest in the product. The phenomenal rise in sales of Ty Beanie Babies was very lucrative for retailers who got in early on the trend. And while some of the older Beanies have retained (or grown) in value, many of the newer pieces are now usually found at retail or less just a few months after release. It's important to realistically assess where a trend or fad is in the cycle. Get in at the beginning and there are profits to be made. Tap in on the tail end and you'll soon be dealing with a lower-priced commodity.

Note: Is the market on the brink of saturation? Sometimes it's a fine line between a satisfied market and a saturated market. Often, it takes experience to be able to make the call. A satisfied market may have room for one more product of its kind, while a saturated market does not. As you gain experience in product sourcing, you'll develop a sense of when a market is close to being saturated.

Tip: If a market is close to saturation and prices are beginning to spiral down, it's time to seriously consider selecting another product and entering a different market. There are millions of products and many, many markets to sell in. Trying to position a product in an already saturated market is a hard road to travel and one that need not be taken.

3. Does the product have a related line of products that you can cross-sell? Do the related products have a higher profit margin? For example, you may sell a line of digital cameras that bring in a moderate profit margin. However, the camera cases, lenses, tripods, photo printers, printer paper, and digital imaging software that you sell as "add-on" products command a much higher profit margin. With a product line such as this, you'll want to stock the primary product, even though it does not carry your desired profit margin. The cameras attract the buyers to your store, while the related accessory sales generate the majority of the profits. This is a traditional retail strategy: stocking products with a slim margin because they attract customers who buy additional products with a much higher profit margin.

4. Is this product a "meat and potatoes" product or an ancillary product? Every retail business must carry several meat and potatoes products—products that are the staples of their business. Meat and potatoes products sell steadily and with a substantial profit margin. In some cases, they may bring in the bulk of the revenue. Ancillary products, on the other hand, are not expected to bring in the bulk of your sales money. You may stock these products to round out a product line, produce additional sales, or act as lead generators to gain new customers. Don't count on low-volume, low–profit margin products to be your meat and potatoes product line or your revenue will suffer.

5. Is anyone selling this product or a related product? Unless a product is completely new to the marketplace and you're one of the first sellers in the game, selling a product that no one else is selling can mean you have a dud on your hands. Usually, if no one else is selling a product that has been available for a while, it's because there was no profit in it. Every once in a while you'll come across an item that's brand new *and* has pent-up demand. This is an excellent X factor! But if a product has been available for a while and there's little or no demand, chances are you won't be able to sell it profitably either.

6. Does the profit margin of the product match the goals for your business? We frequently see people veering off the track on this one. If you have a goal of a small part-time retail business, the volume of product sales and the product profit margins you need to reach those goals will be much different than the seller with a business goal of $500,000 per year in sales. If your financial goals are to make *$1,000 per month in profit*, you need to select products that will *bring a profit* of just over $32 per day. However, if your company's goals are $10,000 *per month in profit* the products you need to select to achieve that number will be quite different. You'll need to choose products with a higher profit margin or that you can sell in higher quantities to hit those target numbers.

7. Is the product a distraction? If you're trying to source a product with a $50-per-unit profit margin, don't get distracted by products that only offer a $5-per-unit profit margin. While these products may have a place in your overall strategy long term, if they do not meet your short-term goals, make a note of them in your Product Sourcing Notebook for further evaluation at a later date. If your goal is to source a line of fashion-forward watches that are moderately priced with a $75 profit margin per watch, don't veer off the track by spending your inventory capital on close-out watches with a $10 profit margin per item (unless you're choosing to sell this watch as an ancillary product, as we discussed earlier). Ultimately, the more focused you are on sourcing products that support your business vision and strategies, the faster you'll reach your sales goals.

8. Does the product fit your business model? Right up there with getting distracted by the right product at the wrong time is getting distracted by a product that doesn't fit your overall business plan. The seller who specializes in automotive tools may come across a great deal on wedding gowns, but in an automotive tools store there's probably no market for wedding gowns. While this example is extreme, it's important to analyze who's coming to your store to shop and if the products you're considering have a *crossover* market in your buyers. For example, if your store sells cosmetics, a good crossover product could be fragrances, or possibly even ladies handbags. A good crossover product likely wouldn't be short-wave radios.

9. Will this product sell on auto-pilot? Sometimes a product practically sells itself. It may not have a huge profit margin, but it could be easy to sell, fast to package, and quick to ship. We call these products mini-profit machines. If something sells consistently and easily with a steady profit, it's a good stream of income to have. For example, selling unique one-of-a-kind blown glass lamps requires a more labor-intensive approach and a more specialized advertising strategy than selling a natural spectrum desk lamp. The blown glass lamp will most likely bring in a higher profit margin per unit, but the time and effort required to sell, package, and ship the lamp will be significantly more than selling pre-boxed lamps that all look the same. While you certainly shouldn't forgo the more labor-intensive product, selling the desk lamp in addition can provide your business with a nice mini-profit machine. String together several mini-profit machines and you can build a strong sales engine. Remember, it's easier to make $5,000 per month with multiple product streams of income than it is to find one product that alone generates $5,000. These little money machines can be as profitable in the long run as the blockbuster sellers that require more working capital and offer less steady profits.

10. Does the vendor offer quantity discounts that would lower your cost for the item? If a vendor is motivated to do business with you, they're very often willing to do some pricing negotiation or offer special shipping promotions. Frequently, the price you start out with when buying a product wholesale isn't the price you end up paying long term. As you establish a relationship with your suppliers and order more products with them, they'll come to value your business and will in turn do what they can to make the proposition more lucrative for you...and them. Look at the big picture when selecting your inventory. Volume discounts, shipping promotions, or additional products added to your order can all make a product or product line a more attractive proposition for you.

11. Is the product part of a larger picture? You may be evaluating a product to sell in which you have mild interest, but it's a gateway to a larger product line that you want to explore in the long run. Holden, an eBay PowerSeller, had always dreamed of selling high-end speedboats. Because his was a start-up business, he didn't have the funding at the beginning to purchase boats for resale so he decided to begin his business by selling boating accessories and clothing. This gave him an entry point into his desired niche and allowed him to build a reputation online with more moderately priced products before he entered the high-end speedboat arena. After almost three years of selling boating products, Holden was ready to make the leap to his dream product—speedboats. Looking back, he believes he made exactly the right choice by entering his desired niche product line slowly. He still deals with almost all of the vendors he started out with and has added many new ones to his supplier list as well. Keep in mind that entry products are a good way to test out a vendor, build a relationship, and explore further the opportunities of doing additional business with a company while paving the way to expand your business fully into your desired niche market.

12. Can your business afford this product? Some products have great profit potential, but if it means tying up all your inventory capital, it may not be the right time to make a purchase. When you find a profitable product line, it's very easy to get caught up in the excitement and rush to place a large order. However, if you must overextend yourself to purchase your inventory, it's usually the wrong time to make the purchase. While there will come a point in every business where in order to move to the next level you must look at expanding beyond your current financial model, when you're starting a company it's good business acumen to make the best use of your resources. As we talked about earlier in this chapter, costs play a major part in your profit margin. Overspending today with the hope of big profits tomorrow is seldom a win-win situation.

13. How much should you trust your instincts? As you become more experienced in product sourcing, you'll develop your product sourcing

instinct—that sixth sense that tells you when a product that looks good on paper still isn't right for you. Or, in the opposite case, when a voice inside of you keeps telling you that even though a product doesn't look good on paper, it's still an inventory item you should add. Sometimes, you'll be right on. Other times, you'll be completely wrong. But each occurrence will prove to be a learning situation and every time will move you closer to having better product sourcing instincts.

As you can see, there are many X factors that can make a product a strong seller or one to steer clear of. Knowing how to see past the numbers and evaluate a product for its X factors will give you a significant advantage in your product sourcing endeavors. After putting your potential products through the "Science Test" and the "X Factor Test," you'll now have a good indication of whether or not a product has profit potential. However, keep in mind that all merchandise buyers make mistakes from time to time. Even the best and brightest working at Nordstrom or Saks 5th Avenue sometimes make the wrong call. When this happens, it's important to learn from the situation and move on to the next product. By using the strategies in this chapter, you'll have the skills at your disposal to pick winners on a regular basis.

Evaluation Tools

Good product sourcing is a direct result of having a repeatable system and the right tools. Nowhere else is this more true than when it comes to doing product evaluation research. While many of your efforts will require the manual review of web sites, auction listings, or a competitor's store inventory, some of your research can be quickly and effectively systematized by using the tools discussed next. In order to operate a successful, professional business, you'll need to have these research tools at your disposal. Not only will they save you time and money, but utilizing them may constitute the difference between making an educated product selection decision and choosing your next product in the dark.

eBay Searches

If you're an eBay seller, there are a host of research tools out there available to you. In this section, we'll focus on two of our favorites that we use on a daily basis and which provide excellent results. A third, which is excellent for both eBay research and other online venues, will be covered in the next section. First, let's start by doing some research on eBay itself, using the data that eBay provides for free. Even though it will take some time to manually do this research, do not skip this step! When you spend time on eBay, it's then you're closest to your marketplace and this is where you can get a bird's-eye view of the true profit potential of your product.

To research an item on eBay, you first want to look at the current listings for the item on eBay. To do this, go to the Search box at the top of any eBay page and type in the name of the product you're researching. A search of current listings will give you an idea of what is happening in the marketplace today. Review the listings to see how many there are for the product you're considering selling and to get an idea of what the current bidding activity is on this line of merchandise. Take note of how many items are listed, which listings have bids, and how many bidders there are for each item.

Tip: When doing your research, be sure and search for the product using a variety of relevant keywords. For example, if you're researching Magellan GPS systems, rather than searching only for "Magellan GPS" you should try a variety of additional keywords such as the make, model number, and style of the Magellan GPS system you're researching. Using different keywords in different variations will allow you to pull up a broader scope of listings to evaluate.

The next step in your research is to do an eBay Completed Items search for the product you're considering selling. A Completed Items page (see Figure 6-1) is where you'll find a wealth of information that will tell you whether or not your product has profit potential. eBay provides you with two weeks' worth of data on completed listings and this data is free to all registered users.

Figure 6-1   An eBay Completed Items page

Tip: eBay offers a unique perspective in that you can actually see the amount of interest in a product. When looking at a Completed Items list you can see if there's a high number of listings with no closed sales, if there are a moderate to small number of completed listings with bids on most of the items, or whether the bidding has simply gone wild. This information allows you to put your product evaluation microscope in place and zoom in on the details regarding the product's sales history.

To search a Completed Items page, type in the name of your product in the keyword Search box, found at the top of every eBay page. Once the search results are returned, select the Completed Listings option in the left-hand box (see Figure 6-2), and then sort the list according to the highest price by choosing Highest First in the Sort By box (see Figure 6-3). Sorting the list by the highest ending price allows you to look at similar products that garnered the top selling price. You'll want to review the search results using the criteria outlined earlier in this chapter in the Product Profitability Checklist found in the section "Science: What to Look For." Additionally, while reviewing the search results, take a look at the individual listings that commanded the top final sales prices.

Completed listings

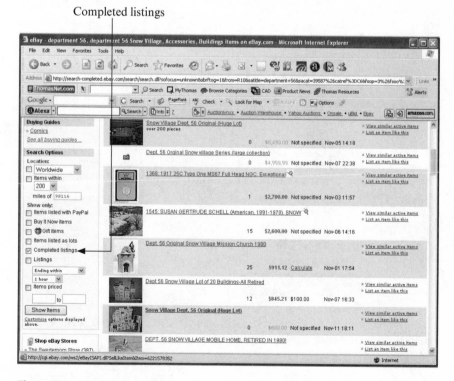

Figure 6-2   eBay's Completed Items gives you a snapshot of market demand for a product.

Sort by

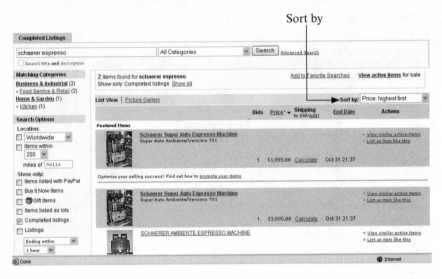

Figure 6-3   Sorting by highest price shows you the items with the highest final sales price.

Note: Keep in mind that when reviewing the sales price of items on auction sites like eBay, you must always look at the *final sales price* of an item, in addition to the price the item is currently being offered for. Looking at a Completed Items page for final sales prices will give you a snapshot of what actually *happened* with the sale of a particular product—as opposed to a Current Listings page, which only shows you what price a seller *hopes* to sell their merchandise for.

This is a good opportunity for you to leverage your time by scanning the listings to see how the top sellers positioned the product. It should include such information as the following:

- What starting price was the product listed at?
- What pricing strategy did the seller employ?
- What keywords were used in the title?
- What day did the listing end?
- What time did the listing end?

Make notes of this information in your Product Sourcing Notebook to refer back to as needed during your product selection process.

eBay offers a variety of reports that help you track the performance of those products you're currently selling. eBay's Sales Reports and Sales Reports Plus allow you to analyze in detail a product's sell-through success rate, as well as the average selling price of your item and much more. You can learn more about eBay Sales Reports at http://pages .ebay.com/salesreports/welcome.html.

In addition, eBay's Store Traffic Report Basics and Store Traffic Reports, which are available to eBay Store owners through http://pages.ebay .com/help/specialtysites/traffic-reporting-basics.html, provide you with a wide variety of information that will help you evaluate the sales success of products you're currently selling. For eBay sellers, these reports offer critical insight into which products you should continue to sell, and which products should be discontinued in favor of new inventory.

Terapeak

Terapeak (www.terapeak.com/signup/book) allows you to search through 90 days' worth of eBay data and provides you with numerous reports that will assist you in your product evaluation tasks (see Figure 6-4). Best of all, you can accomplish this feat in minutes! It offers access to important sales metrics such as:

- The value of goods
  - Sell-through rate
  - Average sales price
  - Total number of listings
  - Total bids received
  - Categories that items were listed in
- Category analysis
  - Best time and day to sell your item
  - Seasonal trends
  - Total sales rank
  - Listing durations

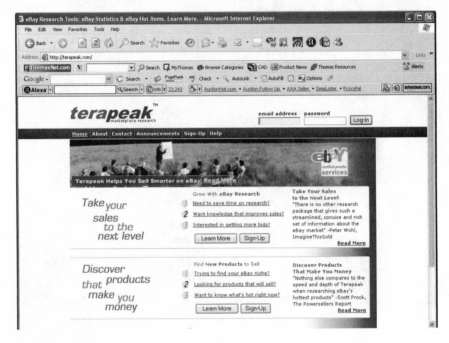

Figure 6-4   A good research tool is a critical ally in your product sourcing endeavors.

- Competitive analysis
  - Market share of the top five sellers
  - Total bids they received
  - Number of sellers competing
  - Market consolidation reports
  - Top seller sell-through rates
- Product analysis
  - Highest volume categories
  - Best bid growth categories
  - Growth trends

In addition, Terapeak offers a number of reports that can assist you in both positioning your products and in establishing effective sales and marketing strategies. The cost to use Terapeak's research tool is $16.95 per month.

Deep Analysis

Another research tool, Deep Analysis by Hammertap, also provides eBay data, but presents it in a somewhat different format. Deep Analysis pulls reports from 30 days' worth of eBay data, and provides information such as the following:

- Sell-through rates
- Total sales
- Most popular items
- Average sales prices
- Average number of bids
- Reserve listing sell-through rate
- Item categories
- Average bids per item
- Most successful sellers

Deep Analysis costs $179 per year, with an annual renewal fee of $49.95. You can test it free for 30 days at http://hammertap.com/deepanalysis/DownloadDeepAnalysis.html.

Other Sales Venues

If you sell in sales venues other than eBay, you'll need to comb the individual sites for the sales metrics that will show you exactly how a particular product is selling. Since you may be selling on your own web site, from a Yahoo store, or from a mall type of store, each individual platform will require slightly different research methods. It's important to take the time to sit down and investigate the research possibilities for your particular sales venues. Only then will you be able to definitively assess your product's selling potential.

The Market Research Wizard

An excellent tool that allows you to analyze the market demand of a product across multiple platforms is the Market Research Wizard, created by Chris Malta's company, WorldWide Brands. The Market Research Wizard (see Figure 6-5) is unique in that it's the only tool that aggregates data from several retail platforms across the Web and analyzes that data in order to provide you with an in-depth sales analysis.

The Market Research Wizard will tell you:

- How much demand there is on the Web for a particular product
- How much competition there is for that product
- Who your competitors are
- For eBay—the auction listings and bids for your product

The Market Research Wizard also provides you with advertising metrics as well as keyword analysis for your potential products, and offers

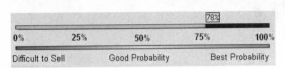

Figure 6-5 The Market Research Wizard allows you to research product ideas across multiple channels.

an easy-to-interpret analysis of your product's potential for success online. You can download a free trial of the Market Research Wizard at www .WorldWideBrands.com/eBay.

The Bottom Line

Ultimately, when deciding whether or not to sell a particular product, you have to ask yourself this question: Can I sell this product at a price that will enable me to be profitable and competitive? If, after doing your research, the answer is yes, then it's time to proceed to contacting your supplier. If the answer is no, then you have two alternatives: lower your direct costs, fixed costs, or desired profit; or consider not selling this product and focus your attention instead on products that have a better profit margin or less competition. Don't get stuck on selling a particular product. Remember, successful product sourcing is a numbers game. For every 30 products you review, one will make the grade. However, when selected for the right reasons, the one that passes the test will bring with it the potential of income and growth for your business.

Summing Up

You now have the skills to choose your next profitable product—and do it time and time again. In the next chapter, we'll add yet another area of expertise to your seller's toolkit: creative product selection. But first, let's review what it takes to discern whether or not a product has the potential for profit:

- The only way you can accurately determine if a product has profit potential is by doing your research. Otherwise, you'll be making product sourcing decisions in the dark.
- No matter how you slice it, the only way to make money in retail is by selling products that people want to buy. Understanding how many people want to purchase a product (*market demand*) is a skill that every retailer must learn.

- If your base cost for your product is too high, and the expenses to sell your product are excessive (labor, advertising, fees, web site hosting, and so on), you won't be able to make a sufficient profit margin on your products.
- Every product goes through stages in market demand. These stages, or cycles, are referred to as the product life cycle and are a critical factor in determining whether or not an item will have a strong market demand.
- Determining an acceptable profit margin per product is something only you as a retailer can decide. In reality, there are no cold, hard, fast numbers that apply across the board to every product or business.
- Once you're in the habit of analyzing all the separate elements that go into a product's profitability quotient, you'll be able to easily see the combination of factors that exemplify a profitable product.
- The science of product evaluation is all about knowing exactly what's happening with pricing and sales volume in the marketplace you sell in. Understanding this information will lead you directly to assessing the market demand for your product and determining its profit potential.
- While strong market demand, high prices, and few competing sellers offer an excellent prognosis for your chosen product, there are other things to consider when evaluating a product for its profit potential. This is called the X factor of your product.
- Ultimately, when deciding whether or not to sell a particular product, you have to ask yourself this question: Can I sell this product at a price that will enable me to be profitable and competitive?

Chapter 7

Creative Product Selection

If you want your business to grow and prosper, differentiating yourself from the store "down the street" is your ticket to success. By using this principle, many sellers have gone from small operations to mega-successes. While selling strategies and marketing techniques play a considerable role in carving out a unique presence for your store, creative product selection is the foundation on which your branding will be built. After all, if you offer the same products as everyone else, and merchandise them in the same basic manner, what impetus will a buyer have to visit *your* store over someone else's?

Creative product selection allows you to put your stamp on your product line. With creative product selection, you have the opportunity to offer products that really set your store apart from the competition. And when you select products creatively, it gives you another very important advantage—the competitive edge. Because creative product selection comes from your unique vantage point, the products you select and the way you select them will be different from every other retailer. Why? Because there's no one else on this earth exactly like *you*!

When Is a Product More Than Just a Product

We often talk to sellers who are very caught up in having a product to sell. They view each product as an entity unto itself. However, when your focus is solely on finding that product, you lose sight of the bigger picture—your overall business strategy. In order to build a *business*, your products must be *relational*, meaning there must be some integration of purpose between the items you sell. Therefore, when selecting your inventory, it's important to assess a product not only on its own merit, but also as one component of your larger business plan.

Not every product will be a product line staple. Some items may serve the function as products you up-sell, cross-sell, or feature to add value to your product line. Or you may choose to add a product to the mix simply to round out your product line. If you sell in a keyword-driven platform such as eBay, you may choose products based on their keyword richness alone. All of these considerations play into your creative product selection. This approach is different than randomly selecting inventory for no rhyme or reason. With creative product selection, you have an understanding of the bigger picture. Every time you place an inventory order, you know exactly what role an item fulfills in your cast of "inventory characters." As you become more adept at this skill, you'll learn to foresee unique and unusual ways to integrate merchandise into your product line and make it work *for* your business.

Cross-Selling

"Would you like fries and a drink with your burger?" The most famous of cross-selling lines comes directly from one of the world's largest food retailers: McDonald's. And while that phrase has often been the punch line for a host of jokes, these cross-selling efforts are no joke when it comes to the positive impact on McDonald's profits. McDonald's sells a lot of sodas and fries that they wouldn't sell otherwise. Why? Because they ask for the sale.

What products do you currently have in your product line that you can cross-sell to customers? If you can't list several, then it's time to do some creative product selection! Cross-selling is a superb way to increase the value of a sale by suggesting an accompanying product. And because of this, you should source your products to ensure that you have an ample supply of available inventory to cross-sell. If someone buys acrylic paints from your eBay store, you should also offer them the opportunity to buy some brushes and a canvas from you. If you sell posters online, before the close of every sale, you should suggest a complementary frame to the buyer. Every time you look at potential inventory, one option you should consider for the product is whether or not it would be a good cross-selling product.

Cross-selling products can produce either a high or low profit margin, and still be good candidates for the job. Computer retailers employ this strategy all the time. A computer may carry with it a fairly narrow profit margin, but the customer who buys a new computer will often need a printer, a backup drive, software, and maybe even a service contract—all items which carry a considerably higher profit margin. When the salesperson offers these items to the customer and they accept, the retailer's profits and profit margin are greatly increased.

Conversely, a high-ticket, high-profit margin item can be an excellent base for cross-selling lower-priced, lower-margin items. Sierra sells high-end manicure kits, lotions, and potions to give you soft beautiful hands. She also cross-sells a significant amount of nail polish. While her primary products, the manicure kits and expensive lotions, both carry a higher price tag and a higher profit margin, the nail polish she sells brings in a nice additional stream of revenue. In addition, she is making her customers happy. When a customer comes to your shopping venue and can get everything they need to complete their purchase and not have to go elsewhere, they feel better about the shopping experience, they are more willing to spend money, and they feel better about you, the retailer. This, in turn, will bring them back to your store again.

One of the cornerstones of cross-selling is that you have to make the primary sale first. Your customer must be sold in their own mind on the principal product they're interested in before they'll consider ancillary products to complement their purchase. But studies show that once they've made that commitment to buy from you, they're more willing to open their wallets and buy more, right then and there. As you can see, sourcing cross-selling products is a very important part of your creative product selection strategies.

Cross-Selling a Service

Cross-selling is not only limited to products. You can even cross-sell a service such as shipping. Amazon.com does this with flair. With every purchase you make at Amazon, you're given the opportunity to get free shipping *if* you increase your purchase to a minimum of $25. Of course, the second book you add usually brings the total order amount to way over $25. Take that one step further, and in the mind of the customer, if they're going to order the two books they want and get free shipping, they may as well order the third book they were considering. This can often bring their order total to three times the original amount. Once the cross-sale is made, however, the customer is happy and the retailer is happy. It's a win-win situation. Think about combining shipping charges for your products. It gives your customers an incentive to buy more and will boost your average sale amount per order. It also makes your customer think they're getting added value, because even though they're buying more, they feel like they're saving more as well.

Up-Selling

Why buy cloth seats when you can have leather for just a little bit more? This is a question heard every day in new car dealerships across the country. The goal of upgrading or up-selling the customer to a more deluxe version of your product is a strategy that will directly affect your product sourcing endeavors. While not a new concept, the concept of up-selling is often overlooked in the day-to-day operations of a retail store. Yet, shifting your customers' purchases to more profitable products can prove to be a valuable strategy.

In simple terms, up-selling is the basic practice of moving the customer from a less profitable item in a category to a more profitable one in the same category. For example, when purchasing a car, after you finally decide on the make and model, you sit down with the salesperson and work out the details. The salesperson's job is to up-sell you into a higher-end package with leather, sound systems, and fancy wheels. If he or she is good at what they do, and offers you the right combination of features, before you know it, you have upgraded from the base model to the more luxurious *and* more expensive deluxe model. The result? A more profitable transaction for the dealership. The same holds true with your retail store.

Up-selling plays right into a basic desire of human nature. We like to have the best. Price considerations aside, there are very few people who, given the choice, would willingly opt for a low-end mundane product over a high-end feature-rich one. And even though some of your buyer's purchases will be price-driven, not all of them will be. And for that group of customers, you'll need products in your line that are suitable for up-selling.

Ideally, in your product line you should strive to maintain different products at different price points so you meet the needs of a wide variety of customers. For example, perhaps you stock a wide selection of bed sheets and comforters, ranging in price from economy pricing to mid-range quality and price. In order to up-sell, you would add to that a number of high-end, high thread count cotton sheets with matching comforters, duvets, and shams. If customers come to your store for the mid-range sheet set, you can now up-sell them to the high-end (and more profitable) Egyptian cotton, high thread count, sumptuous, designer color set.

One of the keys to up-selling is understanding the needs and wants of your customers. The need for this knowledge runs through all aspects of your product sourcing efforts. When selecting inventory for the purpose of using it as an up-sell, the more you learn about your target customer and their buying habits, the better equipped you'll be to select products to up-sell to them. For example, Brenna, a retailer who sells quality children's furniture and accessories, understands her customers' wants and she knows what to up-sell to them. Even though she stocks a line of moderately priced children's furniture, she knows that when parents come in and see the beautiful specialty cribs, dressers, and changing tables that retail from $1,400 to $2,000, they're often hard-pressed to say no to purchasing their baby's dream room. "Because I've learned from talking to my customers over the years that parents and grandparents love these high-end products, I am able to stock them with the confidence of knowing that they will sell. Just from listening to my customers, I can predict which products they will purchase as an up-sell with uncanny accuracy." Brenna has mastered the art of up-selling and you can, too, by reaching out to your customers and asking them what they want to buy. When sourcing products for up-selling, you do not need to make a large inventory purchase up-front. In fact it's better if you test new up-sell products in smaller quantities. Because products for up-selling are more expensive in general, they require a larger financial investment to purchase inventory. Buying in smaller lots and then testing the success of these products allows you to determine if you have selected the up-sell products that appeal to your customers. Once you have the right mix, you can reorder your inventory in larger amounts. As you go through your product sourcing travels, look for products to up-sell. The more products you have to offer your customer, the more lucrative the process becomes.

Can I Cross-Sell When I Up-Sell?

Cross-selling and up-selling are not mutually exclusive. In the earlier example of the store that sells bedding products, cross-selling and up-selling would be a perfect blend. Once your customer has decided to upgrade from the mid-range sheet set to the high-end, Egyptian cotton, 800–thread count set in the unique designer color "lavender lace," you now have an opportunity to cross-sell the matching accessories. Pillow shams, bedside table lamps, wall art, and curtains are all examples of items that you could successfully cross-sell once the up-sell is complete.

The key to cross-selling after up-selling? Knowledge. The more knowledgeable your sales staff is or, in the case of an online seller, the more you connect the dots for your customer with attractive photos of a combination of items, or suggest purchases once they click "Buy" on your web site, the more successful you will be at cross-selling after up-selling. In the case of the online retailer, having a "what's new," "what's hot," or even a "fashion" page to show your customers what products are in style and how they work together will go a long way towards your ability to up-sell and cross-sell your products.

Note: eBay offers sellers the ability to cross-promote their other items to buyers when they check out. To offer your buyers other items for their consideration:

1. Sign in and click the Change Your Cross-Promotions link at the top of any of your current item pages. This allows you to set your own cross-promotion rules, or accept the eBay default rules.

2. Go to My eBay and choose Preferences under My Account on the left. Set up shipping discounts according to your preference.

3. Include your shipping details such as shipping and handling, insurance, and tax in your listing. Cross-promotions are only displayed at checkout when the total amounts are known.

For more information on the eBay Cross-Promotion tool, go to http://pages.ebay.com/help/sell/merchandising-in-checkout.html.

Value-Added Products

Want to keep your customers coming back time and time again? Add more value to your products and your customers will flock back to you for more. Value-added products are a quick, easy, and inexpensive way to give your customers more for their money, and actually allow you to charge more for your products in the process. With every dog dish, dog house, or faux jeweled dog collar she sells, Caitlyn, who designed a web site and built a successful retail business out of a spare bedroom in her home, includes a bar of natural soap with the order—for free. Customers love the added value. People can buy some similar dog products in other stores, but no one else includes a bar of special soap with the purchase. Does this set Caitlyn's business apart in the mind of the consumer? You bet it does. It also leaves buyers with a very good feeling about Caitlyn and her store. Customers feel that Caitlyn wants to make their furry pets a little cleaner, and a little healthier in the process—and for that, they're willing to give her their buyer loyalty. Purchasing value-added products does not have to be an expensive proposition for a seller. Caitlyn buys the natural soap she gives away in bulk so her per unit cost is very small. She doesn't build this added expense into the price of her other merchandise, but other retailers frequently increase the cost of their products when they add value and find that their customers don't blink an eye at paying the higher prices.

Madison, who's making the move from a small brick-n'-mortar store to an expanded online presence, offers a rather expensive value-added product with every NASCAR jacket she sells. With every purchase, her customers can select a framed NASCAR poster. Her strategy has paid off handsomely in a market with strong competition. However, her value-added product does increase her costs. To offset the expense, she has built the costs of the poster into her merchandise prices. *And raised her prices an additional 17 percent on top of that.* The jackets, along with the complimentary posters, sell like hotcakes, even at the higher prices. Madison is able to charge, on average, 27 percent higher prices than her direct competitors. And 17 percent of that is pure additional profit. Why are customers willing to pay more for a jacket they could get cheaper elsewhere? Because in the customer's mind they're getting much more value when they buy from Madison. They're happy to pay the increased price to get a quality jacket, a ready-to-hang, framed NASCAR poster, and great customer service from Madison.

When sourcing your products, look for merchandise you can purchase in bulk which will complement your existing product line. Do you sell children's dresses? Then perhaps you could buy a lot of hair clips in bulk and give a matching set away with each dress. Do you sell expensive kitchen stand mixers? Then offer a matching spatula with each purchase. The important thing to remember with value-added products is that *it must be valuable and relevant to the buyer*. Throwing in a cheap plastic doo-dad doesn't add value to your product. Selecting an item that complements your product *does* add value, however. For years, a small mail-order catalog offered a mystery "surprise" with each order over a certain amount. Customers would get all excited, hoping it was a wonderful item out of the popular catalog. Trouble was, when the customer received the mystery surprise, the surprise was that it was an inexpensive, useless knickknack. And if you placed multiple, separate orders, you'd get the same junk time and time again. This was not adding value to a product, and in the end the practice did nothing to further the relationship with the customer.

The right value-added products also give you one of the most important advantages you can ever have as a retailer: a USP (unique selling position). A USP is what sets you apart from your competition. With a value-added product, you can create a USP that no other retailer can match. Let's say your competition starts offering a spatula with the purchase of every kitchen stand mixer ... all you need to do at this point is change the value-added product you're offering. Make the switch to measuring spoons or whisks. With a value-added product you'll always stay one step ahead of your competition and give your business a unique selling position with which to attract customers.

Value-Added Information

Living in an information society is a boon for the retail entrepreneur, because value-added information is an easy, inexpensive way to increase the perceived value of your products dramatically. Jackson, a budding businessman, found he was able to increase his prices 25 percent across the board when he started adding value-added information to each purchase. His value-added product? An instructional baking DVD. For every baking dish, mixing bowl, and bundt pan bought in orders totaling over $30, Jackson includes his baking basics DVD—an information product that Jackson made himself. While the DVD production qualities are not hi-tech, the information is top-notch, featuring tips, recipes, and Jackson's own baking secrets. Jackson's cost to produce this DVD is just under $3 per unit, a very small cost compared to the revenue the DVD generates. Jackson knows that some customers place an order with him just to get his DVD. In fact, he's found this approach to be so successful he's already at work on creating a second DVD to sell with the new high-end grills he plans to offer later this year. Jackson's success is a strong testimonial to the power of value-added information.

Creating value-added information does not need to be difficult or time-consuming. The information only has to be relevant to the product you're selling. One savvy eBayer created a "planting by the month" calendar and included it for free with each gardening tool she sold. Customers loved the information. The one-page, double-sided 12-month calendar had three suggested plantings, broken out by region, so no matter what area of the country you lived in, you had some suggestions for what to plant and when. The calendar was created in Microsoft Word and then printed and laminated and included with each order. The value-added information allowed this eBay seller to remain competitive when other sellers came into the marketplace and attempted to undercut the prices of her gardening tools. Her customers continued to pay more, strictly because of the value they felt they were receiving with the planting calendar.

Every product you sell lends itself to a companion value-added information product. Think out of the box; get creative. What information would your customer want to know more about in relation to the product that you sell? Tips booklets, "how-to" brochures, cheat sheets, CDs, DVDs, and eBooks all present opportunities for you to include value-added information with your products.

Rounding Out Your Product Line

How well rounded is your product line? Do you have a wide spectrum of products in your niche or are there gaping holes in the array of merchandise you offer? One of the things that customers value most, right after quality, is selection. Even if they're shopping in a niche market store for the same products over and over again, they like the *idea* that there are other products in the store to choose from.

If you deal in selling high-end sewing machines and imported fabrics online, you may not feel it's necessary to sell thread. Your customer, on the other hand, may see it differently. When they arrive at your store with the intent to purchase a machine and maybe cross-sell over to some beautiful silk fabric, they might not stop to buy thread. Just the same, they know it's there if they want it, and this fact adds a level of professionalism to your store in the buyer's mind.

Imagine entering your own store, but from your customer's perspective. Do you carry a diverse assortment of goods in your product line? If you aren't sure whether or not your product line is well rounded, visit a local retailer who specializes in the same type of products you carry. Or take a look at your online competition. What are they carrying? Are there items you need to source in order to have a more well-rounded product line? While not all of these items may sell well, they're still important to have from an impression standpoint. When practicing creative product selection, keep in mind that a well-rounded product line is always part of the big picture.

When Nathaniel, who recently entered the entrepreneurial world, opened his online store his original business model centered around selling hand tools for the do-it-yourself home remodeler. One day, he came across a retail display store in his city that was going out of business. They were offering fixtures, furniture, and track lighting, all for pennies on the dollar. Operating from the perspective of "you make your money when you buy, not when you sell," Nathaniel knew he was looking at some great deals, but didn't think any of it fit well with his existing product line. Nevertheless, he went to his favorite coffee shop to mull it over. He sat for a while and tried to think from his customer's perspective. "If I was a buyer, coming to my store to buy tools, what else would I buy?" He went through the store's inventory in his mind and decided that track lighting would be an obvious choice. If people are remodeling their homes, he thought, chances are they're replacing their lighting. Nathaniel went back to the store and purchased 12 track-lighting systems. Within two weeks, they had all sold. Nathaniel has now expanded his store to carry not only track lighting, but also light fixtures, cabinet hardware, wall-mounted accessories, and more.

Because he was able to see a potentially new product from a different view, Nathaniel introduced a product line to his store that other sellers may never have considered. It's often said that the most creative people see what everyone else sees, but look at it in ways most people do not. Nathaniel embodied that philosophy completely. A shift in your product sourcing perception can help you understand the potential of a product in a different way, which in turn can create a new profitable direction for your business.

Loss Leaders

Have you ever gone to the grocery store with the intent to buy a 59-cent can of tuna advertised in the weekly special, only to leave 30 minutes later with a basket full of groceries and a $48.50 tab? If so, you've experienced the effectiveness of a "loss leader." A loss leader is a product that a store will offer below costs, to draw customers into the store, in the hopes that they'll stay and buy additional, higher–profit margin items. Loss leader selling is a strategy that has been in place since the beginning of retail and is one that every seller should employ.

You may be asking yourself, "Why would I want to lose money, just to get people to visit my eBay store?" The answer to that is simple: because it works. Loss leaders are the bait, the appetizer, the carrot that you dangle in front of your customers in order to attract them to your store and inspire them to browse through your other offerings. Loss leaders are a powerful tool to use in combination with cross-selling and up-selling. If you go to the grocery store to buy that discounted tuna and right next to it is a fresh-baked loaf of tempting sourdough bread, and right next to that is a big jar of mayonnaise (which you just happen to be running low on), how many of us are going to grab the tuna, turn on our heels, and leave? Very likely, only the most budget-conscious among us would do so.

When you're doing your product sourcing, look for products to be used as loss leaders. They don't have to be big or fancy products, only things that are popular enough to attract customers into your store when sold at a deep discount. Keep in mind that you can't have an entire store filled with loss leaders! At that rate, your store would go broke. But you can have one or two loss leader promotions running at a time. Track your results. If certain products are successful, note them, and add more items later if necessary.

Advertising Darlings

Would you sell a product at a break-even cost just to provide your business with some good advertising? If you want to bring in more customers, you would. Certain products are "advertising darlings"—products that everyone wants. These are the ones you'll find on all the top ten lists, featured in the media, and rolling off the tongues of shoppers as they look for them with anticipation. Often, these products are expensive to source, especially if they're hot items and new to the market. Some sellers may bypass these items because of the low-profit margin potential, but remember, creative product selection is all about looking at the big picture.

When the highly touted Nintendo DS was released in late fall 2004, most small retailers were hard-pressed to find them wholesale for a volume purchase that they could afford. Those who realized the advertising potential of these hot commodities headed right out to their local retailers and snapped up the stock. The first sellers to hit the online market place with "retail resales" made a fortune as customers drove prices up. But after a while, prices leveled out and profit margins became much slimmer for those who'd purchased the product retail with the intent to resell. So why were sellers still buying them in droves, knowing that in some cases they would only break even? Advertising. Everyone was looking for the Nintendo DS. Even if they didn't want to buy one, people at least wanted to see it and find out what it was about. If you carried one in your store, you were bound to attract customer traffic. And lots of it. Plus, while those customers were there, checking out the newest gaming phenomenon from Nintendo, they would also see what else you carried in your store and, in many cases, make a purchase.

Carrying a product just for advertising purposes can be a heads-up way to bring a lot of buyers into your store. Once there, you now have the opportunity to show them all the other fabulous merchandise you carry. Keep in mind that you do need to carry products that are relevant to what you sell. If you sell women's lingerie, carrying a Nintendo DS in your store likely wouldn't turn your customers into lingerie buyers. However, if you sell in the game and electronics market, stocking the Nintendo DS could be a powerful advertising tool.

Keyword-Rich Products

The vast majority of online shoppers search for the products they want to purchase by doing keyword searches (for instance, they search the Internet, eBay, or Yahoo for the products they want by using the words or keywords that describe them). If you sell in an online venue, it's critical you make sure you include keyword-rich products in your product-line mix. Now, while we're not advocating sourcing products based on keywords alone, sometimes a keyword-rich product that brings traffic to your online store may turn out to be a very important component in the success of your business.

Let's say for example that you sell major league baseball–branded products. Clothes, accessories, and home décor are all part of your store. Most of the year, you only carry the products licensed to certain teams, but as World Series time approaches, you make sure to carry products for those teams who may have a chance of going "all the way." Part of the reasoning behind this, of course, is because those products will sell well. But another part of the strategy is because they're keyword rich. If the New York Yankees are going to the World Series and you carry New York Yankees merchandise, just as with the advertising darlings we discussed earlier, these keyword-rich products will bring a lot of buyer traffic to your store. Once there, you have an opportunity to cross-sell your other merchandise to them.

Stocking keyword-rich products is especially effective during various holiday seasons. You may not normally carry Christmas ornaments, but during the holiday season, having a few good keyword-rich Christmas ornaments, such as Disney or Christopher Radko ornaments, will bring a lot of buyers into your store who wouldn't otherwise have stopped by. Keep in mind that, as with the advertising darlings earlier discussed, you do need to carry keyword-rich products that are relevant to what you sell. An automotive supplier most likely would not attract the kind of traffic they want to their eBay store by selling Disney baby products.

Note: In Chapter 4, we discussed Search Term Suggestion tools. These tools are also excellent to use in helping you source keyword-rich products.

Product Bundles

Would you:

- Like a method for creative product selection that allows you to compete in your market and win every time? And in a way that no one else can touch?
- Like to use a strategy that studies show has a growing appeal to consumers?
- Like a way to create your own "product" without ever having to manufacture a thing?

If you answered yes to all these questions, then a product bundle is the perfect creative product selection strategy for you!

A product bundle is a "product" that you put together which is made up of components of your choosing. It's the best way to compete in your market-place, blow away the competition, and have complete control over what you sell and the price you sell it at. Consumers continue to favor value-priced offerings, and bundling gives them more reasons to buy products and services. Bundling individual items can significantly lift sales and margins for any business, and is good for both retailers and customers. In fact, if you combine products, you can sell twice as much.

One enterprising seller created a very successful product bundle for home networking. Rather than selling the individual components separately, he put together 500 feet of Cat 5e network wire, a crimping tool, a punch-down tool, some RJ-45 modular plugs, network jacks, and instruction sheets and then advertised it as a Home Networking Kit.

Customers love it because of the immense value it provides them. With his Home Networking Kit they get

- Everything they need to network their home computers
- Instructions
- One-stop shopping, which saves them time and money
- Compatible components

- Reduced shipping costs
- The benefit of his knowledge and expertise. He researched the best components for this kit. He's done the work up-front and the customer reaps the benefits.

What is the benefit to the seller of using this strategy?

- He's created a product that no one else offers.
- Even if someone copies his idea, he can always add to or modify it, thereby staying one step ahead of his competition.
- He'll make more profit on the kit as a whole than he would selling each component individually.
- He sets himself apart from the other sellers with his USP (unique selling position).
- He has complete control over his product and his price because no one else is selling a kit like his.
- He can change or modify his kit at any time.
- He's setting himself up as an expert for the product. Someone who takes the time to put together a kit such as this generates customer confidence in their knowledge of a particular area.

And another great benefit of putting together a product package or bundle? It can be a lot of fun! If you like to get creative with the merchandise you sell, this technique is the answer. You are limited only by your imagination as to how you create your product bundle.

With a little creativity and by thinking outside the box, you can come up with an endless stream of ideas for creating product packages. The following are just a few examples:

1. **Gardening kits**   Garden tools, gloves, seeds, and a garden book.
2. **Book bundles**   Cooking-themed bundles, hobby-themed bundles, craft-book bundles, etc.
3. **DVD/book bundles**   Selling a DVD or DVD set with the accompanying book can make a great gift idea.
4. **Holiday decorations**   Create your own holiday exclusive by bundling together themed holiday decoration bundles.
5. **Children's toys**   Create themed packages with toys, books, and accessories. For example, you might create a package that includes Harry Potter Legos, a Harry Potter action figure, and a Harry Potter sticker book. Individually, these items may garner good interest, but packaged as a bundle, they can be a breakout seller.

Note: Offer to gift-wrap the preceding bundle in Harry Potter wrapping paper and watch your bundles fly off the shelf!

Product bundles lend themselves to any type of product, and sometimes any type of service. There isn't one product that this idea won't work for. Have fun with the idea and be creative! You may find yourself with a whole new line of "products." To find out how to create a product bundle, visit www.whatdoisell.com/bundle.

Components

The opposite of product bundling is component selling, which some product lines can be adapted to very well. Do you sell a product that lends itself to any kind of do-it-yourself kit? Bella, an eBay PowerSeller, had plans to sell silver jewelry online, but after researching her potential product line she decided that the market was too competitive. Talking to a friend one day, Bella mentioned her dilemma. In the course of the conversation, her friend made a comment that she'd been thinking about taking a jewelry-making class and *making* her own silver jewelry. This gave Bella an idea and she quickly went home and researched the market potential for selling jewelry findings. All of the components—the silver findings, semi-precious stones, and the various tools that went into making your own jewelry—were selling well online, and the market was not oversaturated. Bella soon got into the business of selling components instead of the finished product. Her business is thriving because she was in the Product Sourcing Mindset *and* she used creative product selection to see a product in a different light.

Do you sell anything that lends itself to component selling? A few years ago, mini–remote control cars were hot. But there was an entire other side to that trend—*building* your own mini-remote racers. While some sellers were successfully selling the cars themselves, other sellers were making just as much money selling the components. Component selling is a way of looking at product sourcing from the ground up.

Lifestyle Stores

Creative product selection allows sellers to look at products in a different light and gives them the opportunity to create a unique selling position for an otherwise basic item. And nowhere is that statement truer than in the case of lifestyle stores. Lifestyle stores are the true embodiment of niche selling, but with a twist. A lifestyle store caters to specific lifestyle traits that consumers identify with. For example, a lifestyle store that sells products related to *organic living* might carry an entire range of merchandise such as clothes made from organic cotton, cosmetics made from organic plants, blenders that will make healthy organic shakes, books on organic living, mattresses made from organic materials, and more.

What is the appeal of this type of store? As we discussed earlier in this book, the latest consumer research shows that consumers, now more than at any time in history, want to identify on an emotional level with the places they shop. They look to the places they shop to reinforce their identity, values, sense of self, and even self-worth.

A person fully engaged in living an organic lifestyle will look to a lifestyle store to help them achieve their goal of organic living. For the customer, the store is a partner in their quest for an organic lifestyle. In addition to looking to the store to provide them with products and services that support this lifestyle, they also look to the retailer to provide them with new products and services that they have yet to discover. A lifestyle store then becomes an advisor, a resource, and, above all, a very desirable place to shop. Let's look at another example of a lifestyle store—a handcrafting lifestyle store. Who would the target customer be? This target market could be anyone who's passionate about creating traditional handmade arts and crafts. This could be a person who's weary of the fast-paced high-tech world and wants a hobby that serves to "slow things down" for them. All of the traditional crafts would fall under this umbrella. Needlepoint, sewing, crocheting, beading, embroidery, and so on are all traditional crafts.

A lifestyle store on eBay that caters to the consumer who loves traditional handcrafts could offer a combination of the following types of products:

- Needlepoint supplies
- Sewing supplies
- Knitting supplies
- Crocheting supplies
- Beading supplies
- Embroidery supplies
- Books on living a simpler life
- eBooks on how to start your own knitting circle or sewing circle
- Furniture, special lamps, and accessories to enhance the time you spend crafting
- Unique one-of-a-kind patterns
- Hard-to-find imported materials for the preceding crafts
- Custom-designed products made by artisans that embrace traditional crafting methods
- Music CDs to listen to and enjoy while working on your projects
- Instructional DVDs
- Gift certificates to your store for those who want to give them as gifts to someone who enjoys the traditional crafting lifestyle
- Subscriptions to craft magazines
- Greeting cards geared towards traditional crafters
- Artwork made from traditional crafting materials

In fact, you can create a lifestyle store around virtually *any* kind of product.

Tip: For strategies to create a lifestyle store go to www.whatdoisell.com/ lifestyle.

Now let's look at some other ideas for lifestyle stores.

- Time-saving products
- Space-saving products
- Luxury products
- Products that pamper you
- Pets
- RV enthusiasts
- High-end baby products and accessories
- Home do-it-yourselfer products
- Nonmainstream sports enthusiasts
- American history products
- European style
- 'Tweens products (preteen products)
- A baking store
- Family entertainment
- Boating enthusiasts
- Home makeover stores

When it comes to creative product selection, lifestyle stores offer a vast expanse of ideas and possibilities!

A lifestyle store then becomes an advisor, a resource, and, above all, a very desirable place to shop.

Summing Up

There are multiple reasons to choose a potential product, and with creative product selections you have a variety of options to pull from. Before we move on to some tips for building your long-term business, let's review the cornerstones of creative product selection:

- Creative product selection allows you to put your stamp on your product line. With creative product selection, you have the opportunity to offer products that really set your store apart from the competition.
- Source your products to ensure you have an ample supply of available inventory to cross-sell.

- Up-selling is the practice of moving the customer from a less profitable item in a category to a more profitable one in the same category.
- Value-added products are a quick, easy, and inexpensive way to give your customers more for their money, and actually allow you to charge more for your products in the process.
- Value-added information is an easy, inexpensive way to increase the perceived value of your products dramatically.
- When practicing creative product selection, keep in mind that a well-rounded product line is always a part of the big picture.
- A loss leader is a product that a store will offer below cost to draw customers into their shop in the hope that they'll stay and buy additional, higher–profit margin items.
- A product bundle is a "product" you put together that's made up of the components of your choosing. It's the best way to compete in your marketplace, blow away the competition, and have complete control over what you sell and the price you sell it at.
- A lifestyle store caters to specific lifestyle traits that consumers identify with.

Chapter 8

Building Your Long-Term Business

Webster defines the word *consistent* as "marked by harmony, regularity, or steady continuity." Would you like to build a business that is regular, continuing, and marked by harmony? While anyone can become a sporadic seller and make some money, it takes special skills and strategies to generate a consistent income. The skills needed to make that money do not directly relate to *how much* money you want to make. Rather, they have to do with the process of being able *to generate a steady income over and over, month after month,* with reliability and regularity.

In this chapter, we'll look at the product sourcing skills needed to build a business for the long term. We'll show you ways to keep your product lines fresh and to perpetuate the growth of your business using the kinds of professional strategies employed by top retailers. In addition, we'll discuss some very important entrepreneurial skills that will directly impact your product sourcing efforts. Why the emphasis on these areas? Because in the final analysis, the success of both your product sourcing *and* your business starts with you!

Your Business

Success in business does not happen by accident. While it's true that sometimes sellers stumble upon a niche or a product line that propels them successfully into the retail arena, if their business is to continue to thrive and grow, they must implement the time-tested, proven principles of every profitable retail business. If you want to maximize your effectiveness and your product sourcing efficiency, as well as expand your business potential, combining the following business strategies will provide you with unparalleled results.

Begin with a Plan

Long-term successful product sourcing begins with a plan. The same applies to your business. You must first know where you're going in order to get there. Define your sales goals and then source the products you need to achieve them. When you have a monthly sales target in mind—say, $5K, 10K, or 50K per month—you can work "backwards" to build a product line that will meet those revenue goals. If your goal is to sell $5K per month, you know you must keep sourcing a variety of products until you find the mix that generates an income of $5K per month. If you have established goals for both your business and sales revenue, you have a measurable target to work from. Otherwise, you'll find yourself languishing in your product sourcing decisions—not knowing whether or not a product you're considering is worthwhile or if you should pass it by.

Your plan does not need to be set in stone. Revise and refine it on a regular basis. Make it a living document. Post the plan next to your computer, don't file it away in your drawer. If you source products without a plan, you'll soon discover you're torn in several directions because you have nothing to work towards. Make a plan and use it as your map, and it will make all your product sourcing decisions easier and better for your business in the long run.

Do—Don't Dream

It's great to have an abundance of wonderful ideas. But ideas only make money for you if you act on them. Having a list of hot niches in your Product Sourcing Notebook is great, but only to the extent to which you act on them. Many entrepreneurs we speak to have a variety of profitable product ideas, but are hesitant to put them into place. They want to wait until they're absolutely sure they're on the right path, and so they wait. Meanwhile, other sellers come along and act on those very same ideas and become extremely successful. When acted upon, *one average* idea will make far more money for you than ten "blockbusters" that were never implemented. Action breeds more action. Do something now. Do something today. The vitality of your business depends on it. As Ray Kroc, one of the legendary founders of McDonald's, once said, "If you're not a risk taker, you should get the hell out of business."

Fail Fast Forward

Are you afraid of making a mistake? Picking the wrong product? Losing money? If you answered yes to any of those questions, then it could be hindering your product sourcing efforts. Every retailer makes mistakes when they select merchandise for their stores. Without these buyer mistakes, clearance bins across the country would be bare. You'll make mistakes, too. It's guaranteed. Some will be big, others small. You'll make them as a newbie, and as a veteran. The important thing, however, is what you do *after* you make those mistakes. "Fail fast forward" and you won't be afraid of making mistakes. You'll learn from them and move on. If you fear product sourcing failure, your efforts will stagnate. Allow yourself enough leeway to make product sourcing mistakes, and permit yourself the victory of learning from them.

Business or Hobby?

There is an old adage in the entrepreneurial world: "Treat your business like a business and it will pay you like a business. Treat your business like a hobby and it will cost you like a hobby." Building a sustainable business requires employing some key strategies that will give you staying power. Over and over again we see sellers who catapult themselves to success. Others struggle from month to month, never knowing if they're going to have a good sales month or a bad one since they aren't able to count on a set range of income. What is the difference between sellers who make a regular income and those who don't? The sellers who make a regular income online treat it like a business. The sellers who don't treat it like a hobby.

- The business-minded entrepreneur spends time each day working on their business.
- The hobbyist works if and when they feel like it.
- The business-minded entrepreneur tracks the market, sales, and product sourcing results and learns from that information.
- The hobbyist takes a shot in the dark and hopes for the best.
- The business-minded entrepreneur knows exactly where their business stands at all times.
- The hobbyist has "a feel" for how things are going.
- The business-minded entrepreneur knows that it takes time, work, tweaking, testing, and learning to build a profitable long-term business.
- The hobbyist wants it to happen "right now" and when they get bored or frustrated, they abandon the "business" to move on to the next one—unfortunately, usually with the same results.

Consistency

Part of generating a consistent income is *being* consistent. Too many business owners rely on how they *feel* at a given time to determine what to *do*. For example, imagine it's Monday. You have set a goal that Monday is your day to call suppliers. Frequently, however, you don't really feel like calling suppliers—and would much rather update the graphics on your web site instead. What do you do? Do you postpone the calls or sit down and make them? The answer to this question will determine how fast and how stable your business becomes. Unfortunately, many entrepreneurs would put off calling the supplier. "I'll do it later," they think. And this is exactly where their business starts to falter. Every great business story can be traced back to consistent efforts.

Don't feel like calling suppliers? Do it anyway. Think today isn't the day to track your sales? Do it anyway. Cataloging and listing inventory got you down? Do it anyway...and do so on a *consistent* basis. Consistent actions produce consistent results.

"Treat your business like a business and it will pay you like a business. Treat your business like a hobby and it cost you like a hobby."

Your Products

Take one part product sourcing + one part planning + one part people and you have the formula for a thriving business. Within that blueprint are some potent tools that will give you the seller's edge. What follows are some key tactics to building a solid and profitable product line. There's no need to implement these all at once. Remember, your business is always a work in progress. But hit these milestones as you go along and you'll find your business attracting customers, generating sales, and building momentum.

Building One Thing at a Time

How many products and product lines are you currently trying to launch? If the answer is more than one, you could be undermining your efforts. When trying to source and launch multiple products or product lines simultaneously, your energy gets scattered and you start to go into the "needle in a haystack mode," losing your effectiveness. Instead of looking for multiple profitable products to push, look to select one moneymaker at a time. Then, proceed to add in any cross-sell, up-sell, or expansion products. As time goes on and you become an experienced retailer, you'll have the skills to focus on building a few successful product lines at once. But if you find yourself getting overwhelmed and not maximizing profits for one product, it's time to go back to the basics and start with one at a time. Once you're able to get one product up and running and to make it profitable, you have the knowledge to repeat that process over and over again.

Mini-Profit Machines

Not every product you sell has to be a grand-slam homerun. Often, you can do just as well, and sometimes even better, with mini-profit machines. A mini-profit machine is a product that sells on a consistent basis without you having to give it much thought. These products sell on auto-pilot, and, in fact, practically sell themselves. Do they have the highest profit margin of your line? No. Are they the glamour products of your line? Probably not. They're just nice little streams of income that, when multiplied with several mini-profit machines, make up a respectable slice of your business revenue.

A Steady Supply of Inventory

Out of stock! Backorder! These are words that no consumer likes to hear—especially if the product in question is one they really want. Maintaining your inventory levels is crucial in order to build a long-term business. While there will always be times when you run low on stock of a popular item despite your best efforts, having a good selection and a steady supply of inventory is required to make the sale. Inventory supply relates back directly to tracking: knowing what products are selling well and how quickly they're selling. This will allow you to place reorders for merchandise before you sell the last unit of your best-selling item.

Variety Is the Spice of Business

How often would you shop at your favorite store if they never offered anything new? After a while you would probably go in search of fresh merchandise somewhere else. While it's important to have a stable line of products in your store, adding fresh new merchandise keeps customers coming back for more. It also attracts new buyers and entices repeat customers to try them. Too many times, sellers get stuck in a rut. Then one day, they wake up to find their sales have slowed and have no idea why. Even if you sell in a niche, you want to continually add a new assortment of products and services. In addition to making your customers happy, this practice also gives you the opportunity to test out new product lines. Once you pick a winner, you can branch out from there on *that* product line. Adding new merchandise to the mix regularly also seriously benefits you as the seller. It keeps you fresh and energized about your business. And when the owner of the company is enthusiastic about their product line, the customers feel that way too.

Identifying Multiple Suppliers

Having an alternate supply source for your mainstay products is critical in the event your primary supplier cannot fulfill your inventory order. If you buy directly from the manufacturer, you may not have the option of a second supplier. But at least *some* of your products should be obtainable from multiple suppliers. That may mean a brand substitution or having to pay a slightly higher per unit cost. Nevertheless, it's always good to have a supply chain option for those rare times when you really need it.

Diversifying Your Product Line

Do you have a mix of higher and lower priced products? Do you have top selling products and slower but steady selling products? While most people think it would be a dream to carry all hot sellers, to build a large customer base and have a consistent income you should round out the top sellers in your business with steady sellers that may not create as much cash flow but that are responsible for bringing people to your store.

If you sell trendy merchandise, keep in mind that while hot trends can make you a pile of cash (if you get in at the beginning and ride it to its peak), the faster and stronger the trend arises, the quicker it usually burns out (and sales drop off). Add trendy items to your mix, but be sure to balance these with tried-and-true sellers. Adding new products to your offerings on a regular basis will make your business grow, garner new customers, and keep *you* energized about your efforts.

Build Relationships, Don't Just Place Orders

We've talked a lot in this book about your relationship with your customers. But did you know that building a relationship with your suppliers is just as important? If you want to find out about new products before everyone else does, negotiate the best deals, and get in on the great promos, you have to build relationships with your suppliers, not just place orders. As with success in the corporate world, it is oftentimes "not what you know but who you know" that matters most.

The more suppliers you really get to know, the more you'll learn about other suppliers in the business. Vendors themselves can be great resources for other wholesale options. If you are looking for a particular product and it isn't carried by your primary supplier, they're always happy to refer you to a source that can help you out. Once you've established a personal connection with a supplier, you'll then move out of the realm of "just another order" to that of a VIP account or valued customer. Learn your vendor contact's name, and maybe a little about them. They'll likely do the same with you. And in doing so, they'll become immensely helpful to you in building your business.

Network

Who is in your seller's network? Do you have a mix of suppliers, trend spotters, shipping experts, and entrepreneurs that you interact with on a regular basis? Do you participate in any professional organizations or trade associations? While entrepreneurs often start their own business because of their independent streak, it's for this very reason that they can become isolated. In order to get new ideas, learn tips and tricks, and even churn over new product ideas, you have to establish a network of people you can connect with on business-related issues. This can be as simple as an informal group of individuals. Take some time and make a list of the top 30 people you would like to network with. What line of work are they in? What is their area of expertise? Once you have this information down on paper, you'll be amazed at the amount of resources you have in your current inner circle. When it comes to business, two heads are better than one, and 30 heads are certainly better than two. Start building your network today. There is power in numbers.

Three in the Pipeline

Every successful seller always has *at least* three products or product line ideas in the pipeline. This means that even if you have a great-selling batch of products, you must constantly be on the lookout for products to add to your store. You never know when a product or market is going to reach the saturation point or you'll have an influx of selling competition. When that happens, you need to be ready to move fast and implement new merchandise into your product offerings.

One of the biggest killers of consistent income is experiencing a dropoff in sales of your mainstay products and having nothing to replace those sales with. By always knowing what the next products are that you want to sell or add to the mix, you can begin to ramp up your business in other areas as soon as you see sales decline with any of your existing merchandise.

Testing and Tracking

There is no substitute for testing and tracking when it comes to evaluating the success of your products, sales strategies, and marketing techniques. All the projections, opinions, and advice in the world cannot take the place of testing and tracking. The key to building a successful business is identifying your success and then repeating it. What products, marketing strategies, and sales techniques pull in the most sales? Identify those and then repeat that process again with a different product that has the same successful qualities. *Testing + Tracking your results = Money in the bank.*

Consumables

One category of products that you should seriously consider adding to your product line is that of consumables. A consumable is something that a buyer will purchase, use, and then need to replace. For example, skincare products, pet food, and batteries are all consumables. Products that buyers come back to buy month after month are an excellent ingredient in your recipe for successful retention. Once you've made that initial sale of a consumable product, you now have the opportunity to make that buyer a customer for life. And while it may take some thinking to come up with a few consumable products that fit with your product lines, once you do hit on one that generates repeat sales, you'll find it's definitely worth the effort.

Depending on Yourself

Successful product sourcing, a lucrative business, a profitable product line ... it all begins with you. Master the following five traits of successful entrepreneurs and you'll have the foundation you need to succeed.

1. *Don't underestimate the power of drive and dedication.* Without fail, those sellers who have the most drive and dedication are the ones who will succeed in building a profitable, long-term business. Nothing can replace the results of persistence. Everyone has the opportunity to "build it right." It may take several attempts and iterations of an idea before you hit on the one that works. "There is no substitute for hard work," stated Thomas Edison. He was someone well acquainted with this time-honored value. For many months, he toiled to produce the first light bulb. After 10,000 tries, he succeeded.

2. *Be willing to start small.* Do you want to be a Platinum PowerSeller consistently selling $25K per month in goods? Then first you need to master consistently selling $1K per month in merchandise. While it's important to have long-term goals, the first step is to consistently achieve financial goals of a smaller scale. James Dyson, creator of the phenomenally successful line of Dyson vacuum cleaners, began with a seed of an idea in 1979 while vacuuming his UK home. Five thousand prototypes later, Dyson was ready to launch his product. Five years later, sales of Dyson vacuum cleaners had skyrocketed to reach 50 percent of the UK floor-care market and went on to become the best-selling vacuum in the U.S. But before Dyson achieved such astronomical success, he first had to sell one vacuum.

3. *Focus, focus, focus.* Achieving a $500-per-month sales goal requires focus. So does reaching a $25,000-per-month level. Focus is what will keep you on the right path. Lose your focus and you dilute your business building power. Keep focused on your goals and on the tasks necessary to achieve them. If you find yourself getting off track, refocus and start your engines again.

4. *Technician or entrepreneur?* Are you the technician or the entrepreneur for your business? In his book, *The E Myth Revisited*, author Michael E. Gerber states that the entrepreneur surveys the world and asks "Where's the opportunity?" The technician looks inwardly, defines his skills, and then says "What can I sell them?" The potential for success comes from developing the skills to meet that opportunity. It's when the two converge that you're propelled into action with spectacular results.

5. *Avoid paralysis by analysis.* Entrepreneurs often spending too much time thinking and not enough time doing. Going back and forth on product lines, not wanting to put a stake in the ground and commit to an inventory purchase, trying to find the "right" product the first time out

all stall your progress. The most successful retailers are those who are "doers." Doers take action. Doers don't wait for all the facts to come in before they give something a try. As a child, this most likely came naturally to you. Most children simply focus on what they need to do and get on with it. Somewhere into adulthood, we learn to think and pause, think and pause, afraid to take action. If you're in the mode of "paralysis by analysis," waiting to take action before all the "votes" are in—you're shortchanging yourself and your potential business income. Do it now ... perfect it later.

Summing Up

Congratulations! You've completed the first part of this book, which outlined the multifaceted path of product selection.

You're now ready for Part II, which deals with setting up your business and locating suppliers for all your creative product ideas. Before doing so, however, let's review the components of product sourcing and business success:

- While anyone can become a sporadic seller and make some money, it takes special skills and strategies to make a consistent income.
- Successful long-term product sourcing begins with a plan. The same applies to your business. You have to know where you're going in order to get there. Define your sales goals and then source the products you need to achieve them.
- Not every product you sell has to be a grand-slam homerun. Often, you can do just as well, and sometimes even better, with mini-profit machines.
- If you want to find out about new products before everyone else does, negotiate the best deals and get in on the great promos. You must build relationships with your suppliers, not just place orders.
- Every successful seller always has *at least* three products or product line ideas in the pipeline.
- There's no substitute for testing and tracking when it comes to evaluating the success of your products, sales strategies, and marketing techniques.
- While it's important to have long-term goals, the first step is to consistently achieve financial goals of a smaller scale.
- Achieving a $500-per-month sales goal requires focus. So does reaching a $25,000-per-month level. Focus is what will keep you on the right path. Lose your focus and you dilute your business building power.
- If you're in the mode of "paralysis by analysis," essentially waiting to take action before all the "votes" are in, you're shortchanging yourself and your potential business income. Do it now ... perfect it later.

PART II

WHERE TO FIND
PRODUCTS TO SELL

Chapter 9

Getting Legal

Are you an e-commerce business owner, or do you just "play one" on the Internet? There's a big difference between the two, and that difference determines how successful you'll be in your online ventures.

So far in this book, we've talked about creating a mindset that helps you decide what products you should sell on eBay. That's an extremely important foundation for successful eBay sales. Now we'll talk about how to use that mindset to its full potential, by creating an eBay business that goes far beyond casual online selling. We'll talk about securing your eBay experience to a launch platform that will actually allow you to earn your entire living online—if you're really willing to work at it.

We'll also talk about becoming a legal business.

Yes, we know. This is the part that no one wants to think about. Legal stuff, tax issues, paperwork, licenses. Yuck. Just when you thought you found a way to make money that didn't involve government paperwork, all that scary stuff you didn't want to think about reaches out and grabs you from the pages of this book, right? It's just not fair!

Sorry, but we do need to think about it, and talk about it. People who do not take the time to form a legal business generally do not succeed in any real way on eBay, or anywhere else in the business world.

The number of people who absolutely refuse to form a **legal** *online business is exactly equal to the number of people who have* **no chance** *of real success in online business.*

Many people absolutely refuse to form a legal business, thinking it's too much work, or that they don't want the government involved in their private lives, or that they simply can't afford the expenses involved. We've heard every excuse in the book, and then some. These people mope along selling old vinyl albums and whatever else they uncover at neighborhood garage sales, earning a few bucks a month—maybe even a couple of hundred, if they're lucky.

You'll never see those people earn a real, full-time income online, however. They'll never replace their day job with a genuinely successful online business.

If you really want to succeed in business, you must first own a business, and you can't truly own a business until you fill out the paperwork to form one. Fortunately, tackling that paperwork isn't nearly as hard as most people think it is.

We're not telling you that you need to form a legal business just for the sake of having one. There are many very important reasons why your business cannot succeed without becoming legal.

If you don't have a legal business, you can't get a tax ID.
If you don't have a tax ID, you can't buy products from
real wholesale suppliers.

The most important reason to have a legal business is this: *You cannot buy wholesale products from real wholesale distributors unless you have both a legal business and a sales tax ID.* Period, end of sentence.

Becoming a "Real" Business

You see, when you decide to sell products on eBay, you've decided to become a retailer. You're the person who will sell durable goods (products) to the end consumer (the person who will actually own and use the product). That makes you a retailer, whether you like it or not.

There's an exclusive club out there that all successful retailers belong to, from Wal-Mart all the way down to the guy who just bought a new house uptown because his online business is growing by leaps and bounds. Membership in that exclusive club has many privileges. They include, but are not limited to, the following:

- The ability to buy the products you sell online at the lowest possible prices— from real wholesalers—which greatly improves your profit margins.
- A great deal more credibility with your potential online buyers (customers), which increases your sales.
- The ability to open a business bank account and collect payment in your business name. This allows you to accept money directly from your customers' credit cards.

Those are only *three* of the privileges of this exclusive club. There are *many* more, and they are all worth it. Membership in this club opens the door to building a genuinely thriving, successful business, which we can personally tell you is the greatest thrill ride we've ever experienced.

How do you become a member of the club? Simple. *File a legal business name and get a sales tax ID*. This little bit of paperwork is not much to pay for something that may very well turn into the most thrilling business venture of your life, is it?

The single most common point of failure for people who try to succeed selling products online may very well be the failure to take the few short steps needed to form a real business. So, let's not count you among those people who fail, shall we? You're here to make this work, so please don't let a little thing like some minor paperwork stand in your way. You need to get it done. We'll talk about just how to do it at the end of this chapter.

For the moment, though, let's discuss in detail those three important privileges we just mentioned. These are things you must understand about owning a legal business before we can go any further into product sourcing.

The Ability to Buy Products from Legitimate Wholesalers

If you've decided to create an online business that could not only replace your day job but make you quite comfortable financially if you work at it hard enough, you need to *streamline* all the different processes in your business. As your business grows, there will be more and more work to do—more customer service issues to answer, more auction-style listings to create, more advertising to put together, and (most importantly) more money to count! These are all processes that will take up your time. Streamlining a process simply means you make it as easy and efficient as possible so you spend less time on it, and have more time available for everything else.

Product sourcing, of course, is the act of actually finding products to sell online. It's one process within your business and it needs to be streamlined, just like all the others. Running all over town hitting garage sales, visiting local stores, buying overstocks, and doing all those other things that people do when they're a casual online seller will become impossible to carry out. There won't be enough hours in the day for it all once your business gets busy.

In order to streamline your product sourcing, you need to find and work with steady, reliable, renewable sources of quality products that you can sell through your online business. That means that you need to start working with wholesale suppliers of your products. Once you have steady, reliable sources through which you can acquire your products simply by placing a phone call or sending an e-mail, you can cut a tremendous amount of time off your product sourcing efforts.

The most successful online businesses all use dependable, renewable sources of wholesale products.

People who run successful online businesses know this, and do it. It's part of what makes them successful. Therefore, it's important to streamline your product sourcing by working with wholesale suppliers of the products you sell. It's equally important to work only with *legitimate* wholesale suppliers of those products. When you work with legitimate wholesalers, you get the best possible prices, and earn the greatest possible profit. In order to work with legitimate wholesale suppliers of products, however, you must own a legal business and have a sales tax ID. See how that all came back around to the "you must have a legal business" theme?

Please remember the following two things:

- A legitimate wholesale supplier cannot sell you anything unless they have a copy of your business license and sales tax ID. If they sell to you without these things, they run the risk of losing their *own* business license. No wholesaler is going to run that risk for anybody.
- Any company that calls itself a product supplier of any kind, but does *not* ask you for your business license and sales tax ID is *not* a real supplier. They are a "middleman." That's someone that gets in between you and the real supplier, and makes a profit by raising the prices you pay for your products. We'll get into lots of detail on middlemen later in the book. For now, keep in mind that you never want to work with a middleman. It's like taking money out of your pocket and throwing it away.

Let's talk next about *why* real wholesalers are required to have a copy of your business license and sales tax ID. In the U.S. and most other countries, this has to do with sales tax. Put simply, 45 out of the 50 U.S. states require that sales tax be paid on all purchases of durable goods. *Durable goods* means just about anything except basic food products. (Wholesalers in the five U.S. states that don't have a sales tax will still require that you have a legal business name in order to buy products from them at wholesale prices.) So, somewhere along the line, someone is supposed to pay sales tax on virtually all durable goods sold in the U.S. That someone is, of course, your buyer—the end consumer. As the business that sells the product to the end consumer, you're the retailer. That means you're the lucky one who gets to collect that sales tax from your buyer!

Using a Black & Decker toaster as a product example, let's discuss why the retailer is the one responsible for doing this. First, Black & Decker manufactures the toaster. Black & Decker will make tens of thousands of these toasters, and will sell them by the truckload to wholesale suppliers all over the country. Can Black & Decker charge sales tax to the wholesaler? No, because the wholesaler is not the end consumer. So, Black & Decker sells truckloads of toasters to many licensed, legitimate wholesale suppliers without collecting sales tax.

Next, a wholesale supplier is going to sell some of those toasters to you, the retailer. Can the wholesale supplier charge sales tax to you for that purchase? No, because you're not the end consumer either. So, when you buy products from legitimate wholesalers (for the purpose of reselling them to your retail customers) the wholesaler does not charge you sales tax. Finally, you'll sell the toasters one at a time to your online customers. The sale you make to your customer is the point where you, the retailer, must collect sales tax from your customer.

The main reason the retailer is the one responsible for collecting sales tax is because the manufacturer and the wholesaler really have no control over which state or county the product will be sold to the end consumer in. The toasters might be manufactured in North Carolina. The manufacturer may sell them by the truckload to a wholesale supplier in California. That wholesaler in California may in turn sell a few of them to you, the retailer, located in central Florida. Finally, you, the retailer, might sell one toaster to your online customer in southern Florida.

Because the manufacturer and wholesaler do not control where the product is sold to the end consumer, they cannot possibly know what *sales tax rate* will apply to the sale. Most retailers charge their customers the sales tax rate that's in effect in the retailer's own county. That's the most proper thing to do. So, if you're operating your online business from your home in Lake County, Florida, your sales tax rate for Lake County is 6 percent. That's what you would charge your customer in southern Florida when they buy a toaster from you.

It's important to note that currently you only have to charge sales tax to your customers who live in your *own home state*. According to a 1992 ruling by the U.S. Supreme Court, a business must only charge sales tax in states where that business has a *physical presence*. If your business is located in Florida, you would only charge sales tax on Florida sales. The same is true of all other states, though at the time of this writing the U.S. government was trying to create a type of universal sales tax that would cross state lines. It could be many years before this kind of thing is actually implemented, however—if ever.

Each state and county has its own sales tax rates and rules, thus the one that's in effect in the retailer's county is the one that generally applies. So, because sales tax must be collected by you, the retailer, whenever you make a sale in your own state, every legitimate wholesale supplier you work with is going to need to see a copy of your sales tax ID. They cannot sell to anyone who can't *prove they're legally able* to collect sales tax in their own state.

Many online sellers believe that they're better off flying under the radar, selling items without a legal business or a tax ID, and not charging sales tax. Again, if we're talking about simply selling items from garage sales once in a while, people may choose to take their chances and hope they don't get a letter from the IRS. However, if you're planning on putting together a real eBay business that offers a serious chance of financial success, your enterprise must be fully legal so you can work with real wholesalers. Your profit margins depend on it!

Greater Credibility with Your eBay Buyers

Another important thing to consider is how credible your online product listings look to your customers. Online sales are largely a matter of trust. When you walk into a physical store in your local mall, look a sales clerk in the eye, and hand over your money for a product you purchase, you're making a transaction you can feel a certain degree of confidence in. You know where the store is, you have a receipt in your hand immediately, and you can return and complain, get a refund, make an exchange and so forth, should you need to.

However, for people who buy products online, this kind of personal interaction doesn't exist. Convincing someone to see you as an honest online seller can be difficult. As huge as the e-commerce market is (currently 150 *billion* dollars and growing), it would be much larger if that trust issue didn't get in the way. People are fearful of their credit card information being stolen. They hear stories about those who bought products online and never received them. They wonder if they're getting ripped off by bait-and-switch tactics—seeing a picture of one item during an auction, and getting something completely different.

Your online customers need to be able to trust you simply by looking at your web store or auction. The more professional you look, the more sales you'll make.

You get the idea. Trust is important in online sales. Presenting yourself online as a real, professional, legal business will go a long way toward gaining your customers' trust. Actually *becoming* a real, professional, legal business makes it easy to present yourself as one! For example, ask yourself which eBay seller you'd rather buy a radar detector for your car from: an eBay seller whose ID is stinky_jones_40827, or an eBay seller whose ID is Radar_Electronics_Inc?

Which one of those eBay sellers strikes you as the one more likely to deliver a *new* product to you, in good condition, and on time? Which one of them do you think you could contact with a warranty issue, and actually get help from? Which one do you think is more likely to still be around to answer your questions a month from now? The answer's obvious, isn't it? When you have a legal business and can present yourself as a professional company, you're going to make far more sales.

Make sure, however, that you let people know what your business name is. Don't form a legal business called "Stapleton Product Sales, Inc." and then use an eBay seller ID like "Jim_Stapleton" or create an online store called "Jim's Place." Instead, use something like "Stapleton Sales Inc."

Place your business name on your Auction-style listings and/or your online store. Use your About Me page when working on eBay, which is a very good place to tell potential buyers about your business. In fact, use your business name as many times as you can in your store. Just don't overdo it!

If you want to succeed online, you need your customers' trust. An online customer will trust a professional sounding business name over a casual eBay seller ID or store name any day of the week.

Collecting Payments Under Your Business Name

Once you have a legal business, you can then open a business bank account. Instead of paying "Mary Smith" for their eBay purchases from your store, your buyers can pay "Smith Enterprises."

Needless to say, that also goes a long way toward making your customers feel comfortable in buying from you.

Without going into a great deal of detail, having a business bank account also offers you many other benefits.

For example, when you apply for an account with a legitimate wholesaler, their application form will most likely ask whether you have a business bank account. You stand a better chance of getting that wholesale account if you do.

Using PayPal to collect payment from your eBay buyers is often the most sensible thing to do when starting out. However, if you use PayPal, they may solicit your customers to become PayPal members, sometimes during the transaction itself. This can interfere with your sale process. Many people elect to use a merchant account other than PayPal for this and other reasons. If you *do* decide to use a merchant account to collect your customers' credit card payments, you *must* have a business bank account.

As your business grows, you can establish credit lines and apply for credit cards in your business name, but you can only do that if you have a business bank account. And you can't open a business bank account without a legal business name.

Forming a Legal Business

Now that we've done our best to help you understand that you really do need to form a legal business in order to realize the full potential of your online business, let's cover the basics regarding how that's done. This isn't hard since it's not expensive and it doesn't take that much time.

This example has to do with business in the United States, but there will be similar processes no matter where you live.

Filing Your Business Name

You need an official business name that's recognized by your state government. You can do this in one of two basic ways:

- **Filing as a Corporation**   You can file as a corporation with your state. A corporation is a business structure that protects your personal assets, should your business ever become involved in a lawsuit. A corporation costs a little more to file, and takes a little more time to maintain, but it provides you with important protections. For example, if you were ever to get involved in a product liability lawsuit (if someone was hurt by a product you sold them), your corporation could be sued, but your private holdings (your home, your car, and so on) couldn't be touched. We are not attorneys, so please consult a professional if you have any questions regarding corporations. Many people start out in business by filing as a basic corporation. For more information on filing corporations, check out *Tax Loopholes for eBay Sellers* by Diane Kennedy and Janelle Elms (McGraw-Hill, 2005).
- **Filing Under a Fictitious Name or DBA**   This is a simpler way to register your business name legally, but it doesn't afford you the protections that filing as a corporation does. In some U.S. states it's called a fictitious name. That means that if your name was Mary Smith, you could register a name like "Smith Enterprises," and the state would recognize that Smith Enterprises is a legal business belonging to Mary Smith. In other states, it's known as a DBA (Doing Business under an Assumed name), which means exactly the same thing as a fictitious name.

No matter how you decide to register your business, your state will have a web site that explains how to do it, and that teaches you about each different type of business registration. For example, the state of Florida's web site for this purpose is www.SunBiz.org. To find the site in your own state to help you with this, go to Google.com and type something like **Oregon start a business** (depending, of course, on the name of your state).

On your state site, you'll be able to read about the different benefits offered for filing as a corporation or as a fictitious name, you can download and print the proper forms, and you can find out how to contact someone who can answer questions for you. Another way to reveal where your state's business web site is (and to ask questions of a live person) is to call your local County Clerk's office. They can both tell you this information and also help you file your business papers.

Getting Your Sales Tax ID

In almost every state in the U.S., you're required to have a sales tax ID in order to sell products at retail. We've been over the reasons why you need this.

Some states call it a sales and use tax certificate, some call it a seller's permit, while others have yet some other name for it. Again, your state business web site will tell you what they call it and how to get it. In Florida, we can get a sales tax ID in about 15 minutes, and for less than $10, *after* we've filed our legal business name.

Please note that this is different from a federal tax ID, commonly called an EIN (Employer Identification Number). If you file your business as a corporation, you'll end up with an EIN. This does not take the place of your sales tax ID, although some wholesalers will accept it as proof of a legal business. You should, however, still obtain your sales tax ID from your state in order to be fully compliant with the law.

Summing Up

Now that we've gone over why it's important to have a legal business name and a sales tax ID, and how to go about starting that process, let's touch on the high points of this chapter once again to review.

- Successful eBay business owners know they need to have a legal business.
- As your business gets busier, you need to make sure your processes are streamlined so you have time to run your business without getting bogged down in any one process too much.
- Product sourcing is best streamlined by working with legitimate wholesale suppliers.
- You cannot work with real wholesalers without filing as a legal business and having a sales tax ID.
- Any product supplier that tells you that you don't need these things is *not* a real wholesaler, and will hurt your profit margins.
- Even in states that have no sales tax, real wholesalers will require that you be a legal business before they can sell to you.
- Becoming a legal business gives you much greater credibility with your potential customers, and increases your sales.
- Becoming a legal business allows you to open a business bank account. This also increases your credibility, provides the opportunity to get business credit, and helps you get accounts with real wholesalers.
- The two most common forms of filing as a legal business are as a corporation and as a fictitious name. Your state will have a business web site where you can read about these options, download and print forms, and sometimes even file your business online. Your County Clerk's office can tell you how to find your state business web site.

Chapter 10

Why Wholesalers Exist, and Why
You Should Use Them

In home-based e-commerce, sellers source products in a variety of different ways, especially when selling on eBay. This book has touched on many of those different methods already. From garage sales to local area sources to liquidation lots and more, there are a tremendous number of creative ways to source products for an online business.

However, as mentioned in the last chapter, if you're ready to move beyond the casual seller stage to a point where your eBay business becomes your full-time income, you need to start working with legitimate wholesale suppliers. That doesn't mean you can't still source locally when you have the time. That's fine. Plus, it'll add some unique variety to your product selection from time to time. Just the same, you'll still need a steady backbone of easily renewable products when it comes to earning a full-time income on eBay.

Streamlining Saves Time and Creates Larger Profits

Why is streamlining so effective in building your business? Well, as we discussed in the previous chapter, it all has to do with time. There are only so many hours in a day. If you spend too many of those hours on your product sourcing, you'll eventually hit a point where you max out the amount of money your business can make in a day simply because you're spending too much time physically acquiring the products you're selling. To grow into a business that's only limited by the number of buyers in your product market on eBay, you need to make your business operation as lean and mean as possible by streamlining your processes, and that includes your product sourcing.

*There are only so many hours in a day. If you spend
too many of them on product sourcing, you'll max out
the amount of money your business can make in a day.
In order for your business to keep growing, you need to
streamline your processes.*

Let's say you're currently sourcing your products by going to local factory outlet stores, buying products at a discount, and reselling them on eBay. In order to do this, you need to drive out to these stores, meet the people in charge so you can get the best possible deal every time, pick out the products on their shelves that your Product Sourcing Mindset tells you will sell well, then buy the products and get them home. You have to take individual pictures of these products, then you've got to make sure you have the right size and types of shipping materials so you can get the items out the door once you make the sale.

Keep in mind that you may be holding down a day job at this point as well, so the time you spend on your eBay business is limited. As your business grows, you can easily spend more than half your work effort sourcing products this way. That's time that could be spent coming up with new product ideas, researching your market, working on your advertising, improving your listings and eBay store pages, providing timely answers to your customers' e-mails, and much more. Those are all elements of creating a successful business. So, the more time you spend physically running around town sourcing products, the less time you have to build your business. Working with a steady, readily available source of your main products is the best way to avoid that problem.

Manufacturers Don't Usually Sell Directly to Retailers

Although most people don't understand why, that steady source previously mentioned is almost always going to be a factory-authorized wholesale supplier. People write to Chris's company, WorldWide Brands, all the time and say, "I'd rather go right to the manufacturer and buy from them. Why should I go through a wholesale distributor?" One gentleman wrote recently and said, "I buy things online (as a consumer) directly from Sony all the time. Why shouldn't I be able to buy directly from Sony at wholesale (as a retailer)?" This has to do with a common misconception about manufacturers. Most people are (understandably) of the opinion that a manufacturer would jump at the chance to sell their products to you and me (online retailers) at wholesale. You'd think they would see it as a way to sell more products.

Well, that's not the way it works, for many good reasons. To the gentleman who asked about Sony, yes, it does seem like he's buying products directly from Sony as a consumer when he goes to the Sony web site. However, that's actually something of an illusion. It's a harmless illusion, though, and isn't meant to fool anybody on purpose. When he goes to "Sony" on the Internet and buys consumer goods, the web site he visits is actually SonyStyle.com.

Yes, it's owned by Sony, just like many manufacturers that have retail outlets on the Internet. However, the man who wrote me was interested in buying at wholesale so he could resell those products to his online customers, which isn't the same thing.

When he buys consumer goods from SonyStyle.com, he's most likely buying from a division of the Sony company that's set up to sell to consumers at retail.

SonyStyle is a terrific web site, and an excellent place to buy Sony products as a consumer. However, when manufacturers set up systems like this, they are a separate "unit" of the manufacturer. They will have their own offices, staff, and delivery system, probably very far away from the manufacturing facilities. It has nothing to do with buying products at wholesale for resale. The vast majority of manufacturers have their hands quite full just manufacturing their products. That's a very full-time business just in itself.

Manufacturers Don't Need to Reinvent the Wheel

Let's try a little role-playing now. Let's say you've invented a revolutionary new eyebrow plucker. This little machine is really cool. You set it for the shape you want your eyebrows to be, slap it on your forehead, and press a button. Your invention does all the plucking for both eyebrows at once, and your eyebrows are instantly crafted to the shape you want. Of course, it's a little painful, and one of the settings still leaves your eyebrows looking as if you're perpetually surprised, but you're working those problems out. You want to rent a small building and start manufacturing your new eyebrow plucker.

In order to do that, you first have to go through the lengthy legal process of patenting your invention. Then you have to find suppliers of raw blocks of surgical-grade steel, and buy and set up machines that will form and stamp out the parts of your eyebrow plucker. Since you're not an engineer, you need to hire someone to create the printed circuit board that goes into your plucker. Then you must buy and set up the equipment that actually makes that circuit board in your little factory, or contract with an outside electronics company to do it for you.

You also need to create an assembly line process, work out quality control, and then create some plastic "foreheads" that you can test your invention on before boxing each one up. But wait! You can't box them up without going to a graphic artist who's going to create a logo for you, and then build the color screening that will be printed on your boxes. Of course, you need the boxes, too, so you must contact a packaging expert who'll design your box and internal packaging, and afterward you'll need a box manufacturer to die-cut the custom boxes and packaging for you.

That's just a small example of what you need to do as a manufacturer. There are a thousand other details a manufacturer must work out in order to create a product and turn it out on an assembly line, ready to sell.

Then one night, you come home tired and frustrated from working so hard on your manufacturing process, you have a bruise on the right side of your forehead, and half your right eyebrow is missing, and as you get out of the car, you run into your neighbor, Mike. Mike wonders why you look so bedraggled. You tell him about your invention, and all the work you're doing to manufacture the product. Then you tell him that you're even more worried about how to get the product to your potential consumers.

Mikes face lights up and he says, "Hey, I work at my family's wholesale distribution company. We wholesale manufactured products to thousands of large chain stores all across the country. We can buy your eyebrow pluckers from you in large quantities, and distribute them for you, and you won't have to worry about that part of it at all!"

Manufacturers don't want to reinvent the wheel by having to build their own wholesale distribution processes when companies already exist that can do the distribution for them.

What Would You Do?

At this point, you can answer Mike in one of two ways:

- **Answer Number One**   "Gee, Mike, I don't know. I think I'd rather spend years trying to create business relationships with thousands of retail stores. Then I'd like to pay for another warehouse where I can store my product, and lease trucks or contract with a freight company in order to deliver the product. I'd also just love to pay a fortune for warehouse employees, delivery drivers, a sales force, a sales office, and basically spend a great deal of time reinventing everything that you've already had set up and running for years in your wholesale distribution business!"
- **Answer Number Two**   "Hey, Mike, that sounds great! Your family's company already has the warehouses, the delivery mechanisms, the sales force, and contacts with thousands of retail stores. I can simply sell my product to you by the truckload, and you can distribute it to retailers all over the world. I can concentrate on my manufacturing operation, and leave the wholesale distribution headaches to you. I think we have a deal!"

See where we're heading here? Product manufacturers have enough to do without reinventing an entire wholesale distribution system that already exists. Manufacturers would be crazy to want to take on that kind of additional load! They can sell their products in huge quantities to existing wholesale distributors and never have to worry about the distribution process at all. Let's take a look now at how Mike's family's Wholesale Supply Company got started, and why.

How One Wholesaler Got Its Start, from the Ground Up...

Way back in the early 20th century, Mike's great-uncle Augustus was an iceman. He owned a horse and wagon, and every day he went to the local icehouse where they made large blocks of fresh-water ice. He'd load up his wagon with these heavy blocks of ice and drive them around the city through a regular route he'd developed. He'd haul the blocks into people's houses, placing them in his customers' "iceboxes," which would keep their food cold until the ice melted.

Augustus spent years establishing his route in an affluent section of the city, and delivered to people who had nice houses and lots of money to spend. One day during the summer of 1916, he stopped at a customer's home and hauled a block of ice up to the kitchen entrance to deliver it. The owner of the home thanked him, but said he'd no longer need his ice deliveries.

The homeowner showed Augustus a newfangled machine he'd just bought. It was a mechanical refrigerator made by someone called the Mechanical Refrigerator Company. It would keep food cold using electricity, and didn't require blocks of ice. Augustus shrugged, and didn't think much more about it, besides wondering what silly contraptions folks would come up with next. Soon after though, a few more customers along his route began to order mechanical refrigerators from the Mechanical Refrigerator Company.

Augustus was no fool. He knew his livelihood depended on the longtime ice delivery route he'd established in this affluent neighborhood. He also knew that news travels fast, and people were so infatuated with new machines and inventions in those days that he might soon be out of work, especially since his ice delivery route was in an area where most of his customers could afford to buy these machines! So, he asked one of his former customers about the Mechanical Refrigerator Company. He found out that the company had only recently begun producing its mechanical refrigerators, and was doing so in a city far away. In fact, his former ice route customers had waited many weeks to receive their new refrigerators.

Opportunities Are Where You Find Them

Augustus wrote a letter to the Mechanical Refrigerator Company and asked them for information about their firm. In the letter, he mentioned he had an ice delivery business in a very affluent section of his city. He had an idea that he might be able to sell some of these fancy machines to people in his city, and earn money that way if the ice delivery business got into trouble.

Over the course of the next few weeks, through his correspondence with people at the Mechanical Refrigerator Company, he was offered the opportunity to buy several of the machines at *a reduced price* each month, and then sell them at his own price to his ice route customers. The people at the Mechanical Refrigerator Company knew it would be better to send one larger shipment of refrigerators to a city, and let someone there market and distribute them, instead of selling and delivering them one by one to customers in a city far away. The Mechanical Refrigerator Company offered Augustus reasonable terms in order to help him get started, so he did just that. He used most of the money he'd saved over the course of many years to order ten mechanical refrigerators.

The people that he'd known for years along his route were already becoming aware of this new machine, and, of course, everybody had to have one. It wouldn't do for the *neighbors* to have a refrigeration machine and for *my family* not to have one, said many of them. His first shipment of ten mechanical refrigerators sold very quickly, and at a good profit. He then used his ice wagon to deliver them to his new refrigeration machine customers.

Augustus's new business grew quickly, and soon retail merchants in many of the city's stores were asking him where they could get these refrigerators. Augustus placed larger and larger orders with the Mechanical Refrigerator Company and soon began selling the machines a dozen at a time to retail stores. Along the way, he purchased more delivery wagons, rented a building in which to store his ever-growing stock of refrigeration machines, and hired a couple of men to help him run his warehouse and make deliveries.

A Growing Business

As news spread by word-of-mouth throughout his part of the state, Augustus made trips to nearby towns and cities and made deals with local retailers there as well. The Mechanical Refrigerator Company was very happy with Augustus's sales of the machines, and granted him a large "sales territory," promising him that no one else would be allowed to wholesale their refrigerators in that territory.

By 1923, the Mechanical Refrigerator Company held 80 percent of the U.S. market for home refrigerators. Augustus was so good at wholesaling the machines that the Mechanical Refrigerator Company recruited him to help get other wholesalers in his area of the country involved in distributing the machines. They made Augustus a "Master Wholesaler." That meant that for the entire southeastern part of the country, all mechanical refrigerators were delivered to Augustus's warehouses, and he in turn sold and delivered them to *other* wholesalers, who sold and delivered them to the retailers in their own sales territories.

Augustus had gone from a local ice delivery man to being a master wholesaler of one of the hottest-selling products in the country in just a few years. He had warehouses all over the southeast, delivery trucks, and sales-people, who would travel around to various retail and wholesale businesses, all of which made the Mechanical Refrigerator Company very happy.

You see, the Mechanical Refrigerator Company was manufacturing the products, and that's all they had to worry about. They no longer had to sell them and deliver them individually to each customer. Augustus and people like him had built up a wholesale delivery system all over the U.S., and all the Mechanical Refrigerator Company had to do was ship a few massive loads of machines to a few master wholesalers around the country. The master wholesalers sold and shipped them to the wholesalers, the wholesalers distributed them to the retail stores, and the retail stores distributed them to the customer.

This constituted an entire massive business infrastructure that the Mechanical Refrigerator Company did *not* have to spend time, money, and other resources to create.

Over many years, Augustus's wholesale company grew into many different product lines from many different manufacturers. By the time neighbor Mike, a relative of Augustus's family, was born, the company was wholesaling all kinds of products all over the world.

Of course, this is a fictional story, but it illustrates not only how many of today's largest wholesale companies got started, but *why* manufactur-ers would much rather sell to wholesalers rather than directly to retailers. That's why wholesalers exist, and why you'll rarely get to buy directly from a manufacturer.

Small Exceptions to the Rule

Notice, however, that we said *rarely*. There *are* manufacturers of prod-ucts that will sell to you directly, and there are reasons for that. The main reason is that the manufacturers who will do so are usually small companies.

Back when Augustus first approached the Mechanical Refrigerator Company in our little fictional account, he had to correspond with them for a while, start small, and convince them that what he was doing was good for them. In those days, many manufacturers did sell directly to the public, although wholesale certainly was not a new concept. Today, though, many times it's the *manufacturer* that has to convince the *wholesaler* that it's worth the wholesaler's time to carry their new products.

Today's larger wholesalers can boast the advantage of already having a tremendous sales force, warehouse capability, and a distribution network of retail contacts in place. Wholesalers are very aware of how much their warehouse floor space is worth by the square foot since it relates to their distribution power. So, when you invent a new eyebrow plucker, chances are it would have taken you years to get a really large wholesaler to use their infrastructure and sales connections to distribute your products if neighbor Mike hadn't been a good friend of yours. Even though Mike is a part of the family that owns the wholesale company where he works, he will still have to convince some people at his office if his company is going to carry your new product. Why?

- *It has no current customer base.* This wholesaler can't just take over distribution of the product for an existing group of customers you already have. It has to start from a point of zero sales, and build a market from there.
- *Your product has no brand awareness.* Nobody's ever heard of the Instant Electromatic Eyebrow Plucker. There's no advertising campaign on TV, no news articles, no magazine ads, no nothing. It's an unknown product.
- *It's not a proven seller.* Because of the two points just mentioned, there are no sales trends that the wholesaler can use to decide whether it's worth it to them to use their valuable floor space to stock your product and try to sell it.

Many times, it takes years for small manufacturers to create enough brand awareness of their product to convince a large wholesaler to carry it. The products that wholesalers actively go after and want to distribute are those that have made some big media splash somewhere, or are already very well known in their markets.

If you do work directly with a manufacturer, it will probably be an unknown product brand. Well-known brand-name products are always purchased through a wholesale supplier.

That's why if you do find a manufacturer who's willing to sell directly to you, the retailer, you'll notice that the products are relatively unknown, and you won't recognize the name of the company. They're hoping that the sales they get from *your* marketing of the products will help to make people aware of the product and the brand, and eventually they *will* be courted by some large wholesale distribution company.

So, for the vast majority of your purchases as a retailer, you'll be dealing with wholesale suppliers. Legitimate wholesale suppliers are very stable and will supply a steady stream of reliable brand-name products for you to sell on eBay. When you do find a manufacturer who's willing to sell to you directly, that's great, but keep in mind that the prices they charge you will most likely *be* wholesale prices anyway, not manufacturer discounts.

If a manufacturer sells to retailers at the manufacturer's discount pricing, and then they suddenly get a deal with a large wholesaler, they're going to have to switch you, the retailer, over to buying from their new wholesale supply partner. They will then tell you that you can no longer buy from the factory, that you must now instead go to XYZ Wholesalers to get their products. If they've been selling to you at the manufacturer's price, you'll suddenly have to start paying the wholesaler's markup, and they may very likely lose you as a customer. So, most manufacturers who sell directly to retailers *already factor in* a markup that a wholesaler would charge anyway so they can avoid that problem in the future.

Buying directly from a small manufacturer can have its pitfalls, too. Small companies can rarely keep up with a fast-paced sales season, like the Christmas holiday. They're more likely to run out of stock and take longer to make more items. They're also more likely to go out of business suddenly.

It's great to deal directly with a manufacturer, but be careful if they're a small company. Larger wholesale suppliers are much more stable and reliable. It's important for you, as a home-based online retailer, to work with the most stable and reliable wholesalers you can find. A small manufacturer might seem to be a great find, but if the inherent unreliability of a small manufacturer causes you problems in filling orders, it's just not worth it. If you do decide to work with a small manufacturer, just be sure to keep in constant contact with them regarding their stock levels and new product availability.

Summing Up

Overall, you'll find very few opportunities to work directly with manufacturers anyway. The suppliers you'll work with the most are legitimate factory-authorized wholesalers. So, remember the following:

- "Local sourcing" at garage sales, discount stores, and so on is fine when first starting out, but to build a real business income you need to streamline your processes, including product sourcing.
- Streamlining product sourcing means working with steady, reliable wholesale sources of the products you sell the most.
- You can still add unique peripheral items to your online sales through local sourcing when you have the time to do so. It never hurts to spice up a typical product line with a few out-of-the-way items.

- Legitimate wholesale suppliers are an important part of the delivery system between the manufacturer and the retailer. It makes no sense for manufacturers to sell directly to retailers, because they would have to reinvent that entire distribution "wheel" that already exists with wholesale suppliers.
- If you do find a manufacturer that will work with you directly, they're most likely very small. Take care to work with them closely so your customers' items don't end up on backorder simply because the manufacturer isn't big enough to deliver on time.

Chapter 11

Middlemen, MLMs, and Other Dangerous Things

When you're getting into business on the Internet, whether on eBay or somewhere else, you're going to find a tremendous number of people who are perched there like a flock of vultures, just waiting to swoop down on your wallet. They'll promise you overnight riches using their "amazing systems," or claim that for $39.95 they'll sell you an e-commerce business system that will make everything easy.

Many of them look very legitimate. In fact, many aren't necessarily doing anything illegal. They're just selling you junk information that really doesn't work. Or, they're "hooking" you for $39.95 so they can call you back later and tell you that you *really* need to pay them as much as *ten thousand dollars* to make their "amazing systems" work to their full potential. We've seen that happen personally, many times.

People don't really believe the claims of most commercials they see on television, so why are they so eager to believe infomercials? Infomercials are simply longer commercials!

Some of these people run "Internet business" seminars all over the world, and pay for late night TV infomercials. They also usually spend a tremendous amount of advertising money on the search engines so that their easy business system ads are always in your face.

It's Simple Common Sense

Don't listen to them. Don't believe them. They've fooled tens of thousands of people into wasting millions of dollars on their schemes. A real eBay business takes time, patience, a commitment to learning, and a good deal of hard work to build.

That's true of any business, and we all know that. It's just common sense. Sometimes, though, common sense flies out the window when someone promises to fulfill our hope for the American dream for 40 bucks. We promise you that 40 bucks will go down the tubes—and a lot more of your money, too—if you let the Get-Rich-Quick people in through the door.

In truth, there's a whole subset of Get-Rich-Quick schemes aimed at product sourcing—an entire little industry on the Internet that makes its money by fooling you into thinking you're getting something you're not. They break down into three major categories:

- Product sourcing middlemen
- Product sourcing MLMs (multi-level marketers)
- Junk product sourcing information

Let's look at them one by one, shall we?

Product Sourcing Middlemen

We've mentioned middlemen before, so let's describe exactly who they are now.

In the last chapter, we talked about why wholesalers exist, and why you need them. The product supply chain, from manufacturer to retailer, is supposed to go like this:

1. Manufacturer
2. Wholesaler
3. Retailer

Many people have the mistaken impression that the second link in the chain, the wholesaler, is a middleman, because they are in the *middle*, between the manufacturer and you, the retailer.

As discussed earlier, that's not true. The second link in the product supply chain is there for a very important reason: manufacturers don't have the infrastructure to actually sell and deliver small numbers of their products directly to you, the retailer. Real wholesalers *provide* that infrastructure (warehouses, order systems, delivery trucks, account representatives, and so on) *for* the manufacturer.

So, link two, the wholesaler, is a legitimate wholesale supplier, not a middleman.

Here's an example of where an illegitimate middleman fits into that supply chain:

1. Manufacturer
2. Wholesaler

3. *Middleman*

4. Retailer

A middleman is someone who takes *your* place in the product supply chain, and bumps you *down* a link. They try to make you believe they are the second link in the chain (a wholesaler), when they are really the third link (a *retailer*). Sometimes, it's worse than that, though. You could end up dealing with a fake supplier who is actually three or four links down the chain.

How does that affect you? It hits you where it hurts—right in the profit margin. For every link you, the retailer, drop down in that chain, your "wholesale" prices go *up*. You need to be buying your products from the wholesale supplier that works directly with the product manufacturer. Otherwise, your profit margin will suffer.

Creating a Monster

Let's take a look at how a middleman *becomes* a middleman.

One day, Unscrupulous Bob is surfing the Internet, trying to come up with a new way to be unscrupulous. After all, that's why he's called Unscrupulous Bob. He believes, like so many on the Net, that the only way to make money online is to cheat other people out of it.

He comes across one of the product sourcing middlemen that are so common online, and being Unscrupulous Bob, he immediately recognizes this scheme for what it is, and realizes that he can set up his *own* scheme that works the same way. (Unscrupulous people not only lack scruples, they are also not very original or creative. For the most part, they simply copy other schemes and scams, and make them their own.) So, Unscrupulous Bob sets out to make himself a product sourcing middleman.

From the computer in his bedroom, he finds himself a *real* wholesaler of home décor products. He contacts that wholesale supplier, Acme Home Décor, and tells them he's a retailer who wants to sell their products. For all Acme Home Decor knows, he's telling the truth, so they give his business a wholesale account, which is what real wholesalers do. Unscrupulous Bob can now order Acme Home Décor products at wholesale. He downloads images of about 3,000 products from Acme's web site that Acme wholesales, and then he downloads Acme's wholesale price list and adds 30 percent to all 3,000 prices on the list.

Once he's got the prices "marked up," he builds his own web site. Instead of building a retail web site that sells to the public, like he's supposed to, he builds a web site called U-Bob's Wholesale Décor. He fills this web site with images of Acme Home Décor's products, and places the marked-up prices on the products. Then, Unscrupulous Bob starts advertising on the search engines, telling people that *he* is a real wholesale supplier.

The First Victim

Pretty soon, along comes Unsuspecting Andy. Now, Unsuspecting Andy is new to e-commerce, and is just starting an eBay business. He's decided to sell home décor online, which is a good-selling product line. Unsuspecting Andy goes to a search engine, types in "wholesale home décor," and up pops U-Bob's Wholesale Décor site.

Unsuspecting Andy is thrilled. According to the U-Bob web site, he can buy 3,000 different home décor products at incredible wholesale prices, and make an overnight fortune on eBay. He signs up for an "account" on the U-Bob site instantly, and spends a truckload of money, ordering enough products to fill half his garage.

Unscrupulous Bob takes Andy's order, and snickers to himself. Then, Unscrupulous Bob puts Andy's money in the bank, e-mails the *real* supplier, Acme Home Décor, and places Unsuspecting Andy's order. He uses Andy's address as the delivery address.

Unscrupulous Bob just made 30 percent on that big product sale to Andy, simply by taking Andy's order, and forwarding it to the *real* wholesaler.

Andy *will* get the products he ordered, but he paid too much for them. When he tries to sell them on eBay, he's going to find out that other eBay sellers, who work directly with the *real* wholesale supplier, will be able to easily beat his prices. Unsuspecting Andy is now stuck with half a garage full of products that he can't make a profit on.

Does any of this sound farfetched to you? Believe us, it's not. There are an amazing number of web sites on the Internet put up by people who claim to be wholesale suppliers, and those people do exactly what Unscrupulous Bob just did. In fact, they do it all day long, and it doesn't bother them a bit. They're product sourcing middlemen: people who make money at the expense of others through deception.

If you're thinking that something like this could never happen to you, you have a *lot* of company. Most people don't believe they could be taken in this way. However, it's a fact that even experienced online sellers get fooled by people like U-Bob. He and his buddies create extremely convincing sites, and sometimes even raise venture capital to "legitimize" themselves by spending lots of money on print and television advertising. They look and sound *very* real.

Another favorite product sourcing scheme used by the unscrupulous and unprincipled is the multi-level-marketing plan. Let's talk about that.

Product Sourcing
Multi-Level-Marketing Schemes

Earlier, we talked about the fact that it's bad to be bumped from the third (retail) link of the product supply chain down to the fourth link by allowing a middleman to get in between you and the real wholesaler.

We also mentioned that you could find yourself two or three links below *that* level on the chain. Taking you for that ride way down to the lower links is the specialty of the product sourcing MLM (multi-level marketer).

People have been falling for this kind of thing forever. They talk about it on the news—everybody from *20/20* to *60 Minutes* exposes them—and yet still people fall for it every day. Whether it's the old "Airplane Game," where everyone puts $200 in the pot, and then you each get four others to do the same, and so on until you advance to the "Pilot's Seat" and get all the money, or it's the multi-level "wholesale suppliers" on the Internet, it's all based on the same thing.

An MLM scheme is a food chain. When you enter it, you are on the bottom of that food chain. Ask any amoeba, small insect, or bit of plankton floating around the ocean, and they'll tell you that the bottom of a food chain is not a good place to be!

How It Works

Here's an example of a widespread MLM operation already in existence on the Internet. There's a big supplier of imported off-brand merchandise in the U.S. that sells some decent products, but which doesn't carry any well-known brand-name items. Their line consists of several thousand widely varying products—mostly decorative figurines, home accents, and giftware. Again, you won't recognize any of the brand names...it's all imported merchandise, most of it probably from China and the Pacific Rim. We'll call this pretend company XYZ Wholesalers.

You can sign up with XYZ Wholesalers directly and sell their merchandise on your web site for a hefty monthly account maintenance fee, but you'll soon find that the products are difficult to sell—for one very good reason.

Would you open a shoe store in a local mall that already has 50 other shoe stores in it? Of course not. In other words, you must look at your potential competition before deciding on what products to sell.

They already have *tens of thousands* of people who are all trying to sell this exact same merchandise on the Internet. That kind of competition, plus the fact that there are so many more people (millions of people!) already trying to sell giftware in general on the Net, will make it impossible for you to make any real money.

Here's the interesting part, though, which makes this situation an MLM scheme. Joe Reseller comes along and signs up with XYZ Wholesalers as a retailer, and now has the right to sell their products on the Internet.

XYZ Wholesalers knows that Joe is not going to make all that much money trying to buck all the competition that's selling their relatively few products on the Internet, so they send Joe three "wholesale" price sheets.

The "amber" price sheet contains the prices that *Joe* can buy products for, and then resell them online. These are the lowest prices available from XYZ Wholesalers. Joe sets up his own eBay listings, and then sells the products directly to the public using the amber price sheet as his wholesale pricing.

The "hunter green" price sheet contains all of the same products, but they're marked up considerably in price. XYZ tells Joe that *he* can bring in his *own* Internet retailers, claiming to actually *be* a wholesaler himself, and sell the products to them for the prices on the hunter green price sheet. XYZ Wholesalers actually *encourages* the kind of unethical behavior that Unscrupulous Bob displayed in our previous example of middlemen.

In other words, XYZ gives Joe *permission* to pretend to be a real wholesale supplier, and gather his own little army of unsuspecting worker bees to sell for *him*. Joe's worker bees go out and set up their *own* online auctions and eBay stores, thinking that Joe is a *real* wholesale supplier, and they send their orders to Joe. Joe simply turns around and sends his worker bees' orders directly to XYZ, and they fill the orders. Once again, it's like a soap opera: Joe is *not* a real wholesaler, but he plays one on the Internet.

MLMs are like giant hives of worker bees, all buzzing around each other in circles, with no place to go.

The "baby blue" price sheet is the third one that Joe got from XYZ, and it has even *higher* prices. Guess what Joe does with this one? He passes the baby blue price sheet on to the worker bees who think *he* is the real wholesaler, and tells them that they can bring in their *own* resellers, and claim to be wholesalers *themselves*!

Joe's unsuspecting worker bees then recruit their *own* unsuspecting worker bees, and that second level of worker bees under Joe's worker bees all create *their* own online auctions to sell all these same wonderful products, never knowing that they're buying from a fake wholesaler under *Joe*, and *those* fake wholesalers are buying *from* Joe, who is a fake wholesaler *himself*.

Joe is the only one buying from the real wholesaler. He's collecting orders from *two levels* of worker bees underneath him, and passing them all on to XYZ, who fills the orders. So, the more worker bees Joe gathers, the more worker bees *those* worker bees gather, and it all passes upward along the chain to Joe, and finally to the *real* wholesaler.

Uplines and Downlines

The preceding scenario has what's known in multi-level marketing (MLM) as an *upline* and a *downline*. In this situation, the following are the downlines:

- Joe and both levels of worker bees under him are XYZ's downline.
- The two levels of worker bees under Joe, who use the hunter green and baby blue price sheets from Joe, are Joe's downline.
- The worker bees who use the baby blue price sheet are the downline for those who use the hunter green price sheet they got from Joe.

The following, on the other hand, are the uplines:

- XYZ Wholesalers sits at the very top of this "pyramid," and collects membership fees, monthly account fees, and product orders from everyone. They are the only real wholesaler in this picture, although all the lower-level worker bees think they're also buying from real wholesalers.
- Joe has XYZ Wholesalers as his upline.
- The hunter green price sheet users have Joe and XYZ in their upline.
- The worker bees who use the baby blue price sheet are at the absolute bottom of this food chain. The hunter green price sheet users, Joe, and XYZ are *all* in the baby blue worker bees' upline.

There are tens of thousands of these downline worker bees out there on the Internet, all creating sites that claim to be real wholesale sources, trying to put *you* on *their* product sourcing downline. They all want you to believe that they're real wholesale suppliers, and some of them are very good liars with very convincing sites.

Junk Product Sourcing Information

One of the most important things you'll need for your eBay business is information: how to use eBay, how to collect money from your customers' credit cards, where to find products to sell, and so on. Nobody is born knowing all this stuff. You have to learn it, which means you have to rely on someone else, somewhere, to teach it to you or to write down the information that you need so you can read it and learn it.

When you're looking for information on product sourcing, there are people out there who are more than willing to lie to your face, promise you riches beyond your wildest dreams, and then leave you with information that will not only *not* help your business, but will actually *damage* your business. Indeed, bad information can actually cause your business to fail completely.

Many of the people who do this are outright scam artists who are actively and purposely trying to cheat you. Some of them are simply lazy, and are looking to make a fast buck selling substandard, outdated information, not caring who they hurt in the process. Some others actually think it's "okay" to cheat you, because "everybody else does it."

Then there are a very few of these small operations in product sourcing information (only two or three, actually) who do try to put together halfway decent information, but they don't have the time and manpower to maintain that information, and it quickly becomes outdated and useless. That cheats you and your business as well; their efforts aren't malicious, of course, just irresponsible.

It's Not Just Bad Info, It's Damaging Info

How can bad information damage your business? Mostly in the form of lost time. The money you spend on the information isn't really the thing to worry about here. Most of the bad information is cheap to begin with. Some of the scammers have realized that cheap information is recognized as bad, though, and will actually jack up their prices and charge you premium money for the same worthless junk that others sell for two or three dollars.

However, in the end it's really not about the money. The problem, as we said, is lost time. Let's look at an example.

Lionel's Leap of Faith

Lionel decides he wants to start a home-based Internet business. His full-time job doesn't pay all that much, creditors are always calling, it costs money to raise two kids, and his wife hasn't been able to find work in a couple of months. Lionel's not broke, but things could always be better. Besides that, he really doesn't like his job to begin with. So, he takes a *leap of faith*, and decides to invest his money in *himself* and his desire to start a home-based Internet business.

Lionel decides he wants to sell on eBay. He starts out by selling a few things from his attic, as well as items he picked up from garage sales around the neighborhood. He quickly realizes, though, that if he's going to make real money in the long run, he needs to find a steady, reliable source of the products he wants to sell, and pay genuine wholesale prices for them, so he can make a good profit.

Lionel has heard that drop shipping is also a low-entry-cost solution for getting a real wholesaler to ship brand-new products directly to his customers for him, so he doesn't have to buy a bunch of products up-front and ship them from his home. That sounds pretty good!

Over the years, he's become a fairly experienced eBayer, so naturally he turns to eBay to search for information on drop-ship wholesalers. He does a search on drop shipping on eBay. What he finds looks exciting to him: auction upon auction that sport all kinds of "guaranteed genuine" lists of drop shippers and wholesalers! Better yet, many of them are only $5—what a great deal!

Always remember that good information costs
money to create. If you buy **cheap** *information,*
you will **get** *cheap information.*

So, Lionel spends a few bucks on something called *The Best Product Sourcing Guide in the Universe*. The name sounds so impressive he's convinced it must contain oodles of great information. Besides, the auction promises him guaranteed, genuine sources that will make him thousands of dollars in a matter of days. The seller of that information claims to have built this and used it himself, and it works wonders.

Lionel gets his hands on the information, and lo and behold ... there are hundreds of listings of "wholesale" company names there, categorized by the kinds of products they wholesale. Lionel is anxious to jump right in, so he goes to the sporting goods category, and sees a listing for what sounds like a large sporting goods wholesaler. It includes a phone number, so Lionel calls it. The number rings a couple of times, and then Lionel gets a recorded phone company message telling him "this number is no longer in service."

"Well," thinks Lionel, "companies do change their phone numbers. Or, maybe it was printed wrong in the information." So, he sends an e-mail to the address listed in his handy-dandy product sourcing guide.

He waits a couple of days for a reply, and then decides to send another e-mail. In the meantime, he's busy getting other aspects of his business ready to go in order to start selling products on eBay. A week goes by, and Lionel still has no reply. By this time, he's getting frustrated. So, he calls the Chamber of Commerce in the city where *The Best Product Sourcing Guide in the Universe* has told him this sporting goods wholesaler is located, and asks about the company he's been trying to contact.

The nice lady at the Chamber of Commerce tells him that the company went out of business nearly two years ago. (That, by the way, actually happened. There was a sporting goods drop shipper in Pennsylvania that went out of business almost two years ago, and yet is still listed in many of the junk drop-ship lists on eBay, as are hundreds of other useless listings.)

Now Lionel is getting a bit upset. He's just wasted a week of his time that he could have used creating auctions for sporting goods products. He's not going to give up, though, so he goes back to *The Best Product Sourcing Guide in the Universe* and finds that there are several other sporting goods "wholesalers" listed. This time, he calls them all. He gets two more disconnected numbers, one number is answered by a lady who says "Sherri's Hair Salon, can I help you?," and one answering machine that tells him that Jo and Bill are not in, but if he's calling about the 1983 Buick for sale, it's still available and they'll call him back.

At this point, Lionel realizes that he's been the victim of a junk information scammer. You see, it's not good enough to simply have information. The information must be honest, accurate, and up-to-date, otherwise it's *useless*. Many people buy one of these junk lists you find for sale for a few bucks on eBay, for example, thinking that even if the information is mostly bad, there are bound to be a few gold nuggets in the cow flop. Some of that information must lead to real wholesalers, right?

Let's give you a different kind of example of how that kind of thinking will hurt your business, even if there are a few gold nuggets.

Bad Info Affects Your Life Every Day

A couple of months ago, Chris Malta's family physician made a referral appointment for him to see another doctor for a minor checkup. He hadn't been to this other doctor's office before, but his family physician's receptionist gave him an address that was way on the other side of Orlando. The address she gave him was in Altamonte Springs, about a 45 minute drive for him. When the day came, he set off for this doctor's office. He drove all the way there, arrived about ten minutes before his scheduled appointment, found the office building, and discovered that the doctor's name was nowhere to be found in the building's registry.

He got on his cell phone and called this new doctor's office. The receptionist told Chris that they had recently moved to Ocoee, Florida, which was actually only about 15 minutes from Chris's house!

There was no way he could make it all the way back from Altamonte Springs to Ocoee in the five minutes he had left before his appointment, and the doctor was tightly booked, so they made him reschedule for another day. So, because Chris had gotten outdated information from his family physician's office, he used a quarter of a tank of gas, and wasted nearly two hours of time he could have used much more productively.

Now, we know that doesn't sound all that terrible, but think of it this way: What if he repeated that same fiasco with several hundred doctor's appointments, and only made it to an actual doctor's office a handful of those times? That sounds a lot worse, doesn't it?

That is exactly what happens to you when you buy junk information. Of the potentially hundreds of "wholesaler" listings in those bundles of garbage, you're going to spend time trying to contact each one. Let's be generous and say that ten companies out of a list of 300 are real, genuine drop shippers. How many days, weeks, or even months do you think it's going to take you to go through lengthy contact processes and sift through all the junk to find the few real ones?

Losing at the Waiting Game

When using junk lists, you'll be making phone calls and waiting (possibly forever) for return calls. You'll send e-mails and wait hours, days, or weeks for responses that will never come. All that wasted time could have been used productively on building your business if you simply had 100-percent honest, accurate, up-to-date information. That $5 you spent on that cheap list will actually cost you hundreds or even thousands of dollars' worth of lost time. We call that the "save now, pay later" plan, meaning you end up paying a *lot* more than you save.

If that's not bad enough, just wait until you *think* you've finally found a real wholesaler, and it turns out to be a middleman like Unscrupulous Bob, or a product sourcing MLM like the kind Joe was tangled up in. Once again, it's not good enough to simply have information. The information must be honest, accurate, and up-to-date, otherwise it's useless.

Time is money. Truer words were never spoken. You'll find out after spending time spinning your wheels chasing down useless leads from junk information that the time you wasted has cost you a lot. It may even put you out of business.

Learning to Separate the Good from the Bad

Whenever and wherever you find the name of a company that's supposed to be a wholesaler, be very careful. Learn to recognize the signs of a middleman or MLM, such as:

- Any wholesale web site that does not give you a full company name, address, and phone number to call (which they'll *answer*).
- Any supposed wholesaler that does *not* ask you for a business license and sales tax ID.
- Any wholesale web site that makes claims about how much money you can make using their services.
- Any wholesale web site that makes claims about how much money *they* have made with their products.
- Any wholesale web site that you notice is marketing the same products as *another* supposed wholesale web site.
- Any web site claiming to be a wholesaler that tries to sell you other services besides strictly wholesale products.

If you come across a wholesaler that you're not sure about, there are some things you can do to help you decide if they're legitimate:

- *Call them.* If someone answers and says "Hello?" without using the business name, you aren't talking to a real business. You should be able to get hold of an operator who can direct you to an account representative. Ask the account rep all the questions you like until you're satisfied.

- *Go to www.Whois.net and do a search on the company's web site domain name.* If the results tell you that the site is registered to an individual name, chances are you're dealing with a middleman. If it's registered to a company name, that's not proof necessarily, but it's a good sign that they might be legitimate.
- *Search the Internet using the web site name, and then do a search using the company name.* If anyone has had trouble with them, you'll find out quickly.
- *Search the Better Business Bureau web site at www.BBB.org for any complaint history.*
- *Contact the Chamber of Commerce in the city or town where the business claims to be located, and ask about them.* Even if they're not a Chamber Member, someone there should be able to give you some idea about them.

Summing Up

The Internet is a place where anyone can easily pretend to be anyone or anything else they want you to think they are. Let's sum up a few of the most important points you'll need to remember if you want to avoid unscrupulous people who will take your money and leave you with nothing to show for it.

- There are a tremendous number of people who have created a thriving "industry" online that makes money by fooling others into thinking they're real wholesale suppliers.
- These unscrupulous types all get in between you and the real suppliers. Plus, each middleman that gets in the way raises your "wholesale" prices a little more. You can't earn money on eBay when dealing with middlemen, because they leave you no room for any real profit margin.
- A junk information industry exists that makes its money by selling people fake, outdated, and useless lists of wholesale companies. Not all wholesale information sellers are like this, but the vast majority are.
- Learning to spot fake suppliers and bad information, as described in this chapter, is one of the most critical tasks you face if your business is to succeed.

Making sure you're dealing with a real wholesaler can make or break your eBay business, so be sure you know who you're dealing with.

Chapter 12

How a Real Wholesaler Works

The most misunderstood term in the e-commerce industry is the word "wholesale." Ask a hundred different people to explain it to you, and you'll get a hundred different explanations. Many people think they should be able to buy directly from a product manufacturer. That's almost never going to happen, for reasons we discussed in Chapter 10 of this book.

Many people also think that "wholesale" means "the best possible price you can buy a product for." That's not actually correct, either. The wholesale pricing you get will depend on several different things, the most important being the size of the order you place.

How the Product Supply Chain Works

As we've mentioned previously, there are three basic links in the product supply chain, as far as online retailers are concerned. These constitute the following.

Step One: Manufacturing

The product has to be made. That's what a manufacturer does. However, manufacturers are busy enough just making products. Most don't want to be bothered with having to distribute them around the world as well. Which leads us to ...

Step Two: Distribution

The manufacturer may make 50,000 units of the same product every week. A retailer like yourself might only want to carry ten units of this particular product. Since it would take forever for the manufacturer to sell the product in ten-unit increments, they need someone *else* to take those 50,000 units, break them up into much smaller quantities, and *distribute* them to retailers.

That's what a wholesale supplier does. They take big piles of products from manufacturers, turn them into little piles of products, and sell the little piles to retail businesses.

Step Three: Consumer Sales

Once the products get distributed to retail sellers, the next step is selling them to the consumer. As an eBay (or other online) seller, you buy "little piles" of products from wholesalers, and reduce them to just one product sale at a time.

Now, the first link in the chain is a pretty simple concept. We know what a manufacturer does. We may not know exactly how they do it, but we know that they make the product, plain and simple, and that's all we need to know. We also know about the third link—selling the product to the customer. That's what you do. Even if you're not quite expert at it yet, you know that you buy a product from a wholesaler for $50, and sell it to your online buyer for $75. You keep the difference, and that's how you earn your money.

An Example of How the Process Works

All of the confusion in this process seems to surround link two: the wholesale supplier. When it comes to what wholesalers really do and how their business works, and especially how their pricing works, most people just don't get it. Well, we'll try to set the record straight here. As an example, we'll use an actual wholesale company that Chris helped set up a few years ago. That's right, he's actually one of those mysterious wholesale suppliers that nobody understands! By the time we're done here, however, hopefully you will understand it better.

There are three major topics we need to discuss here:

- The physical aspect of wholesale distribution
- How wholesale pricing works
- Wholesale product delivery methods

As we said, we'll use a company that Chris helped to set up as an example to cover all three of these topics. Let's call the business Example Wholesale, Inc.

The Physical Aspect of Wholesale Distribution

The physical part of wholesale distribution (supply) goes like this:

Example Wholesale, Inc. has a warehouse in New York. It has a lot of storage space, an office, a couple of phone lines, computers, fax machine, printers, and so on. They are factory-authorized wholesale suppliers for two sporting goods manufacturing companies. This isn't an easy thing to be. It took months to be approved and authorized by their first manufacturer and over a year to be approved by the second manufacturer. Manufacturers don't authorize just anybody to be one of their wholesale suppliers. They wanted to know that the owners of Example Wholesale could afford to keep buying large loads of their products. They wanted to know how much experience the owners had in the wholesale industry. They checked credit ratings. They checked to see if Example Wholesale would be competing too closely with any of their other authorized wholesale suppliers in that geographical part of New York. They wanted to know what kind of retailers the products would be sold to, and how many retailers Example Wholesale already had available to sell to.

Manufacturers don't want to authorize lots of small wholesale suppliers. They'd rather just authorize and deal with a few larger ones.

Dealing with a few larger wholesalers instead of a lot of smaller ones makes the administrative and logistic work of dealing with wholesalers easier for a manufacturer. It also reduces the amount of money it costs them to ship products to their wholesalers. If they can ship products to five large wholesalers instead of 20 small ones, they don't pay nearly as much money to get those products from the factory to the wholesalers.

When Example Wholesale became authorized by the first manufacturer, they bought truckloads of that manufacturer's products and put them in their warehouse. Then they bought a truckload of shipping supplies. When products come straight from a manufacturer, they aren't in single shipping boxes. They're all wrapped up together in something called *case lots*. Example Wholesale sells both in bulk, and also drop-ships for their retailers. (We'll talk about those methods a little later.)

Since they use both methods of product delivery, though, Example Wholesale had to buy shipping boxes, shipping bags, and shipping labels so they could individually package each product they might drop-ship for online sellers like yourself, who used them as a wholesale supplier.

Example Wholesale also had to open a business shipping account with UPS. In order for UPS to come to the warehouse every day and pick up the products that they ship for their retailers, they needed to pay for, and set up, a UPS shipping account. Thus, they also had to acquire UPS shipping software, a special shipping label printer, and several other things that were necessary for the account.

They had to design and build a web site that made ordering easy for their retailers. Their site is set up so that retailers like yourself can go to the web site, place either bulk orders or drop-ship orders for single products, and have them ship those products directly to you or your customer.

Orders come in through Example Wholesale's web site, and are printed out each morning. Employees in the warehouse have to go through the shelves, picking the products out for each individual order. Then the products are packaged, a shipping label is put on them, and they're set on the loading dock. (Wholesalers call that process "pick and pack.") Once a day, a UPS truck comes by and picks up all those products for shipment.

That's basically the physical part of what Example Wholesale does as a wholesale supply company. Many people understand how that works, although most people don't understand how difficult it is to become a factory-authorized wholesale supplier.

Now for the part that confuses everybody: *wholesale pricing*!

How Wholesale Pricing Works

As we said, Example Wholesale is a factory-authorized wholesale distributor for two sporting goods manufacturers.

Let's call the first manufacturer First Sporting Goods, Inc.

Every few months, First Sporting Goods, the manufacturer, sends Example Wholesale a new *price list*. This list not only has the prices that Example Wholesale pays for the products it buys from the factory, the list will also have *suggested* prices that Example Wholesale should charge its *retailers* for those products. The wholesale supplier doesn't always have to follow those suggested prices though. They can charge a higher wholesale price if they need to. It all depends on their costs for getting the products to you.

The wholesale price that Example Wholesale is supposed to charge its retailers for First Sporting Goods products is really just a guideline so that all of its authorized wholesale suppliers will be able to compete fairly with each other. However, Example Wholesale and the other wholesalers who sell First Sporting Goods products should never stray too far from that suggested price, otherwise they may find themselves no longer in business with First Sporting Goods!

When a wholesale supplier like Example Wholesale buys in large quantities from the manufacturer, the manufacturer charges the wholesaler a "distributor's wholesale price." *Nobody* but a factory-authorized wholesale supplier can buy at distributor wholesale pricing. When Example Wholesale buys truckloads of products from the First Sporting Goods factory, the distributor wholesale price they pay for most of those products is 8 percent less than First Sporting Goods wants them to charge their retailers for the products. So, when Example Wholesale, Inc. sells bulk lots of products to you, the retailer, Example Wholesale makes an 8-percent profit margin. Not much, is it? That's only $80 on a $1,000 order! Wholesale distribution is something that's known as a "volume business." That means that a wholesale supplier has to sell a lot of products to a lot of retailers to survive in the wholesale business.

Wholesalers Can't Survive on Narrow Profit Margins Alone

Of course, there are a few things that help Example Wholesale along. Although they have to live with that 8-percent profit margin on about 80 percent of the products they wholesale, there are special factory deals and other levels of wholesale pricing available to Example Wholesale from First Sporting Goods. The one that's important for us to discuss here is called "keystone" pricing, but most people in the wholesale business just call it *key pricing*.

Key pricing *is the discount edge that wholesale suppliers need in order to make their generally narrow-margin businesses work.*

Key pricing gives Example Wholesale an additional discount on about 20 percent of the products they buy from First Sporting Goods. Those key discounts can range from 15 percent to 30 percent below the prices Example Wholesale usually pays, but they're only available on specific products. So, Example Wholesale makes an 8-percent profit on most of the First Sporting Goods products it wholesales, which isn't much. However, it makes *additional* profits (up to 30 percent) on *some* of the First Sporting Goods products.

Through it all, Example Wholesale sticks to the suggested wholesale price that First Sporting Goods wants them to charge their retailers for the products. Again, they don't have to follow those suggested prices to the letter, but it's best for their relationship with the factory if they do. That extra percentage they get from selling those key-priced products makes their overall profit margin large enough that they can stay in business and make some money as well. If they didn't get key pricing on some of the products they sell, they probably wouldn't be able to stay in business. An across-the-board 8-percent profit margin would not be enough profit to run most wholesale supply companies.

Some wholesalers are a little more eager to earn a quick buck, and will charge you more than the manufacturer's suggested wholesale price for your products. Others may not *get* key pricing from their manufacturers, and will *have* to charge more.

Overall, a wholesale price is really up to the wholesale supplier, following suggested guidelines from the manufacturer.

However, as we've said, those prices never stray very far over the manufacturer's suggested wholesale price, because if the wholesaler charges too much on a regular basis, their retailers won't buy anything, and/or the manufacturer will cut them off. So, wholesale pricing from a *real* wholesale supplier is always within an acceptable range for the product market in question.

Buying Power Is a Factor in Competing Online

Sometimes, as a retailer, you'll come up against competition you just can't seem to beat, even though you're buying from a legitimate wholesale supplier. The large retail chains like Kmart, for example, have more *buying power* than you do. Kmart can go to a company like Example Wholesale and order *20,000* pieces of one particular product if they want to. When that happens, Example Wholesale will charge Kmart less than their standard 8-percent profit margin, because that one order is going to earn them a serious chunk of change even at a lower profit margin.

So, Kmart and the other big retailers of the world can sell the same products for less than you can, because they have much more initial buying power, and can negotiate special price breaks from wholesalers. Those big retailers can only carry so many products on their shelves, though. There are *millions* of products out there to sell, and a big retail store chain like that may only carry ten to twenty *thousand* different products.

The key to working around the big stores' buying power is to sell products that they **don't** *carry. If you want to sell power drills, for example, check out a big store and make a list of the six or seven power drills they* **do** *carry. Then sell one of the dozens of* **other** *models they* **don't.**

Now, let's talk about the two major product delivery methods that wholesalers use.

Wholesale Product Delivery Methods

A wholesale supplier can deliver products to you, and ultimately your customer, in one of two ways. They can sell you a bulk load of products, and ship it directly to you. Then you can repackage the products individually, and ship them to your customers. From the wholesaler's point of view, this is called *bulk wholesaling.*

Some of those same wholesalers who are willing to do so can take your orders for products one at a time, and ship them directly to your customers for you. This is called *drop shipping.* Genuine wholesale suppliers who are willing to drop-ship are actually very rare. Let's talk about both methods.

Bulk Wholesaling

In bulk wholesaling, the wholesaler sells you cases of products, not just one of this, and one of that. All wholesale suppliers are *bulk wholesalers.* That's what they do, remember? They take big piles of products from the manufacturer, and break them up into smaller piles of products that get sold to the retailer.

When Example Wholesale orders products from a manufacturer like First Sporting Goods, the products arrive at Example Wholesale's warehouse in something called *case lots*. That just means that when the wholesaler gets them from the manufacturer, they've packed a certain number of products to a case. Some of the larger products come packed two or four to a case. Smaller ones come packed six, 12, or 24 or more to a case.

If Example Wholesale is going to sell those products to you, the retailer, at a very low 8-percent profit margin, then they have to sell them to you in the same cases they were packed in when they arrived at Example Wholesale's warehouse. The wholesaler *must* be able to take those factory-supplied cases of products, put your shipping address on them, and send them right back out the door in the same case boxes they came in. Here's why ... if Example Wholesale has to break open those cases and re-package a half of a case, or a quarter of a case, they have to pay their employees more money to do that, because it takes them more time.

When it takes the wholesaler's employees more time, it costs the wholesale company more money, and they make less profit. Operating, for example, on an 8-percent profit margin, they can't afford to make less profit! So, when you buy in bulk from a wholesale supplier, you're buying cases of products, packaged just as they come from the manufacturer. In order for Example Wholesale to be able to afford to sell to you in bulk at the low profit margins they make on most of their products, they have to require a *minimum order*. When you order in bulk from Example Wholesale, your first order must be at least $500.

However, for a $500 order, they must charge you 2 percent *over* that standard 8-percent profit margin, which brings their profit margin to 10 percent. If they didn't make 10 percent on a $500 order, they couldn't remain in business. Remember, that's only $50 they're making on that whole order! In order for Example Wholesale to sell to you in bulk exactly at the manufacturer's suggested wholesale price, they require that each order be $1,000 or more. That's the minimum order they're willing to accept from you at their standard markup of 8 percent.

Of course, if you happen to order the few products that Example Wholesale carries that they get factory *key pricing* on, they make a better profit on *part* of your order, and that's really how wholesale suppliers pay their bills and stay in business. Remember, though, that most wholesale suppliers only get that key pricing from the manufacturer on a small percentage of the products they carry.

If a wholesale supplier didn't require minimum orders on bulk purchases, they couldn't remain in business.

Let's imagine for a moment that a wholesaler selling in bulk didn't require a minimum order. Let's say that they took your order for just two of their less expensive purple widgets, and sold them to you at the *manufacturer's suggested wholesale price*. The purple widgets come to the wholesaler from the manufacturer, packed 48 to a case. For the wholesaler to get just two of those purple widgets to you, one of their employees would have to break open a case of the widgets. He would have to take two of those purple widgets out of the case box, and re-package them in a smaller box.

Where does that smaller box come from? The wholesaler has to buy it separately. How about the extra packing materials that will be needed? The wholesaler has to buy those separately as well. And what about their employee's extra time? That's the costliest thing of all for the wholesale supplier!

So, if the wholesaler sold you just two of those purple widgets, at the actual manufacturer's suggested wholesale price of $18 each, they'd make about $2.88 at that 8-percent profit margin. The extra shipping materials and their employee's time to repackage that order cost them about $10. Thus, the wholesaler just *lost* $7.12 on that one order. Obviously, they couldn't stay in business long if they did that!

When a wholesaler sells cases of products to you in bulk at the minimum order amounts they require, the profit they earn makes it just worthwhile enough for them to do it close to or at the manufacturer's suggested wholesale price. They don't have to break open the cases in their warehouse, and it doesn't cost them extra for more packing materials and extra employee time. That's what bulk wholesaling is, and that's why you see minimum order requirements from nearly all legitimate wholesalers when you buy in bulk.

We've mentioned that *drop shipping* is the other way that a wholesale supplier can deliver products for you. Please remember that *real* wholesale suppliers who are willing to drop-ship are *rare*. Drop shipping constitutes a lot of extra administration and cost for a wholesaler, which is why most of them won't do it.

Drop Shipping

When Example Wholesale or any wholesale supplier drop-ships, they send individual products, one at a time, directly to your customer for you. They take care of the packaging and the shipping. That means *you* don't have to keep a garage full of products from a bulk order that you may not sell. *You* don't have to buy packing and shipping materials, and *you* don't have to set up a UPS account, or travel to the nearest shipping location to send your products out yourself.

As a drop shipper, the wholesale supplier is doing a tremendous amount of work for you, and saving you the expense of buying products in bulk, before you sell them. It costs the wholesaler more to do that, though.

Think about it for a minute. When a wholesaler sells a bulk order, they can simply reship case lots of products to you. No picking products off the shelf and re-packaging them. So, they can do that at or close to the manufacturer's suggested wholesale price, depending on how much you order.

When a wholesaler drop-ships, it costs the wholesaler a lot more, and saves you money, because you don't have to do all that work of stocking, re-packaging, and shipping.

Since drop shippers go to all that expense for shipping materials, including paying their employees for the extra time spent, they *must* charge a higher wholesale price when they drop-ship. Drop shippers cover that expense in two ways.

Drop-Ship Fees

A drop-ship fee is usually about $2 to $5. The drop shipper has to charge that fee in addition to the total of each drop-ship order. This is done to cover the extra packing materials they have to buy. For example, a wholesale supplier might charge a $4 drop-ship fee per address. That means that if they ship one product, or five products, to that one address for you at the same time, the drop-ship fee is still $4 for the whole order. Averaged out for their business, they will have learned over the years that a $4 drop-ship fee pays for the extra packing materials they have to buy to ship individual orders straight to their home-based retailer's customers.

Slightly Higher Wholesale Pricing

When a wholesaler sells products in bulk, it doesn't take that long for their employees to re-ship factory case lots, as we've already discussed. However, when they drop-ship for you, their employees have to spend a lot more time on each order. They have to pick the products out of case lots individually, and then spend time re-packaging them for shipment to your customer. That costs the wholesaler money in the form of extra pay to their employees.

In the course of doing business, a good drop shipper will have figured out how much extra money it costs them to do that with each different type of product they sell, and they raise their wholesale price by that much in order to drop-ship their products. In the case of Example Wholesale, they still end up making about that same 8 percent or so on their drop-shipped sales, since the extra money they have to charge you, the retailer, goes to pay their employees; it doesn't go into the company's pockets!

Yes, it costs you slightly more per product to have a drop shipper ship something directly to your customer. However, when the wholesaler drop-ships for you, it means you don't have to spend the time and money to do your own shipping. Remember, time equals money for you as well. When you don't have to stock products and do your own shipping, you don't have to pay for packing and shipping materials.

You also have more time and money available to work on marketing your business, and selling more products. So, when you balance out your business books at the end of the year, you'll probably end up making about the same profits using drop shipping as you would by placing small bulk orders. It all depends on how you want to do it.

A Couple of Drop-Shipping Tips

eBay sellers can end up with negative feedback if they don't deliver a product on time. Online store owners, on the other hand, can end up with customer service complaints, lost customers, and negative remarks about them in online review sites and forums if they don't deliver properly. It's important to remember that drop shippers are taking over the delivery process for you, and you should keep a couple of things in mind.

- When you use a drop shipper, contact them a few times a month and ask about the stock level of the more popular products you sell. They have that information, and can tell you if and when they expect a product to be out of stock. Use that information to judge when you should take a break from selling something that may not be available for a while.
- A good way to avoid unexpected backorders is to actually buy a couple of your best-selling products yourself, and keep them in your home. That way, if you do come up against an unexpected backorder before you can stop sales of a product, you'll have a couple of extras to fill that backorder with.

Summing Up

A good understanding of how wholesale companies actually works will go a long way toward forming and maintaining good relationships with them. Here are some very important points to remember from this chapter:

- Product manufacturers do not want to sell directly to retailers. They're busy enough just making the products. They use wholesale suppliers to get their products to retailers like you.
- Most manufacturers have a suggested wholesale price for the products they make. As a general guideline, wholesale suppliers should always charge only that manufacturer's suggested wholesale price when selling at the proper bulk order quantities to retailers like you.
- Wholesale suppliers who are doing an honest business have a small profit margin on most of the products they sell. Wholesaling is a volume business.

- Wholesale suppliers usually get key factory discounts on *some* of the products they sell. That allows them to make enough money to keep their prices low and still stay in business!
- Wholesalers need to charge minimum order amounts on bulk orders if they're going to stay in business.
- Wholesalers need to charge slightly more for drop shipping if they're to stay in business.
- When you use drop shipping, you pay slightly more for the product, but spend less on packing and shipping materials, thus doing much less work on your end. At the end of your business year, either method should work out to be equally cost-effective.

There you have it. That concludes this basic description of how a real wholesale supplier's distribution, pricing, and delivery methods work.

Chapter 13

Finding Real Wholesalers

W e've already established that you must work with real wholesale suppliers if you want to streamline your product sourcing process and earn the best profit margins on the products you sell on eBay. We've talked about why wholesalers exist, what middlemen and MLMs are, and how real wholesalers work. We've already gone over the cheap lists and junk wholesale information that are being sold for a few bucks online, and how buying the *wrong* information can hurt your business. Now, it's time to start talking about how you can do the research needed to find real wholesalers on your own. But, before we get into that, the first thing you absolutely must learn and understand is where *not* to look for real wholesalers!

Why Real Wholesalers Don't Advertise in the Search Engines

Most people who sell products online automatically start with the search engines when they're looking for wholesalers of products to sell. Believe it or not, the search engines are just about the *last* place you want to look. We know that sounds strange, but it's true, and it's very important to understand why.

Chris Malta talks a good deal about the fact that most wholesale suppliers don't go out of their way to advertise to home-based business owners on the Internet. The most common response he gets from home-based business owners is "They *should* advertise to us on the Net! They want to sell products, right? If they advertise to us on the Net, they would sell more of them!" Well, yes, but that's just not how most real wholesalers see *their* business world. The vast majority of real wholesale suppliers doesn't need or even want to advertise themselves on the Internet. For the wholesale supply industry, there's an entire sales and marketing structure that's been in place forever, long before the Internet ever came to be.

In the real business world, home-based e-biz owners are
not *a wholesaler's ideal advertising target, although many*
will work with us if **we find them.**

Real wholesale supply companies deal for the most part with *large* retailers: Sears, Kmart, Wal-Mart, and so on. These wholesale supply companies have entire sales divisions in place, with salespeople who actually travel to and call on these massive accounts personally. It's been done this way for so long that a real wholesale supplier runs the risk of seriously hurting themselves if they deviate from that strategy. Let's use an example.

The Personal Touch vs. Hi-Tech

Bill Jones is a sales rep for Acme Wholesale Supply. Acme, the company Bill works for, wholesales bicycles. They wholesale many brands of bicycles from well-known manufacturers, from Schwinn to Huffy and more. When people walk into their local MegaMart, for example, they see those huge racks of bikes in the sporting goods area of the store. Those racks contain kids' bikes, adult bikes, and so on. Let's say that MegaMart buys those bicycles for their huge racks from Acme Wholesale Supply.

Bill's sales territory is the southeastern United States, and he's the sales rep (usually called the Account Manager) for Acme Wholesale Supply in that region. It's Bill's responsibility to keep selling bicycles to all the MegaMart stores (and all the other big chains) in that territory, and to make sure that MegaMart doesn't decide to go to some other wholesale supplier to buy their bicycles.

MegaMart, like most medium- to large-sized retail chains, has regional purchasing offices. Bill doesn't have to go to each MegaMart branch store in order to maintain his MegaMart account. All he has to do is stay in contact with a very few MegaMart Regional Purchasing Managers in order to keep those bicycles flowing from Acme Wholesale Supply to MegaMart.

Most of the time, Bill can do this from the comfort of his office. Sometimes, when Acme is introducing a new product, Bill will travel to those regional purchasing offices and meet with the Purchasing Managers personally. He will also do this if he senses that the Purchasing Managers may be considering buying from someone else ... it's his job to make sure those accounts stay with Acme. Bill does the same thing with all the other medium to large retail chains in his territory that buy from Acme. He also calls and visits retail stores that do not buy from Acme to try and get them to start buying bicycles from Acme Wholesale Supply.

One day, his boss calls a special sales meeting. Bill and his fellow Account Managers all file into the conference room at Acme, and sit down over coffee and bagels for this meeting. His boss introduces Andy Smith, from the company's IT (Internetworking Technology) department. Andy Smith is the guy responsible for the computer networks at Acme.

Andy is very interested in creating an enhanced web site for Acme Wholesale Supply. Andy has convinced Bill's boss to listen to his proposal for putting most of Acme's account management (sales) work online, which will cut down on the need for a personal sales force, like Bill Jones and his co-workers. Andy claims that it's the future, and Acme needs to take their marketing into the 21st century. Andy says that if Acme advertises on the Internet using keywords like "Wholesale Products," they can attract many more retail businesses, and increase their sales.

So, the boss tells Bill and his fellow Account Managers that Acme is considering doing much of their sales work through the Internet, and wants the Account Managers to tell him if there is any reason why they should not do that. Most of the Account Managers in the meeting turn white as a sheet, realizing that some of them may be out of work if this project is approved. Bill Jones, however, has been around for a long time, and this kind of talk doesn't bother him a bit. In fact, he's been expecting it.

He leans back in his chair, taps his pencil on the table, and says, "Boss, let me tell you why that isn't going to work."

Bill's boss nods to him to continue.

"Boss, you and I have been around this business for a long time. We both know that the most important part of large-scale wholesale is the personal touch. I know my clients. For example, take Mike Adams at the MegaMart's purchasing office in Atlanta. He's been married 11 years. His wife's name is Joan. He has two kids, Ellen and Mike, Jr. He loves to play golf. His favorite course is only a couple of miles from his office, and when I go to see him, we always get out for at least nine holes. Mike loves a good steak, so I always take him over to Charlie's Steak House near the golf course after we play. He's a science fiction fan, mostly into *Star Trek*, so I always send him the newest Hallmark *Star Trek* Christmas ornament every holiday season. When we talk on the phone, he always has something to say about the Atlanta Braves, so if I'm calling him during the season, I check to see how the Braves are doing first.

"Mike has been buying from me for six years, ever since he took over the purchasing job there. Two of our competitors have tried to get to him in the past *two* years, and Mike and I have always come to an understanding that keeps us number one in his book."

Bill leans forward in his chair, and levels his gaze directly at his boss. "Let me make three points," he says quietly.

"Point Number One: Mike is just *one* of my clients. I work that way with *all* of them. Can Andy Smith from IT build you a web site that can do that?

"Point Number Two: While we're busy destroying the personal relationships we've spent years building with our clients by referring them to an impersonal web site, our competitors are still going to be out there in person playing golf with people like Mike in Atlanta. We're going to lose business.

"Point Number Three is this," Bill continues. "How many new employees do you want to hire to handle incoming new account requests from every mom-and-pop operation in the country who wants a better price on bicycles? You advertise this company openly on the Net as a wholesaler, and you open the door to a huge number of very small new accounts that will never end up buying anything significant."

Five minutes later, the meeting is over, and Andy Smith from IT is suddenly the one worried about his job.

The Internet has many other uses besides simply advertising in the search engines. Large, established, smart wholesalers will only use a web site as an informational tool for clients contacted through other means.

You see, Andy Smith *can* build Acme a web site that attracts retailers and automates many sales processes. However, it will depersonalize a hands-on, personal Account Manager system that wholesale suppliers have used for as long as they can remember. The big wholesalers don't want to let that happen. It's too much of a gamble to abandon a system that's served large wholesalers for as long as they can remember.

They also realize that this advertised web site approach will attract thousands of very small retailers.

Andy would have been better off to suggest a site that showcases Acme's products, but refers prospective clients to Bill and his fellow account reps, and does not open the door to a tremendous amount of small business traffic.

They May Not Advertise to Us, but Many Will Still Work with Us

The fact that wholesalers don't purposely look for home-based e-biz owners doesn't mean that there's anything wrong with home-based Internet businesses! Again, this is simply the way most of the big wholesalers view their world, and you have to understand that in order to make progress with them. Acme is a large wholesale supplier, and an excellent business for any small retailer, like yourself, to work with. However, Acme is not *actively looking* for *small* retailers. They make money by working with the big retail chains, and doing a very large volume business. Remember that we talked about wholesale being a *volume* business in the last chapter. A real wholesaler's primary concern is getting and keeping *very large* accounts.

Don't despair! There are many real wholesale suppliers who will work with small retailers. Acme is probably one of them. It's just not usually in their best interest to help *you* find *them*! The big brand-name wholesalers of the world just don't go around spending time and money advertising themselves to an audience that they feel won't be a significant part of their overall business.

That's why, as an online retailer, *you* have to go to *them*. Wholesalers don't go out of their way to make it easy for the home-based business owner to find them. However, they *can* be persuaded to work with you if you can just find them and ask.

Why Fake Wholesalers Do Advertise on Search Engines

The search engine keywords "Wholesale," "Wholesale Products," "Drop Shipping," and so on attract a huge number of people who own or are starting home-based Internet businesses. That's because people who are relatively new to e-commerce are not yet aware of these wholesale scammers and sellers of substandard information. Most people simply do not know that search engines are the wrong place to look for real wholesalers.

While 98 percent of the world's real wholesalers do *not* advertise there (for reasons we just discussed), those search engine keywords are the sweet spot for middlemen, MLM schemes, get-rich-quick con artists, and sellers of junk information. We mentioned before that you can find a very small number of genuine wholesale information sellers there. However, for the most part, you need to stay away from the top results in the search engines if you're researching real wholesalers.

So, Where Do You Find Legitimate Wholesale Suppliers?

When Chris Malta first started selling products on the Internet back in the 1990s, he asked the same question. He wanted to find wholesale drop shippers for his new online business, and started wondering where to look for them. He thought he had the answer back then, just like many people think so now. His first instinct was simple: hit the search engines, and search for "Wholesale Drop Shipper." So he did just that. Yahoo returned about 60 gazillion hits touting a popular book supposedly filled with hundreds of drop shippers. This thing was all over the place. Can't go wrong there, Chris thought, so he happily zapped 12 bucks over the Net to one of the countless resellers of the popular book. He stood patiently next to his mailbox for a couple of weeks, waiting for his shiny new hardbound copy of the book that would make him rich. When it finally showed up, he almost gave it to his son, thinking it was a copy of the boy's elementary school newsletter. In short, it wasn't much help. Those listings that did have phone numbers, Chris called. Some of them didn't know what he was talking about. Some were willing to drop-ship, but Chris didn't think he was going to make a fortune selling fake vomit and dribble glasses on the Web. The rest were either used-book sellers, or they wanted Chris to mail money to a P.O. Box so they could send him some *other* information that would make him rich. *Sigh.*

Okay, back to the search engines. Chris cleverly dodged all the people who wanted to sell him a "complete turnkey web site package with products ready to sell." He wanted to put *his* kids through college, not *theirs*.

---

*Complete, ready-to-use Internet business packages that include products to sell are **not** real businesses. They are simply a way for someone else to turn you into their commissioned salesperson.*

Chris finally located someone who claimed to be the owner of an import company that drop-shipped hundreds of great products. Chris paid 50 bucks for a "membership," and got a no-name catalog in return, with a "wholesale" price list. "Great!" he thought, "here we go!" He searched, and found, many of these products for sale on the Web on other sites. The products were identical, but guess what? Their retail prices were the same as Chris's "wholesale" prices. In other words, Chris had zero profit margin. The guy he signed up with was an MLM scammer, just like Unscrupulous Bob from Chapter 11, and he was now $50 richer. Chris was still nowhere.

With a grim sort of last-ditch determination, Chris dug, and he dug, until he found the *real* source of this no-name catalog he had paid the MLM scammer 50 bucks for. It was a manufacturer and importer in Texas, and they were actually the source of the products! He set up an account with these people and began selling their products. A little later, he found another company ("3,500 products you can sell on your own web site" ... that will sound familiar to you if you've spent time searching the Net for wholesalers!) and spent weeks sifting through more resellers who were *posing* as that source until he found *that* original supplier outside of L.A. Chris sold products from these two companies for about six months, and actually did about $12,000 in sales, but he wasn't happy. The products were imported knock-offs. He wanted the shiny new name brands that look so cool on your web site, and that everyone wants to buy. After dealing with about the umpteenth customer who wanted to return his patched leather made-in-Kuala-Lumpur backpack because he wasn't happy with the quality, Chris had had enough. It was name brand or bust!

After another exhaustive search of the Web, he found a company that offered hundreds of name-brand products that they would drop ship. The stuff was great! Everything from Panasonic to Shop-Vac! They sent him the catalog, and he spent two weeks working on his site, replacing most of the knock-off stuff with the "Holy Grail of name-brand products." *Then they sent Chris the price list.*

They had done it to him again. The "wholesale" prices he was supposed to purchase this stuff at was, in most cases, higher than other sites were *selling* it for! Another middleman. Needless to say, Chris was very unhappy. It seemed that he would never locate the kind of wholesale suppliers he needed.

Going Straight to the Source

When Chris was a kid, and his mother was angry with someone, she would go right to the top. He clearly remembers her forcing her way through to the President of a bank when she was furious about having to wait six days to cash a large check. The banker experienced The Wrath of Mom, and she walked out of the bank with $30,000 in cash that same day. So, Chris decided to try going straight to the top. Nothing left to lose, right?

He went to the Westclox web site, since that was one of the lines he had wanted to resell from what turned out to be a middleman earlier on. Turns out Westclox was owned by General Time, Inc., in Atlanta, GA. So was Seth Thomas Clocks. He found the number for General Time, and asked for the Sales department. He explained his situation, and asked if they could refer him to any wholesaler who could drop-ship their products for him. "Oh, no problem," said Jason, the salesman, "we can drop-ship single units for you right from the factory." It took Chris a full 90 seconds to crank his jaw back up off the floor.

After about ten minutes on the phone, Chris was well on his way to establishing an account directly with General Time. Talk about wholesale prices on name-brand products! This was the real thing! They sent him catalogs, price lists, and all the info he needed to get started immediately. For *free*! As we've said before, rarely will you get a chance to work directly with a manufacturer, if ever. Manufacturers make products; they generally do not wholesale them. So, you have to find the real wholesalers. Chris actually got lucky with General Time. Finding the company was when Chris figured out something he feels he should have known right from the start (given his background in wholesale and retail). There *are* people who know *exactly* who the real wholesalers of every product made on Earth are. It's so simple he was embarrassed he hadn't figured it out sooner. Who is it? The *manufacturers* of the products! After all, they're the ones who factory authorize those real wholesale suppliers in the first place.

So there it is, folks. That's all you have to do. Ask the manufacturer of the products you want to sell who their authorized wholesalers are. They'll tell you.

Who Is the Manufacturer?

Ah, we'll bet you were just waiting for a catch, weren't you? Well, there is one, but it's just a small detail. In order to contact the manufacturer of the products you want to sell, and ask them who the real wholesalers are, you have to know who the manufacturer is first! That's not always as easy as it sounds.

You can't just assume you know who the maker is, even if it's a popular brand-name item. RCA products, for example, are manufactured by Thompson Consumer Electronics. You wouldn't know that without looking at the owner's manual of a product, or the serial number sticker on the back. Thus, you need to go *all* the way to the top of the manufacturing chain; not just to some subsidiary brand name.

Virtually every product made will have some kind of information on it or be packaged with a label that identifies its manufacturer.

If you have a hard time figuring out who the manufacturer of a product is, your best bet is to simply *buy* one of the products you want to sell, or take your Product Sourcing Notebook to your local mall and inspect a demo product on the store shelf if you can. Take a look at the box, the owner's manual, or any warranty papers that come with it. Check out the model and serial number stickers on the back of the product. Somewhere, you'll find the name of the product's manufacturer. Then, all you have to do is call them.

Manufacturers Are Your Gateway to Information about Wholesalers

To find out the true wholesale supplier of a product, all you need do is ask the manufacturer.

- Call the manufacturer, identify yourself using your legal business name (remember that little detail?), and ask for the Sales department. Tell them your company is interested in retailing their products, and you need to speak with a sales rep.
- They'll likely tell you they're a manufacturer, and don't sell directly to retailers. Tell them that you understand that, and that you're just looking for a recommendation for a wholesaler of their products.
- It may take some time to get through to a sales rep. In fact, you may have to leave a message. If you don't hear from them within a couple of days, call again. Stay on their back until you speak to someone personally.
- When you do get through to a manufacturer's sales rep, you can ask at this point if they will wholesale products to you direct from the factory. The answer 99.9 percent of the time, however, is "No, of course not." That's okay. Tell the sales rep that you would appreciate a list of wholesale suppliers that he or she recommends.

The manufacturer's sales rep has that information, and should not have a problem e-mailing it to you. Then, you can start calling those wholesalers. We'll talk about what to say to them, and how to deal with them, in the next chapter.

Summing Up

As home-based business owners, we have to live with the fact that we are *not* the desired "target market" for most real wholesalers, and real wholesalers don't go out of their way to advertise to us. Here are some things to remember from this chapter:

- Search engines are not a good place to look for wholesale suppliers. While you can work on product sourcing *ideas* there, you won't find many legitimate wholesalers using search engines.
- Real wholesalers are not openly advertising to home-based Internet businesses, because larger accounts are more important places for them to spend their advertising dollars.
- Search engines are the sweet spot for product sourcing scammers. Don't believe anything that sounds too easy!
- The manufacturers of the products you want to sell are the people who know where the *real* wholesalers are. All you need to do is find out who makes the product, and ask the manufacturer to recommend a wholesaler.

Chapter 14

Working with Real Wholesalers

Now that you know how to find real wholesalers of just about any product made, it's time to actually contact them and try to set up an account. The account you're trying to set up will allow you to buy products from the wholesale company, and resell the products at retail to your eBay business customers. This process will be the same no matter how you found your wholesale supplier, but we're going to assume here that you found them by asking the product's manufacturer for a list of their authorized wholesalers.

Making First Contact with Wholesalers

Start calling the list of wholesale suppliers you got from the manufacturer. When you get an answer, ask for the Sales department. In the last chapter, you were asking for the Sales department as well, but that was different. You were calling a manufacturer, and their Sales departments only sell to wholesalers. All you were looking for during those calls was information on who their wholesalers were.

This time, though, you're going to be talking to the person who is either going to give you a wholesale account, or isn't. Your attitude on the phone during this first contact actually goes a long way toward determining whether the sales rep will give you an account. These wholesale company reps are looking for business-like professionals to sell to. They honestly don't want to waste their time setting up an account for someone that they feel isn't going to place any significant amount of orders with them.

You see, when a wholesale account rep agrees to set up an account for you, there's paperwork and follow-up to be done on their end. It's work for them, and takes time out of their day. Also, they're most likely going to get commissions on the sales they make to the accounts they set up. All things being equal, they would much rather spend their time setting up an account for someone they think is going to actually buy products than someone who they think is an amateur who doesn't know what they're doing.

*Account reps are people you need to impress. They
will decide whether or not you get a wholesale account,
depending on how much money they think their company
will make from your purchases.*

Remember, *you* are the one who needs the goodwill of the account rep, not the other way around! Here are some very basic things, as a home-based business owner, that you want to remember when you call a wholesale account rep for the first time:

- Don't make "first contact" business calls from a cell phone. It's annoying to the reps who have to deal with your signal cutting in and out, and it will feel unprofessional to them.
- Make sure you don't have a stereo blasting in the background, or kids screaming and running around the house, or dogs barking. *You want the rep to think you're calling from an office*, not a home. Offices are quiet!
- *Never* call with an attitude. If you act like you're doing the rep a favor by calling them, or if you act like they owe you something, that account rep will most likely blow you off after your second sentence, and then you'll have to move on to another wholesaler. This needs to be a respectful business conversation. That doesn't mean you have to demean yourself in any way. Just be professional, polite, and listen when the rep is talking. I've spoken to many people who've asked me why they can't get accounts with wholesale companies, and while I'm answering that question, they're interrupting me, and treating me like I'm their indentured servant. That's their answer, right there!

Let's remember from previous chapters that most real wholesalers unfortunately still see home-based e-biz owners as a very small market. And, as business owners, we have to understand that it's not just the account rep's time that's taken up by setting new accounts up. The wholesaler themselves spend money on this process as well. They have to pay their account reps, maintain offices, computers, phone lines, and so on, just so they *can* set up new accounts. When the new accounts in question look very small to them, they honestly figure that it's not worth the cost of setting up and dealing with those accounts. They also know that it's a *statistical fact* that most home-based business owners won't follow through with orders once they have an account set up. Nothing against home-based business owners, that's just the way it is.

So, most wholesalers you'll deal with probably have some kind of policy in place about dealing with home-based businesses, and that makes it harder to get the account you want. What makes it harder still is the fact that most real wholesalers have designed their account setup process to weed out, so to speak, the people they don't think they'll make any money from. That isn't new. Such processes have been going since long before the Internet.

In other words, they're going to ask you questions you may not be prepared for right now, and ask you for documentation you may not have yet. You can prepare for those questions, though, and you can get your documents in order before you call, so you won't lose a chance to work with a wholesaler before you even get started.

What to Say When You Call

Let's give you an example of how Chris would start an initial phone contact with a new wholesale supplier that he wanted to work with.

- He calls the wholesaler, and someone named Mike answers the phone.
- He says, "Hello, Mike, this is Chris Malta calling from WorldWide Brands. Can I speak to someone about a new account, please?"
- Mike tells him that he'll transfer him to the Sales department. He does, and Melissa answers the phone, asking how she can help him.
- Chris says, "Hello, Melissa. This is Chris Malta, calling from World-Wide Brands in Orlando, Florida. I got your number from Acme Manufacturers. We're a retailer interested in carrying several of your products. Can you tell me how to apply for a new account?"

Now, please notice a few things here. When Mike answered the phone, Chris didn't simply assume he was a receptionist, and ask for the Sales department. For all he knew, Mike could have been a sales rep himself. So, Chris told him who he was, what his company name was, and what he wanted to do. Even if Mike *is* the receptionist, he may not have let Chris' call go through if he hadn't done that.

Treat Each Person You Talk to As If They're the One Who Could Deny Your Account

At most companies, receptionists are far more than people who simply answer phones. They are the gatekeepers who separate the people who get to talk to someone, from those who *don't* get to talk to someone. They are the ones who can decide to bestow upon you the gift of speaking to a live person, or decide to throw you kicking and screaming into a circular automated telephone system that could take forever to get out of. *Be nice to receptionists.*

People who *don't* get to talk to someone are usually people who don't identify themselves properly, don't sound like a business caller, or act rudely. If Chris hadn't given Mike the information he did, it would have led to more questions.

For example, if he had just asked for the Sales department, Mike would have been forced to ask him who he was, what company he was with, and exactly what he wanted with the Sales department. You see, if Mike lets just any phone call through to the Sales department, he's going to have account reps complaining to him that he's letting through calls that waste the reps' time.

Chris gave Mike all the info he needed, right up-front, so he didn't have to ask any questions. There are certain things you don't want to reveal to the wholesaler right away (like the fact that you're a home business), and any chance you get to avoid initial questions is a good thing! He also spoke to Mike clearly and professionally, in a casual, friendly manner. He wants Mike to think that he's a professional who sets up new wholesale accounts for his company all day long, and twice as often on weekends!

The same exact thing is true with Melissa, the rep Chris got transferred to. The first words she hears from him are the first impression he'll make on her, and he'll never get another chance at that. He wants her to think he knows exactly what he's doing. He gave her a little more information, because at that point he knew he was talking to an account rep. An important part of that extra information was mentioning that he got her company's phone number from one of the manufacturers they are factory authorized by. When you do this, you can also mention the name of the manufacturer's rep you spoke to. The wholesaler's rep probably won't know that person, but it helps if the rep thinks you're calling on a personal referral.

Closing the Deal

Now that Chris is talking to the account rep, there are some things she'll ask right away and some things that he'll have to supply in writing later. When we get to this point, all companies do things a little differently, so we can't go in any kind of order here and expect it to be correct every time. So in the following we'll just list the most common things you'll likely be asked by a wholesaler.

What a Wholesaler Wants

The account rep may ask you a few initial questions over the phone, or they may simply refer you to a page on their web site where you can fill out the information they need. There are still a large number of wholesale companies who don't use the Internet very efficiently, so they may ask you for a mailing address instead so they can mail you the forms you need to fill out.

Business Name and Tax ID

One thing you can be sure they'll want is your business name and Sales Tax ID number. We don't care *who* tells you that you don't need this to buy from real wholesalers. You *do*. That is the number one thing that so many people simply refuse to understand. If you're going to deal with manufacturers and wholesale suppliers, then you absolutely *will* need a business name and Sales Tax ID.

If you come across someone claiming to be a wholesale product supplier that doesn't ask you for this information, they're not a real wholesale supplier. If you come across someone claiming to be a wholesale product supplier who has some kind of explanation as to why they don't require this information, they're not a real wholesale supplier.

As we said earlier, there are two basic kinds of tax IDs. One is called an EIN, which means Employer Identification Number. If you start a business using just a sole proprietorship (DBA, Fictitious Name, and so on) like most people do, you simply file papers with your state and you're in business. You really don't need an EIN at that point. The EIN is *usually* used to report earnings that you pay your *employees*, among other things.

The kind of tax ID you need is a Sales Tax ID. You'll remember from an earlier chapter that a real wholesaler cannot sell you products at wholesale, unless you show them proof that you're authorized by your state to collect that sales tax from your customers. As we talked about before, five states in the U.S. don't have a state sales tax. If you live in one of those states, you obviously can't get a Sales Tax ID there. However, the wholesaler will still require proof of your legal business, and may even ask you for an EIN tax ID.

In a case like that, you can get an EIN for your legally registered business at www.IRS.gov. It's free, and doesn't take long to get. So, if you're in a sales tax–free state, you should look into getting an EIN before contacting wholesalers.

Business Information

The wholesale account application will probably ask you for more information pertaining to your business. These things can include your business address, business phone, business fax, hours of operation, and so on. When you're a home-based e-biz, questions like these can make you nervous. Remember, wholesalers typically aren't over-anxious to do business with a home-based e-biz. So, when you respond to these questions, consider your answers carefully before submitting the application. That application should look professional, and it helps if it looks like it comes from a business location, not a home.

We aren't suggesting you hide the fact you're home-based. You'll tell the wholesaler that before your account setup is completed anyway. It just helps if you can legitimately get further into the account setup process with them before you end up having to tell them that. By that time, your rep will have gotten to know you a bit, and will already be feeling comfortable that you're serious about your business. Thus, they may be more likely to grant you an account, even if the wholesaler generally doesn't work with home-based businesses. We've seen that happen ourselves many times.

If they do ask you that question up-front, be completely truthful with them about it and take your chances. The worst thing that can happen is that you have to go to the next wholesaler of that product on your list. Never lie to people you work with in business.

Entering Your "Business Information"

Some things to remember about the business information you put on your application.

- **Business Address**   Your business address is, of course, your home address. If your home address is 100 Merchants Road (yes, there is a residential road with that name—in the city where Chris grew up!) then it will look to the wholesaler like you have a business office. However, if your home address is 234 Sunny Morning Way, Apartment #5, the wholesaler is going to know right away you're a home-based business. If you're in an apartment, you can replace "Apt" with "Suite," which will help if your street name at least sounds business-like. You may want to consider renting a local Post Office Box in a commercial area, in order to give your business a more professional look. They're cheap, convenient enough, and this isn't the only reason you'll want one. When you deal with your *customers*, it's better if your business address sounds business-like to *them*, too.

- **Business Phone and Fax**   You should put a phone number here that isn't likely to be answered by one of your kids, or by someone who simply says "Hello." When you're first starting out, we know it's hard to justify spending money on a second phone line, so in this case, you can use a cell phone number if you have one. Again, this isn't just for your wholesale account application. Anyone you deal with in your eBay business that you give a phone number to should get a business-like answer when they call you. If it's going to be your cell phone, change your cell phone's voicemail message to something like "Thank you for calling Mary Smith, of Smith Enterprises. I am currently on another line or away from my desk. Please leave a message, and I'll get right back to you."

As for a fax number, if you have one, great. If you don't, just put N/A (Not Applicable) on the account application.

- **Hours of Operation**   When you own an e-commerce business, your *real* hours of operation are 24/7! At least, it'll feel that way. Keep this one simple, though, and say Monday through Friday, 9 a.m. to 5 p.m. Even if you're working the day job at that time, your account rep can still get your professional voicemail, and leave you a message.

Business Status

You might come across a wholesale account application that asks you what the *status* of your business is. That means they want to know if your company is a partnership, a sole proprietorship (one person), a corporation, a retailer, and so on. Sometimes your business will be more than one of those things, in which case you should write them all on the application. You could be a corporation and a retailer, for example.

The wholesaler is probably asking this question in order to determine how solid your company is, and once again that has to do with extending credit. They will consider a corporation that is a partnership to be a stronger business than a sole proprietorship. If you see this question on an account application, you're probably dealing with a wholesaler that's pretty demanding in its criteria for setting up accounts. That's okay, just write in the answers and keep going.

Time in Business

The wholesaler will also probably ask you how long you've been in business. You *have* to tell them you're a new business, if that's the case. Once again, never lie to anyone you do business with. There will always be people out there who'll tell you that a certain amount of deception and underhandedness is unavoidable in business. That's not true. On the Internet, your reputation is critically important, and if you aren't always honest with everyone you deal with, people will find out. Then they'll post it all over the search engines, and everyone *else* will find out.

If you mislead a wholesaler and get caught later, you'll just end up running a bunch of auctions that you can't get products for anymore because the wholesaler found out you lied, and cut you off. Sometimes they're willing to work with new businesses, sometimes they're not. You need to always tell them the truth and take your chances, though, if you're going to establish successful business relationships.

Even so, if you've been at this for say, a few months, you probably don't want to say "four months." You can say "less than a year." If they ask you for the date you started your business, you can just put down the year alone.

Trade References and Bank References

Another question you'll have to answer for most wholesalers is "Who are your trade references?" What a wholesale account application is asking here is "What other wholesalers have you bought from in the past?" For most home-based e-biz owners, that's a tough one, because it's a catch-22. If you're trying to get set up with your first wholesaler, you don't *have* any trade references. But your first wholesaler may not set you up without them.

Along those same lines, they'll probably ask for business bank references. They'll want to know who you bank with, and may ask you for certain business bank account information. What they're looking for is information on banks that may have expended business credit to you in the past. So, they'll want trade references and bank references. Most home-based e-biz owners won't have these at first, but there's a completely legitimate way around those issues which works almost every time.

It has to do with the *reason* they're asking you these questions. Most wholesalers are used to extending credit to their retailers. That means, of course, that you can place orders now and pay for them at the end of the month. It's called Net 30. Thus, you have 30 days from the order date or invoice date to pay them for the products. *However*, if you tell the wholesaler that you *don't want credit terms*, the need for the trade references and bank references *goes away*. You simply tell them that you either want to pay for the products with cash up-front, or by credit card, which is what the vast majority of home e-biz owners do anyway. If they don't have to process your application for an extension of *credit*, they have a much easier time giving you an account.

Later on, when you've worked with a wholesaler for a while, you can *ask* them for credit, and you may get it. Then, *that* wholesaler *becomes* your first trade reference, for when you talk to *other* wholesalers.

DUNS (Dunn & Bradstreet) Number

Dunn & Bradstreet is, for the purposes of this discussion, basically a business credit reporting agency. They do much more, but the main reason a wholesaler may ask you for a DUNS number is so they can pull a credit report on your business. Once your legal business gets rolling, it's a good idea to look into getting a DUNS number and begin building your business credit record.

At this point, though, the wholesaler is asking for this for the same reason they wanted trade and bank references. They think you want them to extend you Net 30 credit. You can make this issue go away in the same manner. Simply tell them you do not want Net 30 at this time, and that you'll pay by credit card as you go.

Estimate Purchases from Current Suppliers

This one is fairly rare, but you may see it from time to time. A wholesaler who asks this is trying to establish potential sales that they may make to you. This number will have some effect on their decision to give you an account, but it will also be used internally by the wholesaler to estimate their own quarterly sales. If you're new, and you don't currently purchase from other suppliers, just write N/A here.

Your Product Mix

When you see this, the wholesaler is looking for information on what other products you already sell. A wholesaler of candles and incense might feel like they're wasting their time setting up an account for a retailer who currently sells radio-controlled cars, for example.

Wholesalers are most interested in setting up accounts for retailers that already have an established customer base, and that already buy products related to what the wholesaler carries. A situation like that makes a wholesaler feel confident you might be placing many large orders with them over a short period of time. That means sales, and that's what it's all about. So, what your current product mix is can be a very important question for them to ask, although not all wholesalers ask it.

The Size of Your Customer Base

Again, some wholesalers will be interested in your current customer base—how many people you already sell to on a regular basis. If you know those numbers, great. If you're new to e-biz and you don't have the numbers, you can always write in "New business." Wholesalers don't necessarily have a problem with a new business, but if they're asking this question, they are probably fairly strict about new accounts.

Your Physical Storefront

Sometimes you'll find wholesalers who want to see information on, or even an actual picture of, your physical storefront. That means they want you to have a brick-n'-mortar store out there in the world somewhere. There are several reasons for that, but mostly it centers around product wholesalers who have physical sales territories to maintain, and they can't step on the toes of those sales territories by allowing people to sell all across those territories on the Internet. If they absolutely require a physical storefront, there's no getting around that one, and you should just move on to the next wholesaler on your list.

Don't Sweat It

These are the basic things that most wholesale suppliers will ask you for in an account application. Overall, this sounds much harder than it is.

Wholesale account reps are people, too. Just be prepared, tell it like it is, and ask them to help. You'll know when it's the right time to tell them that you're a home e-biz owner. Sometimes the right time is during your first conversation. Other times, you'll feel like you should wait for them to ask. If they can set up an account for you, they will. If they can't, there are a lot of other suppliers out there.

Owning a home-based business is a *great* thing. It shouldn't be something you worry about telling people. It's just that, by and large, the traditional wholesale world has not really caught up with the 21st century yet. There are still many wholesale companies that operate out of shoddy dockside buildings, use more pencil and paper than they do computer hardware, and do business the old-fashioned way. Yet, many of those companies are some of the biggest suppliers out there because they've been around for decades. They'll come around to home-based e-biz eventually.

You can be sure that if a wholesaler turns *you* down for an account because you're new or home-based, they're turning down all your competitors, too, so at least nobody you're competing against will have that edge over you. You'll also get turned down for many more wholesale accounts than you get accepted for. Chris certainly did when his online business was new. And that's okay. Just move on to the next supplier on your list, and start again. You *will* find good suppliers you can work with, and if you're armed with the information we just discussed, it will happen sooner than you think.

Summing Up

People who are prepared and act professionally get many more wholesale accounts than those who just make casual phone calls to wholesalers, so please remember the following:

- When you contact genuine wholesalers, *you* need to impress *them*, not the other way around. If they don't think you're going to make them money, they won't bother to give you a wholesale account.
- If you're asked whether you're a home-based business, be up-front about it. If you're not asked, don't volunteer that information until you have to.
- Be prepared with the information a wholesaler is going to want, as described in this chapter.
- Speak and act professionally, as if you do this kind of thing all day long.
- You won't always have all the info the wholesaler wants, and may not be able to provide it since home-based businesses are set up differently than large retail companies. Just give them everything you can.
- Don't get upset if you don't get an account. Most general wholesalers are hesitant to work with home-based businesses. If they won't do it, just move on to the next wholesaler on your list.

Chapter 15

Other Product Sourcing Methods

After working in wholesale, retail, and product sourcing for a very long time, our best recommendation for sources of products to sell on eBay will always be new products from real wholesale suppliers. When you're dealing with wholesale suppliers, you're getting brand-new merchandise that's under warranty. You have an account rep who can handle shipping issues, damaged merchandise, returns, and product liability questions, and who provides images and descriptions of the products you sell.

To us, that's invaluable in streamlining product sourcing, thus bringing the best quality products to your customer, and protecting your business from lost income. There are many people, though, who are interested in alternate methods of product sourcing. We'll go over the basics of three major alternate methods in this chapter: liquidation buying, overstock buying, and importing.

Liquidation Buying

Several large web sites on the Internet deal in product liquidations, and it *is* possible to find good deals that you can earn money on. However, if you're going to consider doing this, you really need to go into it with your eyes wide open, and be very careful about what you're buying. Let's look at the term *liquidation* carefully. To the casual observer, this word looks appealing when it involves product sourcing. To most people, liquidation means "pennies on the dollar." That's usually true, but there are reasons for that, and it's important to understand them if you're going to separate the good deals from the bad.

When a number of products are liquidated, that means whoever owns them no longer wants them. In fact, they want to get rid of them so badly they're willing to accept virtually no profit, or even take a financial loss, to do so. You have to always keep one thing in mind in business. There is *no* free lunch! When you get deals for pennies on the dollar, there is a reason for it, and it generally has nothing to do with the products being a great deal.

When a number of products are liquidated, that means whoever owns them no longer wants them.

Sometimes, the products being liquidated *are* brand new, and a manufacturer simply made too many of them. Or, they weren't that great a seller to begin with, and the manufacturer or wholesaler got stuck with a lot of extras. In our experience with liquidation, though, brand-new products that are still in the box, never having been opened, are more the exception than the rule.

Many times, brand-new products are liquidated from wholesale warehouses because the *floor space* these products take up in the warehouse has become *more valuable* to the wholesaler than the products themselves. The products up for liquidation are not selling well for the wholesaler, and are no longer worth keeping. They want to get that stuff out so they can bring in the products they think will sell much better for them. Think about it ... if a wholesaler with retail connections all over the business world can't sell these products, it's not that likely you'll be able to either.

Most of what gets liquidated by an actual wholesaler is last year's model products, or products that are two or three years old, or even older. Some of them may be store returns. These are products that the wholesaler has taken back from a retail store because the retailer couldn't sell them. Products like these often sit in the back areas of a warehouse for years, and are finally liquidated either to reclaim the floor space or just to get them off the company's books.

Other times, the products being liquidated are *used*, and may have been sitting around some *corporation's* storage room for years. A big company that has tens of thousands of employees (Kodak, IBM, and so on) goes through a lot of computer hardware, for example. Thus, these companies are constantly upgrading computers to newer, more powerful models. That means they end up with storage warehouses full of old computers.

Depending on the company's accounting policies, those old computers will either depreciate until they have a zero value (and will then be thrown away) or they'll be liquidated if the company still attaches some kind of value to them and decides to sell them off. If they're liquidated, chances are they'll end up on some liquidation web site on the Internet. This situation isn't just the domain of the big corporations, either. Everyone from cities and towns to public school systems get rid of all kinds of old, used products like these through liquidation.

The Infamous Breakage Pile

Many years ago, back in the 1970s, Chris Malta worked for a wholesale beer distributor in New York. It was quite an experience, in more ways than one. Back in the '70s, people didn't take drunk driving nearly as seriously as we do now. The men who drove the delivery trucks in those days used to come in to load up their trucks for the day at about 5 a.m. Guess what the first thing many of them did each morning as soon as they arrived?

Yep, they started drinking. In those days, it was actually part of the driver's employment contract that there was to be a keg of beer on tap in the Driver's Room at all times. So, many of the drivers (not all of them, of course) would head straight to the Driver's Room at 5 a.m. and start drinking while their helpers loaded their trucks. This certainly doesn't happen anymore, but it was always amazing to Chris that he never saw a single traffic accident involving one of those big beer delivery trucks while he worked there. Why are we telling you this? Well, we do have a point to make here.

At that beer distribution warehouse, they had what was called the *breakage pile*. This was a large area of the warehouse that was simply a mountain of cases of beer that had broken bottles or cans in them. You see, Chris never saw a driver get into an accident with a truck even though a lot of them drank all day long while driving and working. However, plenty of them had accidents while handling cases of beer during the day! Cases got dropped during deliveries, and bottles and cans inside those cases broke.

When that happened, the cases with the broken bottles or cans inside were thrown back on the truck. At the end of the day, those broken cases were unloaded from all the trucks and thrown on the breakage pile. In fact, during the time Chris worked there, he was actually out on delivery routes occasionally where a driver would purposely pick up a case of premium beer, drop it on a sidewalk, and say "Oops!" with a big grin on his face when he heard a couple of the bottles smash inside the case. Then, the driver would drink a few of the unbroken beers from the broken case since no one ever checked the cases on the breakage piles to see if they were full.

Recycling the Breakage Pile

Once every six weeks or so, the breakage pile would get too big, and start getting in the way of warehouse operations. The company would bring in some part-time help for a few days, and put them to work on the breakage pile. The company had stacks of new, empty beer case boxes for every kind of beer they carried. The guys working the breakage pile would pick the unbroken bottles and cans of beer out of the broken cases, wipe them off, repackage them in new case boxes, and set them on pallets in the warehouse. Those newly repacked cases of old beer would then be sold directly to the public, from the warehouse, for *pennies on the dollar*.

We don't know if you've ever tasted a "skunky" beer, but that's the best word to describe the stuff that had been sitting around in a hot warehouse for six weeks on a breakage pile. Still, people bought it, because it was sold for "pennies on the dollar." You can imagine that this doesn't happen only with beer. In warehouses all over the world, there are breakage piles. On those breakage piles are products that got damaged in shipping, or in handling in the warehouse, or were returned by retail stores after having been broken. Many times the store returns are open boxes that are missing parts. Have you ever bought a product from a local store, and found when you got it home that the box looked like it had already been opened and then taped shut again? Then, when *you* open the box, you find there's a part missing?

That's because some chucklehead who works at the store replaced a broken part for some *other* customer by opening a new box, taking the needed part out, and taping the new product box shut again without all its parts. Then, he put the box back on the shelf for some other poor soul to buy who would think it was complete. That's the exception to the rule with breakage. What the store employee is supposed to do is take the box that's missing the part, put it on the store's breakage pile, and give the customer a brand-new product off the shelf.

Yes, big retail stores have breakage piles, too. They are full of sweaters that are missing buttons, jeans that have broken zippers, TVs that only display the color green, computers with nonfunctioning CD drives, and, well, you get the picture, right? Or, if you end up with that TV, you *don't* get a picture.

Guess what happens to those retail store breakage piles when they get big enough? All that junk gets loaded onto pallets and shipped back to the wholesale suppliers they came from. The store gets credited for the returns by the wholesaler. Then, it all gets thrown on the *wholesaler's* breakage pile, and eventually gets *liquidated*.

The overall point we're making here is that liquidated products are liquidated for a reason. No company will ever liquidate a product that has any kind of reasonable resale value to them. Liquidation web sites classify the products for sale on their sites in several ways. The following are examples of *their own* definitions:

- **New**   These are products that are new in the box and have never been offered for sale in a retail environment. Liquidation sites do not, however, provide any classification that tells you *how old* the "new" products are. They could be this year's product, last year's, or five years old, still new in the box.
- **Used**   This includes products that have been sold, are used, or have been returned (store returns). They usually have noticeable defects. They do not come in the original box, and rarely ever have owner's manuals or accessories that were sold with the product when it was new. Used liquidation products are many times in need of repair.
- **Returns**   Liquidation sites define "returns" pretty much the same way they do used items.
- **Refurbished**   Products that were used by someone and broken, and then rebuilt. They're rarely in their original packaging, and seldom

come with owner's manuals or their original accessories. They'll often show damage or signs of age.

- **Shelf Pulls** These are products that were for sale in stores, but that never sold. They may have multiple reduced-price tags stuck on their boxes, and sometimes don't come in their original packaging or with the usual accessories since they may well have been used as floor models.
- **Salvage** These are products that are broken and that can only be used as a source of parts.

So, basically, only *one* type of product out of the *six types* sold on liquidation sites is anything that we'd want to buy personally: New. Of course, if some liquidator tells you the products you're buying *are* new, be careful to make sure the liquidator is telling you the truth, because liquidation sales are *final*.

The ads for the product lots on liquidation sites are a great insight into what you're getting, if you read them carefully. Here's some ad copy for a random liquidation item we pulled from an Internet liquidation site. This lot was one wooden pallet that contained three TVs and a home theater system:

"These assets are offered 'as-is, where-is' with no returns, guarantees, or claims as to working condition."

In other words:

- The products are in as-is condition. The seller is not telling you whether or not they're damaged.
- The products are "where-is," which means the liquidation price you pay does *not* include shipping the pallet to you. You pay extra for that, and may have to contact a shipper and arrange the shipping yourself.
- There are no returns, guarantees, or claims as to working condition. That pretty much speaks for itself; this lot is straight from some wholesaler's breakage pile.

Here's the bottom line. If you're thinking about buying liquidations, keep in mind that there are some good deals out there, but they're rare, and you have to look carefully. Try to find liquidation lots that you can see pictures of, and make sure they are new, all in their original boxes, and that they've never been opened. Otherwise, you could get easily stuck with an expensive breakage pile of your own.

Overstock Buying

Overstock merchandise is *supposed* to be new, in the box, never-opened products that have simply been left on the warehouse shelves from the previous season. There are many reasons why manufacturers and wholesalers get stuck with some of last year's inventory. Mainly, this would be because the manufacturer produced too much product, or the wholesaler bought too much and the manufacturer won't take it back.

Whichever is the case, we're still talking about products that didn't sell for some reason, and that has to be taken into account when you consider buying them and trying to sell them yourself. Remember that even if you do find genuine overstocks, you'll be dealing in last year's models, which will have already been replaced with *this* year's model. Other eBay sellers will be selling this year's model. Even though it may be more expensive to buy this year's model, buyers may shy away from purchasing "new" products that are outdated or discontinued.

Chris Malta's Experience with Manufacturer Overstocks

Here's an example. Earlier in this book, we told you that Chris had set up a wholesale company in New York a while back for a friend, and worked with him to develop that business. The company was making about an 8-percent profit margin on most products it carried, and up to a 30-percent profit margin on *some* products that it got key pricing on from the manufacturer. Every few months, the company called their manufacturer's account rep and asked if she had any overstock products they could buy out at a low price. Many times she did, but the company never ended up buying them, even though they certainly could've afforded them.

The products she had overstocks on always turned out to be products that the company didn't think anyone would want. They did their research on each product, and it always turned out that very few other people were selling them. You'd think that would be a good thing, because the market would be wide open, right? Not always. In doing market research with WorldWide Brands' Market Research Wizard on those products, the company also found there was very little demand for the products.

Not every product created by a manufacturer ends up being a good seller. The ones that don't have to be gotten rid of somehow!

These were products that the manufacturer had designed and produced, but found that there was very little retail interest in them. *That's why* they were letting them go as overstocks. Because even *they* couldn't sell them. Just something to keep in mind if you consider overstock purchases. If you look around the Net these days, you'll find that many overstock dealers are trying very hard to distance themselves from being lumped in with the word "liquidation," although on many overstock sites you'll see that they have liquidation "departments."

Overstock, like liquidation, is another place where you have to be very careful about who you deal with. I've spoken to many people who purchased what they were told were "overstock" items, only to find very little new product on the pallet they got. Instead, they found they had paid for a pallet loaded with *some* new product, and the rest filled out with goods you would expect from a liquidation breakage pile. Keep in mind that with overstocks, just as with liquidations, you'll be dealing with a "no return, no guarantee" policy.

Pros and Cons

Con artists litter the Internet, as we discussed earlier. Product sourcing is a lucrative realm for such scammers, making no product sourcing market completely safe. Overstock dealers are no different. There are a few good ones, and lots of bad ones. We could continue writing about overstock buying—what to look for, what to look *out* for, and more—but it would end up looking very much the same as the last section on liquidations.

There is, however, one way to make sure the overstock products you buy are always what you expect *without* having to go through web sites that claim to sell overstocks. We recently talked about it, remember? That's right—it's the list of wholesalers you got from the product manufacturers you called.

Most overstock merchandise comes from wholesalers in the first place. In some cases, manufacturers do unload overstock, and may actually do it for you, the retailer. It can't hurt to ask. Talking to the manufacturers and wholesalers you're going to call anyway is a great way to get in on the ground level of overstock buying. Yes, it's more time-consuming than going to an overstock web site, and yes, you would have to set up an account with the wholesaler of the products (or if you're lucky, in the case of overstocks, the manufacturer) in order to get them to sell you overstock products when they have them.

So it's your call. You can risk your money with an online source that claims to provide genuine overstock merchandise, or you can spend more time and effort, but know you're getting exactly what you pay for by finding out who makes the products you want, and then calling the manufacturer and wholesalers directly. As for us, we always go to the *real* source.

Importing Products

If you really want to get the best possible prices available anywhere, you need to buy directly from a manufacturer. However, as we've already discussed, that's not going to happen very often when you're a retailer—but it *can* happen when you're an *importer*.

There are countries in the world today that are producing so many products at such a low cost that the prices are sometimes hard to believe. China, Taiwan, Mexico, Indonesia, India ... you name it, they're opening factories and producing durable goods. In fact, pick up a few products that are sitting on your desk right now. Your stapler, your pen and pencil holder, even your phone. We'll bet you find "Made in China" printed on at least one of them. There is, in fact, a bonanza of low-cost products available in many countries around the world. Most of them end up on store shelves and eBay listings in the U.S.

Even if you're buying from a wholesaler in the United States, chances are the company that manufactures the products is having them made in China, for example. Although a product itself was probably designed in the U.S, the U.S. manufacturer will work with a Chinese business to produce a product. The Chinese business will actually rent space in a building somewhere in China for the express purpose of setting up a factory to produce only those products for that one U.S. product maker. Products made in China are no longer associated with being "cheap" goods, remember. Nearly every major brand name company in the world has at least some, if not all, of their products manufactured at facilities in China.

Imports Take Time

This was the case with the sporting goods manufacturers that author Chris worked with in the wholesale company in New York that we told you about earlier. As a wholesaler, they were buying directly from the manufacturer, and there was more than one time when the manufacturer ran out of some of the products Chris was buying from them. When that happened, it always took at least six weeks for them to get more of that product. Why?

Because when they ran out, they had to schedule another "production run" of those products at the factory in China.

It would take two to three weeks for the factory to make the products, then two to three more weeks for the Chinese factory to get the products on a freighter and ship them to the manufacturing company's warehouse in New York. Then, they had to deliver the product to the company Chris worked with, the wholesaler.

There are people selling on eBay today who actually have products made to their specifications in China and then import them directly. There are also eBay sellers who simply import already existing products from China and other countries. They have to be sure to anticipate how much time it will take to actually deliver those products, and be certain the products are still "in season" when they finally arrive.

Here's something that's important to remember. You will not be able to import name-brand goods. Those name brands are owned by companies here in the U.S. and in many other places around the world. So, please don't believe the common misconception that you can directly import Prada, Gucci, Sony, and so on. You can't, unless you actually approach the owner of the brand itself, and create a working arrangement. That simply does not happen with home-based businesses.

People who claim to be importers able to sell you those big brand names at cheap prices are not importing the real brand-name goods. They're importing knock-offs (fakes) which are illegal on eBay, or they're importing stolen goods (from the black and gray market), meaning they're breaking several laws either way. If you see someone on the Net claiming they can import brand-name products for you at a fraction of the regular wholesale price, run in the other direction!

If you want to sell Gucci, Prada, and Sony, you have to talk to a *factory-authorized wholesaler* of Gucci, Prada, Sony, or whatever other brand name you're considering. With that said, there are two basic ways you can get involved in selling imported products, as discussed in the following two sections.

Dealing with an Import Web Site

Just like the huge number of people on the Net who claim to be wholesalers, there are a huge number of people with web sites who claim to be importers. Some really are; most aren't. Again, you have to be very careful whom you deal with. The same warning signs apply to this type of business that apply to wholesalers. Check out any business thoroughly before you send them any money for anything.

If you're a U.S.-based home e-biz and you work with a U.S.-based importer, you're not actually importing products. The *importer* is importing the products, and they're *reselling* them to you. If it's a genuine importer with a good reputation, that's okay. It's just like working with a factory-authorized wholesaler. However, you can't consider yourself an actual importer if you work this way.

If you're a retailer who's working with an importer who is acting as a wholesaler, then this is the same as if you're working with a factory-authorized wholesaler.

For the best information we've ever found on finding and working with genuine importers, take a look at Ron Coble's web site: www .ImportExportHelp.com.

Importing Products Yourself

Actually, becoming an importer of products and then selling those products on eBay can be a very lucrative business. We know several Power-Sellers who do just that. However, if you're in the startup stages of your business, or even still in your first couple of years, you probably don't want to consider this. It can be *very* expensive, and there is a lot to learn.

Since this book isn't meant to teach direct product importing, and you really need to learn a lot about it before you try it, we'll just cover what Chris Malta's company, WorldWide Brands, went through when investigating this process in early 2005.

- Chris's company actually sent people to China. They spent about $10,000 to send two people there on a fact-finding tour. They went with a PowerSeller that WorldWide Brands knew who already imports from China. While WorldWide Brands' people were there, they toured several factories and attended some very impressive manufacturers' trade shows.
- During that trip, they found a trusted trade contact in China through their friend, the PowerSeller. They knew they'd need someone *in* China to act as their agent when they negotiated with factories and placed orders. There are still some very real language and cultural challenges in dealing directly with Chinese manufacturers, and the best way to go is to work through an agent. Their WorldWide Brands' agent in China is actually subsidized by the Chinese government, who wants him to bring in new business. Thus, his commissions are nominal.
- Here in the States, WorldWide Brands prepared to receive imported goods. They leased warehouse space, complete with an office, phone line, and so on. They set up a computer, a fax machine, and brought Internet access to the office. The warehouse space costs them several thousand dollars per month.

- They spent a great deal of time deciding what their first product imports should be. Chris and his partners at WorldWide Brands knew they'd be dealing with large minimum orders since most Chinese manufacturers only make the products you order, when you order them. The size of your order has to justify enough production time in the factory's schedule to make it worthwhile to the manufacturer. They knew they'd get the best deal if they placed orders large enough to fill an entire shipping container (the trailer on a tractor-trailer rig). So, they prepared to spend between $20,000 and $70,000 per order, depending on the product.

- They learned which seaports were the most cost-effective places to have their shipping containers delivered, considering WorldWide Brands' physical location in Central Florida. Then, they began talking to shipping companies here in the States. Once a shipping container from China gets to a port in Florida, it's WorldWide Brands' responsibility to have a shipping company pick that container up and deliver it to their warehouse.

As you can see from just these basic facts, becoming a direct importer of products is a time-consuming and expensive process to set up, and you need to be in a position to place large orders. We do know some eBay sellers who pool their resources in order to share the expense of this type of operation, but you have to be very careful there, too. The people you choose to partner with are people you'll likely work with for some time. You need to make sure they're going to hold up their end.

So, overall, you can either work with existing importers who actually become your "wholesaler" for imported products, or you can import products directly yourself. Obviously, working with existing importers is much less expensive and time-consuming, but carries the same risks as looking for wholesalers using search engines. Be careful who you work with!

Summing Up

As you can see, there are product sourcing methods other than buying directly from wholesalers. However, please be careful to remember the following points when looking at alternate methods:

- Liquidated products are being liquidated because *whoever owns them now no longer wants them*. Be very careful!
- Most liquidations are last year's models, or may be damaged, returned, refurbished, and even completely broken products. Remember, there are no guarantees and no returns.
- Overstocks are *supposed to be* brand-new products, but many times liquidation-type products slip into overstock lots.

- The vast majority of the liquidation and overstock products you'll find on the Internet are questionable at best, and a complete waste of money at worst.
- The best sources of real liquidated and overstock merchandise are the genuine wholesalers and manufacturers themselves, but you must always be sure that what you're getting is *new in the box* if you want the best products.
- There are good deals to be had in importing if you can find a legitimate importer. But be careful!
- Do *not* believe people who tell you they can get you Gucci, Prada, and so on for pennies on the dollar. Those products are counterfeit knock-offs, and can cost you your eBay account or land you in legal trouble if you're caught selling them online.
- Directly importing products yourself can be lucrative, but the startup costs are very high. Most people who move into direct importing are online sellers who've been working their businesses for a few years and are financially ready to move into this industry area.

Chapter 16

Building Product Sourcing Relationships

A good relationship with your supplier(s) is an important thing to have, for a number of reasons. As we talked about earlier in this book, as a home-based retailer, you must understand that you need your supplier more than they need you. That's not a slam against home e-biz. It's just a fact of life, and facts are what rule the business world. People who can learn to deal with facts, even when they don't like them, are much more likely to succeed in business.

The Care and Feeding of Your Supplier Relationship

We talked earlier about making that first contact with a wholesale supplier. You should be professional and civil, and never treat the account rep as someone who owes you something. These people hold the keys that unlock the door to the wholesale products you want to sell. Even if you come across a rude account rep, take it in stride. If you're going to be in business, you're going to need to learn to deal with rude people without allowing yourself to get upset.

The vast majority of wholesale account reps is very helpful, and will do their best to work with you. Remember, they're people too, and they're just doing their jobs. The best thing that could happen is that you end up on a friendly, first-name basis with your wholesale account rep(s).

The main reasons you want a strong, friendly relationship with your wholesale account rep are the following:

- Prompt attention
- Honest information
- Timely delivery

- Special considerations
- Obtaining credit
- Trade references

Let's go over these one by one.

Prompt Attention

We know that you've been through voicemail systems that drive you crazy. First, you have to sit there and listen while the recording gives you 15 different ways to contact the company you're calling, without calling them. It's obvious that they would rather you contact them any other way than by phone. Then, you sit through option lists, waiting for the one you need. You get to the end of the first list, and have to press 9 so you can listen to *another* list of options, because the first list didn't have the option you wanted.

Then, once you find the option you want, you press that number on your phone, and enter *another* option list that you have to sit through. When you finally think you've found what you're looking for, you get a recording telling you to look up that information on the company's web site. Then the system hangs up on you. This certainly doesn't happen with just wholesale companies. Your doctor's office, your insurance company, your utility company ... they all use these systems now.

In days gone by, you used to be able to just press the 0 key and get transferred to an operator. Well, in most automated systems, that no longer works. Some restart their messages from the beginning when you press 0 now, and some actually hang up on you! When you need to speak to your wholesale rep, it's usually something you need to talk about *now*. If you form a good relationship with that person, you'll probably end up with the person's direct extension number, and many times even their cell phone number. Prompt attention from your wholesale rep is very important for your business, and all it takes to get it is creating a good relationship with the rep.

You don't want to be the person that the account rep groans about when he or she hears your voicemails. If you become that person, you always get shuffled to the bottom of the callback list.

Honest Information

There's a great deal of information that your wholesale rep has that he or she isn't going to volunteer to you on a regular basis. You have to ask, and if the rep likes you, you'll get honest answers, as long as the rep is allowed to give you that info. Some of it is information they can share if asked, and some of it is info that they're not really supposed to share with you ... but they will if they *really* like you. Here are some examples of both kinds of questions:

- *"What will your best-selling products be over the next three months?"* Your rep knows this, based on past sales trends. The answer to this question will help you prepare for each upcoming season, so you can have products picked out and orders placed *before* your competition.
- *"How many of the products I sell do you still have in stock?"* It's very important to stay on top of this issue, so you don't run into backorders. A rep can check those numbers. You may get an answer like "I'd have to check the warehouse and get back to you on that." If they don't get back to you later, you might not have a good relationship with your rep.
- *"What's your restock time on those products?"* Once the warehouse runs out of something you sell, you need to know how long it will be before you can get the item again. If you don't have a good relationship with your rep, they'll give you a standard company line like "four weeks," when it may actually be six or eight weeks.
- *"Which of your best-selling products can I get the best deal on?"* You'll want to have a really good relationship with your rep if you ask this, because he or she might be steering you away from products that may make them more commissions if they answer that question honestly.
- *"How many of these products is your largest home e-biz customer ordering?"* This is a question you really want to reserve until you know you're on good terms with your rep, because they're not really going to want to tell you about other customers of theirs. Reps have actually answered questions like this for me, though, and have given me even more detailed information on my competition, which is always good to have.

You can see from these few examples that being on good terms with your account rep can really help your business. These are only a few of the things you may want to find out during the course of doing business, and you need the goodwill of people who can answer those questions.

Timely Delivery

In the wholesale world, there are big accounts and small accounts. In the beginning, you're going to be a small account. That's okay. Many of Chris' accounts with wholesalers have been small ones, too. Remember, he started out doing exactly what you're doing. When we're small accounts, we tend to get placed on the back burner from time to time. For example, if you ordered 50 widgets yesterday, and a big account orders 400 widgets today, and the warehouse only has a total of 400 widgets, the big account is going to get all 400 of theirs, and you're not going to get any of yours until the warehouse restocks—even though you ordered first. Your account rep can pull your order back from the Shipping department, and use your widgets to fill the big account's order.

Faster and slower shipping methods exist, and there are ways to combine shipped orders to maximize fast delivery and minimize cost. Your rep knows how to do these things, and you want to be sure your rep is willing to do them for *you,* whenever he or she can. When a new shipment of products comes into the warehouse from the factory, and you and a whole bunch of other people are waiting for them, you want your rep to be willing to take your order right off the top of the pile and get them to you quickly, rather than service all the big accounts first and then send you yours last.

Wholesale account reps work hard to keep two kinds of people happy:

- People who have big accounts
- People they really like

If you don't have a big account, be *really* likeable!

Special Considerations

One of the greatest things about having a good relationship with your rep is when you call to talk with them about something, and they say, "Hey, guess what? I've got a really good deal for you if you want it." Now, if you don't work well with your rep, that may just be a push for more sales. However, you'll know when it really *is* a good deal if you work well with your rep.

Chris spent a good deal of time (several years) working with one particular manufacturer's account rep in Pennsylvania. She was a really great person to talk to, he was always straight with her, and he never backed out of a commitment he made to her. Over time, they became very comfortable working with each other. They got to a point where she would actually call *him* when she found a genuinely special product or pricing situation that she could create for someone. With that one rep, he went from being a very small account to becoming her largest account (with her help in finding him special deals) to finally becoming the *exclusive Internet wholesaler* of the products her company manufactures. Without her willingness to point him to special deals, put in a good word for him with her management from time to time, and stand in his corner when he wanted to take over exclusive Internet distribution of those products, it never would have happened.

You never know what kind of special considerations someone might be able to give you until they actually do it, and they'll never do it unless they like you.

Obtaining Net 30 Credit

Something you should always be trying to do for your business is to start, build, and maintain a good credit record. As your business grows, this is going to become more and more useful to you. When you're first starting out, business credit is probably the last thing you're thinking about. You should, however, always keep it in the back of your mind. Someday, when a rep you're on great terms with calls you and offers you an incredible deal that you want badly but can't pay cash for, business credit is going to make that possible.

Your business credit is always going to be tied to your personal credit. There's no escaping that. Even after all his years in business, Chris and his partners still have to put up personal guarantees for large credit lines, and so on. That's because they are a privately owned company, which is exactly what you are.

If your personal credit isn't very good, spend some time each month trying to correct the problems you have with it. You don't have to rush this process. A little at a time, without straining the bank account, is fine. It's going to take a while to get to a point where you can ask wholesalers and other companies to open credit accounts for you anyway.

Don't look at bad credit as a problem you can't fix. Get your credit reports from the three main reporting agencies (Equifax, Experian, and TransUnion) and clean up a little bit at a time. If your credit is good, so much the better, but make sure you keep it that way! Try not to load your personal credit up with too many loans, or credit card balances that are too high.

If you work hard at it, you're going to reach a point when you want to ask a wholesale supplier to extend credit to you. That's usually referred to as Net 30. When you have a Net 30 account, you can order from your supplier, and only pay them once a month for all your orders. This helps you to increase the volume of your business, because you're not limited to the cash you have on hand, or the maximum limit on your credit card, when you order products. You can place larger orders and sell more products when you have a Net 30 account with your supplier.

Expect this to take a good year or so with your first supplier. Net 30 accounts generally aren't even considered for small accounts unless they've been active and have placed a decent amount of orders for some time. During the time you're building up your rapport and your business credit, make *sure* you don't let even one credit card payment come back declined with your supplier. That one mistake can set you back a lot farther than you think. Always be sure you have the money available on your card or in your bank account *before* you place an order.

If and when you do decide to ask for a Net 30, you'll find that it's kind of like taking out a loan for a car. You're going to have to supply a good deal of personal and bank account information, and your credit report will be checked. You may not get a Net 30 account the first time you apply for one. As we said, it's going to have a great deal to do with your personal credit record, but that's not all. The wholesaler is going to want evidence that you're a strong, solid business with the ability to pay a bill even if you suddenly have a problem and can't sell the products right away. Having your account rep standing in your corner always helps in these situations!

Trade References

Earlier in this book, we talked about trade references. Trade references are wholesale companies you have worked with in the past. If you take good care to work well with your first wholesale account rep, that wholesaler will *become* your first trade reference over time.

Then, when you go to apply for accounts with other wholesalers, you can use that first wholesaler as a trade reference. Work well with *that* wholesaler for a time, and you'll have two trade references. Before you realize it, you'll have references and Net 30 accounts built up all over the place, and you won't have a problem getting accounts with any wholesaler you want.

The care and feeding of your relationship with your account rep will lead to great things for your business over time. You're going to find that it's easier to build personal relationships with your rep when you work with a smaller wholesale company, but smaller companies are more reluctant to extend Net 30 credit because they can't afford to take too many financial risks.

Extending Net 30 credit to you is something that suppliers are reluctant to do for home-based businesses. They see it as a financial risk. Building a good relationship with your account rep will help you to get that Net 30, however, in time.

On the other hand, larger wholesalers may be willing to take more of a risk in opening a Net 30 account, but they'll tend to be more impersonal about it, and you may not be able to deal with the same account rep every time. If you do work with a larger company that simply has a staff that picks up the phone and takes orders, try to latch on to one person on that staff and contact them directly every time, even if you have to leave a message and wait for a call back. That personal relationship will pay off for you in the end.

Just remember that it takes time and careful attention to create these important relationships.

Things You Don't Want to Do
to Account Reps

Wholesale account representatives are people who have a specific job to do, and are responsible for certain things within the scope of that job. Over the years, we've heard horror stories from dozens of account reps about people who simply don't understand that a wholesale account rep is not a catch-all for every problem a customer has with their online sales. The following are a few examples:

- An account rep is not responsible for setting retail and wholesale pricing across the e-commerce marketplace. Yet, some people will go ballistic on an account rep if they have problems with not being able to beat their competition's prices online. Product pricing online or in physical stores is not your account rep's problem, and he or she did not create the competitive marketplace we all work in. There are going to be times when you just can't figure out why your competition is selling the same product on eBay at a lower price than you can, even though you get them from a genuine wholesaler. There are many explanations for this kind of thing. Your competitor may be selling last year's model, purchased from a liquidator. Your competitor may be further along in his business, and is getting better price breaks by buying larger quantities using a Net 30 account. Your competitor may be charging a low retail price for the product, and jacking his shipping price up to compensate. Your account rep is not a target for your frustrations about competing in retail pricing. He or she will sell products to you according to the wholesaler's prices and quantity discounts, so don't blame the account rep if your competitors *seem* to be getting a better deal. There's always a reason for someone else selling at a lower price, and it never has to do with your wholesale account representative. As long as you're working with a *legitimate* wholesaler, you're getting a legitimate price. Figuring out how your competitors are selling for less is something you have to do for yourself.
- An account rep *is* the person you need to go through before you'll be allowed to sell their company's products. we've spoken with more than one rep who was shocked to find that an Internet seller would find their company's web site, copy their product images, place the products for sale online, and *then* call the wholesaler and ask for an account and a wholesale price list. The account has to be approved *before* you can begin to market a company's products.
- The number of people who treat a wholesale account rep like a home e-biz tech support line is truly astonishing. This is the number one complaint we hear from wholesalers who decide to sell to home-based e-biz owners, and is probably the number one reason why many will *not* sell to us. A wholesale account rep's time is paid for by the wholesale company. It is valuable time. The wholesaler needs that account rep to be opening new accounts and taking orders. Their account reps are *not* there to explain to home-based e-biz owners how to resize product images on their computer, upload products to their eBay stores, create marketing copy to sell products more quickly, fix problems with their e-mail programs, or anything else that has nothing to do with buying products at wholesale.

So, please keep in mind that a good interpersonal relationship with your wholesale account representative is going to be a very important thing for your business.

Nothing Good Comes Easy

We know it seems like there are a million things that are important to your business, and it's impossible to deal with or even remember all of them. It takes time, it takes patience, and it takes hard work.

Way back in 1848, gold was discovered at John Sutter's sawmill in California. Thousands of people picked up their entire lives and ran for those hills. It was said that all you had to do was pick up a handful of gravel from a streambed, and that gravel would shine with nuggets of gold. Someone started selling "California Gold Grease," which the buyer rubbed all over his body, and then rolled down a hill. The sellers of the product claimed that the buyer would reach the bottom of the hill covered in gold dust, and nothing else.

E-commerce is exactly the same thing. People are still buying "California Gold Grease" and wondering why they're covered with nothing but dirt when they reach the bottom of the hill. There *is* gold in those e-commerce hills, but, as many thousands of people learned in the late 1800s, you have to dig it out of the ground. It's not going to stick to your back just because someone tells you that you can get rich by rolling downhill.

Making your living from your home-based e-biz is *not* impossible. People do it every day—they really do. If you do the work and ignore the misleading shortcuts, you will, too.

Action—Your Next Step

We would like to thank you for your investment of time and attention in reading this book. You now have the product sourcing knowledge you need to move forward and either start or expand your e-commerce business. Use this book as an ongoing tool to help you build your business.

As you continue on your path to a successful e-business, we would like to leave you with this final thought. There is no more powerful combination than knowledge + action. If there is a true "secret" to success, this is it.

Knowledge without action will not produce results, and action without knowledge will most often produce unprofitable results. Take what you have learned in this book and put it into action. Your actions don't need to be perfect, and you don't need to get it right the first time. But you do need to act. The successful entrepreneur takes consistent actions every day towards growing their business. And consistent actions produce consistent results and income.

If you want additional information on product sourcing and find out about more product sourcing resources, please visit both What Do I Sell.com at www.whatdoisell.com and WorldWide Brands at www.worldwidebrands.com.

We wish you the best of success in your journey to a profitable retail business!

Index

About the Authors

Chris Malta is founder and CEO of WorldWide Brands, Inc. (www .WorldWideBrands.com), an eBay Certified Solution Provider. Introduced to wholesale selling by his parents at the age of ten, he has maintained his own successive chain of businesses all his adult life, and has more than 30 years of experience in the wholesale and retail business world.

Chris's company, WorldWide Brands, Inc., publishes the Internet's premier product sourcing directories and creates eBay-certified market research software. He is the writer and host (along with his business partner, Robin Cowie) of "The Entrepreneur Magazine EBiz Radio Show," and "The Entrepreneur Magazine Product Sourcing Radio Show." He is also a contributing editor for "Product Sourcing for eBay Radio."

Lisa Suttora is founder and CEO of What Do I Sell.com (www.whatdoisell .com), an eBay Certified Service Provider that specializes in teaching retail entrepreneurs how to find the products buyers want, locate legitimate suppliers, and sell successfully in the eBay marketplace. Lisa combines her background in sales and marketing with a lifelong love of research and a unique approach in order to bring creative solutions to the question of "What should I sell?"

A contributing editor to "The Entrepreneur Magazine Product Sourcing Radio Show" and "The Entrepreneur Magazine eBiz Radio Show," Lisa has also been a guest on the eBay Radio Product Sourcing segment. Lisa has been a featured speaker on the eBay Live Product Sourcing Panel and is an eBay Certified Consultant.